DATE DUE

NOV 2 – 1994	
OCT 1 7 1996	
OCT 2 0 1999	
NOV 2 2001	

Rousseau's Exemplary Life

ROUSSEAU'S EXEMPLARY LIFE

The *Confessions* as Political Philosophy

Christopher Kelly

Cornell University Press

Ithaca and London

First published 1987 by Cornell University Press.

International Standard Book Number 0-8014-1936-0
Library of Congress Catalog Card Number 86-32961

Printed in the United States of America

Librarians: Library of Congress cataloging information appears on the last page of the book.

The paper in this book is acid-free and meets the guidelines for permanence and durability of the Committee on Production Guidelines for Book Longevity of the Council on Library Resources.

TO JEANNE

Contents

Preface

Jean-Jacques Rousseau's project in his *Confessions* is to transform the way his readers look at the world by offering a picture of an exemplary human life. For the majority of readers, this picture is to be an account of how it is possible to live in a corrupt age; for a few readers, it is to be an illustrated analysis of human nature. My work here is to outline this project, to show how, on Rousseau's understanding, a profound treatment of political and philosophic issues can also be, and in some ways must be, a popular persuasive device.

The attempt to understand the *Confessions* in this way runs counter to the common expectations readers bring to autobiographies. Readers who approach Rousseau's *Confessions* for the first time are likely to do so with the expectation of titillating revelations about the personal life of an infamous man. The book is quite capable of fulfilling such expectations and has done so for generations of readers. Books about the *Confessions*, most of them personality studies aimed at satisfying the same expectations, are less exciting than the original. The authors of these books characteristically seek information lacking in Rousseau's presentation of himself by investigating his correspondence or the testimony of his contemporaries. In effect, they look for a hidden Rousseau to judge his public presentation of himself.[1]

---

1. For a useful biography of Rousseau that draws heavily on his correspondence, see Jean Guéhenno, *Jean-Jacques Rousseau*, trans. John Weightman and Doreen Weightman (New York: Columbia University Press, 1966). For studies of his personality, see Ronald Grimsley, *Jean-Jacques Rousseau: A Study in Self-Awareness* (Cardiff: University of Wales Press, 1961), and Jean Starobinski, *Jean-Jacques Rousseau: La Transparence et l'obstacle suivi de sept essais sur Rousseau* (Paris: Gallimard, 1971).

The present book is guided by the judgment that the *Confessions* is a profound work as well as a personal one. I attempt here to uncover the significance of Rousseau's methods of presenting himself, a significance that emerges only in the light of his less personal philosophic works. Rather than regarding the *Confessions* as merely providing access to the man behind the works, I use it in an effort to clarify the most important issues of Rousseau's thought. Viewed in this light, Rousseau's presentation of himself loses none of its importance if his account of the details of his life are shown to be somewhat inaccurate. It is more important for what it shows about Rousseau's judgment of the fundamental human problems than for what it shows about his life—and in this the autobiographical inaccuracies are just as revealing as the facts.

The first reason for considering the relation between the *Confessions* and Rousseau's philosophic thought is that the influence of that thought has always been inextricably linked with opinions about the man who formulated it. Discussions of Aristotelian or Kantian philosophy seldom turn into discussions of the personalities of Aristotle or Kant, but discussions of Rousseau's thought almost invariably turn into discussions of Rousseau. Unlike most other great thinkers, Rousseau presented his own life as the embodiment or dramatization of the most comprehensive human experiences and dilemmas. It is Rousseau's ability to present these experiences vividly that made him so powerful an influence on his contemporaries and succeeding generations.

Nietzsche, who was no champion of Rousseau, describes this influence. He compares "the man of Rousseau" with other images of human life. The Rousseauian image "possesses the greatest fire and is sure of producing the greatest popular effect." "From [it] has proceeded a force which has promoted violent revolutions and continues to do so; for in every socialist earthquake and upheaval it has always been the man of Rousseau who, like Typhon under Etna, is the cause of the commotion. Oppressed and half crushed by arrogant upper classes and merciless wealth, ruined by priests and bad education and rendered contemptible to himself by ludicrous custom, man cries in his distress to 'holy nature' and suddenly feels that it is as distant from him as any Epicurean god."[2] Nietzsche's picture is characteristically bold and sweeping in its portrayal of the power of an image to transform the world. It gives an indication of the fascination with which Rousseau was regarded by some of the great-

---

2. Friedrich Nietzsche, *Schopenhauer as Educator*, in *Untimely Meditations*, trans. R. J. Hollingdale (Cambridge: Cambridge University Press, 1983), p. 151.

est novelists and poets of the century after him, including Shelley, Stendhal, Schiller, Goethe, Hölderlin, and Tolstoy. Rousseau's ability to present complex and profound human problems as concrete images is the source of this fascination. Because the *Confessions* presents his understanding of human life in the most concrete form, it is one of the works most responsible for Rousseau's effect on the world.

There is another dimension to Rousseau's influence. He affected others by the force of his arguments as well as by skillful use of popular genres. He wished to combine, and to a large degree succeeded in combining, an appeal to the minds of a few great thinkers with an appeal to the hearts of a large popular audience. His books were the only ones capable of forcing Kant out of his daily routine and compelling him to suspend his critical thought for a week at a time.[3] Rousseau combined poetry and philosophy, deep emotion and reflective thought. His images strike and challenge the reader from their first appearance and richly reward further reflection. The second reason, then, for considering the *Confessions* in relation to Rousseau's more systematic thought is to understand the thought itself.

Rousseau himself indicates that the *Confessions* should be read this way. In addition to his many statements about the personal significance of the work, he claims that it has a more general importance. He says that it "will always be a precious book for philosophers" (I, 1154). Rousseau obviously did not make the strict distinction between personal and theoretical writings that most readers are likely to make. In fact, he considered the *Confessions* to be as important philosophically as *Emile*, the *Discourses*, and the *Social Contract*. Thus the *Confessions* demands a reading that considers its own teaching in relation to Rousseau's teachings in the other works. In my approach I argue for this coherence in Rousseau's works. Such an interpretation should not detract from the usual pleasures of reading the *Confessions*, but if it succeeds it will add new and less common pleasures.

One of the pleasing aspects of writing a book is the opportunity its publication gives for thanking those who have assisted in its genesis.

My work on the *Confessions* began with my dissertation for the degree of Doctor of Philosophy at the University of Toronto. The National Endowment for the Humanities provided material support for

---

3. On the influence of Rousseau on Kant, see Ernst Cassirer, *Rousseau, Kant, and Goethe* (Princeton: Princeton University Press, 1945).

the present book in the form of a fellowship. The Newberry Library of Chicago very graciously opened its facilities to me during the fall of 1984 and provided an excellent setting for concentrated work. I also thank Cornell University Press and its readers for their editorial assistance and useful comments on the manuscript.

I have had the extreme good fortune of finding friends and teachers at all stages of my education who were able to teach me much about Rousseau in particular and about the qualities of serious scholarship in general. Joel Schwartz has been an excellent source of advice and information during a long and continuing dialogue about Rousseau and other matters. Among my teachers, Walter Berns, Clifford Orwin, and Thomas Pangle contributed greatly to my ability to write this book. I am among the many students who owe a special debt to Allan Bloom, who supervised the early stages of my work on Rousseau and taught me about the proper mixture of lightness and gravity necessary for the study of the most important questions.

My wife, Jeanne Christensen Kelly, has made many contributions to this book. She has been an unflagging source of support at all stages of its composition. Her constant insistence that I clarify my thoughts and their expression has improved every section. From her I have learned that *inter virum autem et uxorem maxima amicitia esse videtur*. I dedicate this book to her.

CHRISTOPHER KELLY

Baltimore, Maryland

Primary Source Citations

References to works of Rousseau appear in the text in parentheses immediately after the citations. Translations from the French editions are my own. The references use the following abbreviations.

I, 1–000   *Oeuvres complètes.* Paris: Gallimard, Bibliothèque de la Pléiade, 1959–69; references are cited by volume and page numbers. Occasional references to the Geneva edition (1782–89), 33 volumes, are cited as such.

d'Alembert   *Letter to M. d'Alembert on the Theatre.* Trans. Allan Bloom. In *Politics and the Arts.* Ithaca, N.Y.: Cornell University Press, Agora Editions, 1968.

Discourses   *The First and Second Discourses.* Trans. Roger D. Masters and Judith R. Masters. New York: St. Martin's Press, 1964.

D.M.   *Dictionnaire de musique.* New York: Johnson Reprint Corporation, 1969.

Emile   *Emile, or On Education.* Trans. Allan Bloom. New York: Basic Books, 1979.

J.J.   *Jean-Jacques entre Socrate et Caton.* Ed. Claude Pichois and René Pintard. Paris: José Corti, 1972.

S.C.   *On the Social Contract, with Geneva Manuscript and Political Economy.* Trans. Judith R. Masters. Ed. Roger D. Masters. New York: St. Martin's Press, 1978.

Rousseau's Exemplary Life

[1]

Political Philosophy and the Genre of Lives

The Problem of Autobiography

The contemporary scholarly habit of looking into the personal lives of philosophers to gain insight into their thought would seem to justify the study of philosophers' autobiographies as a means to explain their other works.[1] This practice seems especially appropriate in the case of Rousseau, whose works are thought to be so closely linked to his personality. Even the *Social Contract*, which Rousseau deliberately made his most abstract work,[2] begins with the frequent repetition of the first person singular.[3] Because Rousseau himself found it appropriate to present his thought in very personal terms, it seems to violate the spirit

---

1. Works on Rousseau that present his thought in terms of his personality include the following: Marshall Berman, *The Politics of Authenticity* (New York: Atheneum, 1970); Pierre Burgelin, *La Philosophie de l'existence de J.-J. Rousseau* (Paris: Librairie Philosophique J. Vrin, 1973); Bernard Groethuysen, *J. J. Rousseau* (Paris: Editions Gallimard, 1949); Jakob Herman Huizinga, *Rousseau: The Self-Made Saint* (New York: Grossman, 1976); Marcel Raymond, *Jean-Jacques Rousseau: La Quête de soi et la rêverie* (Paris: José Corti, 1962); Judith N. Shklar, *Men and Citizens: A Study of Rousseau's Social Theory* (Cambridge: Cambridge University Press, 1969). This list, which could easily be extended, shows how widespread this view of Rousseau is across generations, oceans, and academic disciplines.

2. Rousseau says that Geneva was the intended audience for his *Political Institutions*, the larger work of which the *Social Contract* was to be a part. He claims that he deliberately wrote the work in an "indirect manner" in order to "spare the amour-propre" of his fellow citizens (I, 405).

3. The first two paragraphs of Book I of the *Social Contract* each begin with the first person singular. I am indebted to Victor Gourevitch for pointing out Rousseau's ubiquitous use of the first person.

of his works to approach them without reference to his personality. Thus Rousseau, perhaps more clearly than any other thinker, illustrates Nietzsche's claim that philosophy is nothing but "the personal confession of its author and a kind of involuntary and unconscious memoir."[4]

Nevertheless, some thoughtful scholars have attempted to impose caution on hasty efforts to reduce Rousseau's thought to his life. Several important interpreters of Rousseau's political thought have given powerful arguments against such a reduction. Ernst Cassirer stated this position most directly: "There are familiar writings in the Rousseau literature which give us in place of the work almost the man alone, and which describe him only in his dissensions and divisions, in his inner contradiction. The history of ideas threatens here to disappear into biography and this in turn appears as pure case history."[5] Cassirer's characterization of this sort of Rousseau scholarship does not exaggerate. It is almost as startling to note the number of psychological and physiological case studies of Rousseau as it is to see the variety of conclusions drawn in these studies.[6] Such studies tend to rely on the *Confessions* for interpreting all of Rousseau's works. Resisting this trend, Cassirer and others have attempted to force a serious consideration of Rousseau's arguments on their own merits.[7]

These attempts to focus on Rousseau's thought have directly or indirectly turned attention away from the *Confessions*. Cassirer's statement does not deny, rather it concedes, the existence of Rousseau's internal dissensions, divisions, and contradictions. Therefore his effort to attend to Rousseau's thought leads to a separation between the autobiographical works in which these internal divisions are manifested and the more obviously theoretical works in which they are muted if not absent. This separation has had the merit of making possible a number of studies of Rousseau's consistency and importance as a thinker, but it has done so only by ignoring a large portion of his work.[8]

4. Friedrich Nietzsche, *Beyond Good and Evil*, in *Basic Writings of Nietzsche*, trans. and ed. Walter Kaufmann (New York: Modern Library, 1968), p. 203.

5. Cassirer, *Rousseau, Kant, and Goethe*, p. 58.

6. For a review of this literature, see Starobinski, *Transparence*, pp. 430–44.

7. For an argument similar to Cassirer's which explicitly claims that the *Confessions* is unnecessary for understanding Rousseau's thought, see Roger D. Masters, *The Political Philosophy of Rousseau* (Princeton, N.J.: Princeton University Press, 1968), pp. vii–x.

8. Noteworthy among the works that approach Rousseau's thought without reference to his personality is Victor Goldschmidt, *Anthropologie et politique: Les Principes du système de Rousseau* (Paris: Librairie Philosophique J. Vrin, 1974).

Cassirer's position has a powerful traditional basis. In fact, autobiographies were sufficiently rare when Rousseau wrote the *Confessions* that there was no need for a specific term to describe this genre. The term "autobiography" entered the European languages around 1800 and gained popular currency only with the post-Rousseau onslaught of works inspired by the *Confessions*. Even the term "biography" began to be used only a generation before Rousseau's birth.[9] Although works belonging to these genres existed even in classical antiquity, famous autobiographical works such as Julius Caesar's *Commentaries* and Xenophon's *Anabasis* concealed their autobiographical character by the use of third-person narrative. Xenophon went so far as to attribute the *Anabasis* to a certain Themistogenes of Syracuse rather than to himself.[10] In these cases, autobiography was masked as biography.[11] This is not to suggest that classical biography was accorded a particularly high status. Both it and autobiography share with all forms of historical narrative a focus on particular events—what someone did or suffered—rather than on what that person might or should have done.[12] Thus they are subject to Aristotle's well-known argument against the significance of history. He argues that "poetry is both more philosophic and more serious than history. For poetry speaks more of universals but history of particulars."[13] Thus historical works, including lives, lack seriousness because they necessarily partake of the accidental aspects of particular events. The authority of Aristotle and the force of his argument partly explain the scarcity of autobiographies by philosophers before Rousseau, for from the standpoint of philosophy the focus on any particular, especially oneself, is not the most serious enterprise. This well-established position supports Cassirer's effort to separate the less serious, personal dimension from the more serious, philosophic dimension of Rousseau's work. Rousseau himself could not fail to be aware of the traditional low ranking of the genre of the *Confessions*.

9. Information on the history of the word "autobiography" is found in James Olney, "Autobiography and the Cultural Moment: A Thematic, Historical, and Bibliographical Introduction," in *Autobiography: Essays Theoretical and Critical*, ed. James Olney (Princeton, N.J.: Princeton University Press, 1980).

10. See Xenophon, *Hellenica*, III.1.2. On the importance of Xenophon as an autobiographer, see Arnoldo Momigliano, *The Development of Greek Biography* (Cambridge, Mass.: Harvard University Press, 1971), pp. 47–59.

11. For Rousseau's judgment on the significance of specifically Christian biography and autobiography, see Chapter 2.

12. For this characterization of history, see Aristotle, *Poetics*, chap. 9.

13. Ibid., chap. 9.

The reactions of the earliest readers of the *Confessions* show their acceptance of both the Aristotelian depreciation of history and the low status of autobiography even among historical works. Today some college freshmen are titillated and, in some instances, mildly scandalized by details of Rousseau's revelations. Some are surprised by what Rousseau says about himself, yet they take for granted the desire to talk about oneself if one can find an audience to listen. In general, however, Rousseau's early readers were as shocked by the very fact that Rousseau wrote about himself. In particular, they were disappointed by his emphasis on his youthful, prephilosophic life.[14]

These observations present us with a question that might otherwise be obscured by Cassirer's separation of the philosophic from the personal in Rousseau. The fact is that Rousseau did choose to write an autobiography. The significance of this decision and its relation to his thought needs to be explained; it cannot be ignored. On the whole, students of political thought and philosophy have left the investigation of this question to students of literature.

Contemporary students of the literary genre of autobiography use some arguments that resemble Aristotle's attack on history and others that are in some respects more radical. For example, Roy Pascal adapts Aristotle's argument to claim that autobiography is completely unsuited for presenting a generalizable theoretical teaching: it "is in fact not at all a suitable vehicle for the exposition of a doctrine, for by its very form we are led to appreciate the ideas and insights expounded in it . . . not in their objective truth, but as true for this particular man, as true of him."[15] This argument implies that Rousseau's very success at stimulating interest in personal experience prohibits any claim of philosophic significance for his work. Pascal begins by agreeing with Aristotle that a work concerned with historical particulars cannot convey a general teaching. He concludes, however, by substituting a notion of personal truth for the factual truth that Aristotle had argued was the characteristic of historical works. According to Pascal the thoughts and incidents

14. Part One of the *Confessions* was first published in 1782, Part Two in 1789. For an account of its initial reception in France, see Bernard Gagnebin, "L'Etrange Accueil fait aux *Confessions* de Rousseau au XVIIIe siècle," *Annales de la Société Jean-Jacques Rousseau* 38 (1969–71): 105–26. For corresponding accounts involving Germany and England, see Jacques Mounier, "La Reception des *Confessions* en Allemagne de 1782 à 1813," *Ouvres et Critiques* 3,1 (1978): 101–13, and Edward Duffy, *Rousseau in England* (Berkeley: University of California Press, 1979).

15. Roy Pascal, *Design and Truth in Autobiography* (Cambridge, Mass.: Harvard University Press, 1960), p. 182.

revealed in the *Confessions* are not factual truths or falsehoods; rather, they are expressions of Rousseau's personality. They are true of, or for, Rousseau rather than being simply true or false. Even falsehoods are true indications of some aspect of his personality. From this standpoint Rousseau appears as a pioneering autobiographer who, in large part unwittingly, began a genre that others have perfected.

Pascal uses his notion of personal truth to criticize Rousseau for naiveté. He finds Rousseau to be overconfident of his ability to understand himself.[16] William Howarth, a recent critic of Pascal's book, adds weight to this charge by accusing Pascal of exaggerating "the extent to which autobiographical poets actually *understand* their meaning and form." Thus, if Pascal, who is said to be too generous in his assessments of the lucidity of autobiographers, finds Rousseau naive, it is not surprising that Howarth finds that Rousseau "stumbles into frantic delusion."[17] Howarth attacks Pascal's notion that a self-conscious revelation of a purely personal truth is possible for anyone. According to Howarth's position, it is not Rousseau's failure to express "personal truth" adequately that is to be blamed, but his attempt to do so.

Some recent examples of autobiographical theory and practice illustrate the significance of this position. What an autobiography seems to promise to do, by its very name, is to present the author's own life in writing.[18] The claim that it is not possible to express a self-conscious personal truth implies that this promise is a delusion. Autobiographies based on this promise must invariably deceive either the author or the reader or both. One scholar who attempts to demonstrate the deceptiveness of this promise is Georges May, who suggests several factors that unavoidably distort autobiography. Some of these, such as forgetfulness or shame, are surmountable in principle if not in practice.[19] Another, the necessity for an a posteriori reconstruction of causality, is simply unavoidable if the written work is to be coherent. According to May, autobiographers are doomed to say too little because of their forgetfulness or shame and doomed to say too much because of their

16. Ibid., pp. 70, 184.

17. William L. Howarth, "Some Principles of Autobiography," in *Autobiography*, ed. James Olney, pp. 112–13; emphasis in original.

18. Although Rousseau does not make this implicit claim by using the term "autobiography," he makes the same claim more explicitly by referring to the work as his "life" (I, 1149).

19. Georges May, *L'Autobiographie* (Paris: Presses Universitaires de France, 1979), p. 77. See also Germaine Brée, "Michel Leiris: Marginale," in *Autobiography*, ed. James Olney.

desire to interpret their past. Thus the most they can do, as James Olney puts it, is to "re-create the past in the image of the present."[20] Pascal may wish to call such a re-creation the personal truth, but it would be more accurate to call it fiction.

These modern denials of the possibility of a truthful autobiography assume an unbridgeable gap between the writer, who lives in the present, and his life, which has been lived in the past. In other words, autobiography is always today's version of yesterday; it is not yesterday itself. A further complication appears with the distinction between the writer and what is written. There is a gulf between author and text just as there is between text and the past to which it refers. Each part of the term "autobiography" (the author, the life, and the written work) reveals its own problem in relation to the other parts of the term. One response to these problems is to look behind the autobiographical text to the author who lived the life. Some critics and biographers look at letters and diaries, psychoanalyzing to find the truth the author concealed or was unable to admit. In the case of Rousseau, such critics evaluate the truth of the *Confessions* against a standard arrived at independently of the *Confessions*. They are content to leave a rigorous investigation of his thought to people like Cassirer, but both parties end by slighting the *Confessions*.

Other contemporary critics who have paid attention to the *Confessions* attack any reliance on information from outside of that work itself. They argue that, far from resolving the problem of distortion in autobiography, such approaches merely compound it by adding the critic's distorting interpretation to that of the author. Rather than propose an alternative strategy for arriving at the truth of an autobiography, these more radical critics insist that the problem is insoluble and that, as stated, it is misconceived. In Rousseau scholarship this radical trend is best represented by the work of Jacques Derrida.

Derrida calls into question the presumed gap between the autobiographical text and the real life of the author. He does not argue that a gap exists but is nonetheless bridgeable; rather, concerning the division between life and text, author and book, signifier and signified, Derrida declares, *"There is nothing outside of the text."*[21] This does not mean that there was never a person named Jean-Jacques Rousseau,

20. James Olney, "Some Versions of Memory/Some Versions of *Bios*," in *Autobiography*, ed. James Olney, p. 254.

21. Jacques Derrida, *Of Grammatology*, trans. Gayatri Chakravorty Spivak (Baltimore, Md.: Johns Hopkins University Press, 1976), p. 158 (emphasis in original).

born in Geneva in 1712, who wrote a book called the *Confessions*. Instead, Derrida's statement implies that an appeal to the so-called real life of Rousseau is an appeal to an interpretation or a linguistically constituted description or text, and not to something that can accurately be called the real Jean-Jacques. Such an interpretation or description, which the critic calls Rousseau's life and uses as the standard to judge the text of the *Confessions*, is itself merely another text with no legitimate status as a standard. As Derrida says, reading "cannot legitimately transgress the text toward something other than it, toward a referent (or reality that is metaphysical, historical, psychobiographical, etc.) or toward a signified outside the text whose content could take place, could have taken place outside of language."[22] Derrida's argument eliminates the possibility of judging an autobiography by reference to the real person who wrote it. According to this view, Rousseau's *Confessions* is not about either the real Rousseau or human nature. Derrida's position also eliminates the possibility of judging a philosophic book by reference to the world it purports to be about, the "metaphysical reality," in Derrida's terms. The consequences of Derrida's argument must be extended beyond autobiographical texts to the philosophic texts read by political scientists and philosophers: the works read by Cassirer refer to something outside themselves no more than the *Confessions* does.

While this line of reasoning removes the gap between author and text that is said by May to make an accurate autobiography impossible, it does not restore the possibility of a truthful autobiography. On the contrary, it makes the autobiographical project, as it is normally understood, pointless.[23] In this respect Derrida does not disagree with, he merely carries to its conclusion, what other modern critics have said about Rousseau. Following Derrida's argument strictly leads one to the conclusion that the categories "autobiographical," "philosophic," and "historical" are meaningless, because they imply the existence of objects outside the text by which it can be clarified and judged.[24] Following his

22. Ibid., p. 158. No attempt is made here to discuss the general significance of Derrida's position. It should be noted, however, that Derrida does not argue merely that Jean-Jacques and the other characters of the *Confessions* are not available to us. The radicalness of Derrida's claim can be seen in his statement that "in what one calls the real life of their existence 'of flesh and bone' . . . there has never been anything but writing" (ibid., p. 159).

23. For another account of the relation between an autobiographical writer and his readers, see Philippe Lejeune, *Le Pacte autobiographique* (Paris: Editions du Seuil, 1975).

24. A useful summary of the understanding of a text which serves as the point of

argument less rigorously leads one to the judgment that Rousseau did not know what he was doing when he wrote the *Confessions*. He was even more naive than Pascal thought and more deluded than Howarth claimed. Whereas Derrida's argument implies that it is meaningless to talk about an author's naiveté or delusion, Derrida himself finds it hard to avoid such judgments about Rousseau. His own reading of Rousseau's works is filled with references to Rousseau's lack of consciousness about what he was really saying.[25] Neither the strict nor the loose reading of Derrida offers any support for a reading of the *Confessions* that helps to shed light on Rousseau's thought. Still, Derrida's approach does accord a sort of unity to Rousseau's works by denying the validity of the criteria used to separate them into different categories. In other words, this approach asserts that none of the works has either a personal or a philosophic significance as these terms are normally understood.

In sum, for various reasons, modern critics have implicitly rejected any claim that the *Confessions* is a philosophic book. First, they argue that, because autobiography is so personal a genre, it cannot present universal truths. Second, they argue that autobiography cannot adequately present even personal truths without distortion. Finally, some say that, because Rousseau is unable to recognize either one or both of these points, he is naive, deluded, or blind in his understanding of his own enterprise. Students of politics, philosophy, and literature may disagree about why the *Confessions* is not a philosophic book, but they all agree that it gives little aid to the understanding of Rousseau's thought.

Confession and Rousseau's Autobiographical Project

Rousseau's own characterization of the *Confessions* resembles Derrida's in that it insists on the unity of his works. It is the reverse of Derrida's in its insistence that all of his works, including the *Confessions*, have philosophic significance. Rousseau by no means makes this claim blindly. It would be a mistake to think that he was unaware of the considerations that have led modern critics to question the possibility of autobiography. His complicated use of a variety of narrative devices,

---

departure for Derrida's position can be found in Roland Barthes's essay "From Work to Text," in *Textual Strategies: Perspectives in Post-Structuralist Criticism*, ed. Josué V. Harari (Ithaca, N.Y.: Cornell University Press, 1979).

25. See, for example, Derrida, *Grammatology*, pp. 201, 215, 242, 243, 246, 268, 302.

such as the splitting of himself into character and narrator or person and author in the *Confessions* and its sequels, indicates his awareness of the problematic relation between an author and his narrative. His awareness of the impossibility of a simple representation of himself in an autobiography can be traced to one of his earliest compositions, a riddle whose key is "portrait":[26]

> Child of Art, Child of Nature
> Without prolonging one's days I prevent one from dying
> The more true I am the greater the imposture I make
> And I become too young by virtue of growing old.
>
> (II, 1133)

Long before he wrote the *Confessions*, Rousseau was aware that a portrait of any sort could have at best the most fleeting accuracy and could resemble its subject only by a sort of deception. His awareness of the necessary incompleteness of an autobiographical portrait is emphasized by his decision to end the narrative of the *Confessions* before it reached the period during which he wrote the book.

The issue between Rousseau and Derrida, then, is not over the possibility of presenting factual truth in an autobiography. Rousseau does, however, disagree about the possibility of broader purposes, such as presenting general philosophic truth in both the *Confessions* and his other works. A first indication of the general issues addressed by the *Confessions* is the title itself. Although Rousseau says very little about the selection of this title, he does give a few indirect indications of its importance. That this choice was not unreflective is indicated by an earlier collection of autobiographical fragments, which he called "My Portrait" (I, 1120–29). His decision to adopt a different title for the *Confessions* indicates at least some reflection on the proper title for the work. At the very least, the final title avoids the dilemma of a portrait in Rousseau's riddle on this word.

Rousseau shows us more of the significance of his title choice by saying what his book is not meant to be. In Book VII he says, "I have no

26. For discussions of this riddle, see Juliet Flower MacCannell, "History and Self-Portrait in Rousseau's Autobiography," *Studies in Romanticism* 13 (1974): 279–98, and Ann Hartle, *The Modern Self in Rousseau's Confessions: A Reply to St. Augustine* (Notre Dame, Ind.: University of Notre Dame Press, 1983), pp. 37, 133. In her argument that the *Confessions* is a portrait, Hartle relies on an analogy with painting and therefore denies the importance of the temporal movement in the book. Rousseau asserts that music can paint pictures through time. The same is true of words. The "portrait" in the *Confessions* is more like a piece of music that must be followed across time than like a painting.

fear that the reader ever forgets that I am making my confession and as a result believes that I am making my apology" (I, 279). In Book VIII he reminds the reader, "I have promised my confessions not my justification" (I, 359). In both cases he insists that he is defending neither his behavior nor himself. His sole interest is in telling the truth. His use of the word "apology" in the first passage is a faint reminder of Socrates' defense at his trial. Rousseau's insistence that he is not making an apology is at least a slight indication of a desire to distance himself from Socrates. Some of the reasons for this distancing are considered in the next chapter.

Rousseau's title is an obvious reference to Augustine's work of the same title.[27] In a piece written to introduce his readings from the *Confessions*, Rousseau shows the religious or sacramental character of his title by saying that he has written his confessions "in all the rigor of the term." He goes on to remind his auditors that by listening they have charged themselves "with the function of confessor" (I, 1165–66). This introduction prepares his listeners for a work written in a tradition that can be traced back at least to Augustine. One should not, however, assume too quickly that a common title betokens a common purpose.

Augustine indicates two interrelated aspects of confessions in his work. First, he writes addressing God directly and asking pardon for his sins. Near the beginning of the book he implores, "Lord cleanse me from my secret faults and spare thy servant from the power of the enemy."[28] Second, as the work proceeds he makes it clear that confession entails more than the revelation of one's sins; it also requires recognition of God's greatness. Accordingly, he says, "The lowliness of my tongue confesseth unto *Thy Highness that Thou madest heaven and earth*."[29] These two aspects are reflected in the structure of Augustine's work as he moves from the discussion of his sins in the first part to a general discussion of God's creation of the world in the concluding books. His self-revelation takes place only for the sake of the acknowledgment of God.[30] In short, the personal aspect of confession is for the sake of a more general, or higher, purpose.

The difference between Rousseau and Augustine begins to be re-

27. Jean Guéhenno argues that Rousseau draws an advantage from leaving this comparison implicit. See *Rousseau*, vol. II, p. 141.

28. Augustine, *Confessions*, I.v.

29. Ibid., X.ii.

30. For an explanation of the significance of confession for Augustine, see Peter Brown, *Augustine of Hippo* (London: Faber & Faber, 1967), p. 175.

vealed even when Rousseau most closely approximates Augustine's formulations. For example, while Rousseau does not address God directly, he discusses circumstances in which he would do so: "Let the trumpet of the last judgment sound when it wishes, I will come to present myself before the sovereign judge with this book in my hand. I will say loudly: here is what I have done, what I have thought, what I have been" (I, 5). This passage does imply some religious intent quite directly, but it does not contain the least trace of repentance or hope for divine pardon. Rousseau makes a single request of God: "Eternal Being assemble around me the numberless crowd of my fellows." Unlike Augustine, he makes the human race and not God the direct audience for his confessions.[31]

This preliminary indifference to divine forgiveness is maintained throughout Rousseau's work, and it leads to a departure from Augustine's second purpose—pointing beyond oneself to God. Rousseau's work contains three specific confessions (*aveux*), one in each of the first three books, and one *confession* in Book VII. There are numerous passages concerning misdeeds or errors that he does not designate as confessions, including his insincere conversion to Catholicism and his abandonment of his children.[32] The first *aveu* concerns something "ridiculous and shameful" (I, 18), but Rousseau expresses no repentance for it. What his confessions have in common is a revelation not of wrongdoing, but of something that has been private or hidden. This characteristic is made clear in the midst of his final confession, when Rousseau declares, "Whoever you may be who wishes to know a man, dare to read the two or three pages that follow, you will know J. J. Rousseau to the full" (I, 320). It is this knowledge that is the object of his book. Rousseau's epigraph is "*Intus et in cute*" (inside and under the skin). By living up to this motto, by revealing his inner character, Rousseau may have a more general purpose in mind, but this purpose does not entail either asking for forgiveness or glorifying God. In choosing the same title as Augustine, Rousseau calls attention to his departures from his predecessor rather than to his agreements. We see the political significance of these departures in Chapter 2.

The assertion of a self-revelation unconnected with an Augustinian revelation of God is a large part of the importance of the *Confessions*.

31. For a useful comparison of Rousseau's and Augustine's appeals to God, see Starobinski, *La Relation critique* (Paris: Gallimard, 1970), pp. 90–91.

32. Rousseau seems to use *confession* and *aveu* as equivalents. For a discussion of confession in Rousseau, see Lejeune, *Pacte*, p. 54.

Rousseau was well aware of the reaction such a personal work would receive from most readers. He wrote in conscious opposition to the view that autobiography lacks seriousness. The *Confessions* is an attempt to establish that self-absorption and self-expression are in fact serious activities. Rousseau is, as Jean Starobinski has said, the great proponent of the modern "myth of an individual experience so rich that it can replace all other possessions."[33] In other words, behind Rousseau's autobiographical enterprise stands the view that personal and individual experience can be at least as serious as the public deeds recorded by historians and biographers or the thoughts of philosophers.

The constant popularity of the *Confessions* is an indication of Rousseau's success at persuading others to accept this new emphasis on internal life.[34] Sales of the book continue to benefit from the taste for autobiographical literature it helped to create. We are so consumed by an autobiographical if not confessional urge that we take it for granted. Not only is the genre well established, its limits continue to expand.[35] The change from antiquity is manifested most clearly in the modern practice of claiming autobiographical status for works that are in fact biographies. Today Xenophon would be encouraged not only to come out of the shadow of Themistogenes, but also to rename the *Memorabilia* "The Autobiography of Socrates," with the addition in small print of "as told to Xenophon." In large measure, to understand the *Confessions* is to understand the reasons that led Rousseau to attempt to bring about this reorientation.

The most direct testimony about the philosophic significance of the *Confessions* can be found inside the book. Throughout the work Rousseau claims that although (and because) the *Confessions* focuses on his unique personality, it also serves as the basis of "the study of men, which certainly is yet to begin" (I, 3). In the Neuchâtel preface[36] he claims that the *Confessions* will always be "a precious book for philoso-

---

33. Jean Starobinski, "The Accuser and the Accused," *Daedalus* 107,3 (1978): 56.

34. See May, *L'Autobiographie*, p. 92.

35. From an extensive survey of autobiographies May found that such works are almost always written by people over forty who were previously known to the public (ibid., p. 25). The first of these findings has been shattered by the now ubiquitous autobiographies of rock stars, actors, and athletes. Perhaps the second will also be demolished as more and more people seek to become famous by exposing the details of their lives.

36. This preface accompanies one of the two manuscripts of the *Confessions*. Rousseau says that he wrote it in 1764, near the beginning of his work on the *Confessions*. For an account of the manuscripts, see Hermine de Saussure, *Rousseau et les manuscrits des Confessions* (Paris: Editions E. de Boccard, 1958).

phers" and that it will force its reader "to make a further step in the knowledge of men" (I, 1154, 1149). These startling claims force the reader to wonder what sort of book Rousseau thinks he is writing and what its relation is to his more obviously theoretical works. Most puzzling of all is the implicit claim that even the earlier *Emile* and *Second Discourse* did not begin the study of men. For Rousseau to justify his claim that the *Confessions* will always be "a precious book for philosophers," he must explain what sort of book it is, how his autobiography is a possible enterprise, and how an autobiography can be philosophic. He must provide these explanations in the face of formidable attacks from the different perspectives of classical antiquity and recent modernity.

To see how Rousseau attempts this project is to see a pivotal point in the modern understanding of what is most important about human life and hence of what makes a good life. To shed light on this project must be the goal of a serious study of the *Confessions*. As we see shortly, Rousseau shows two lines of interpretation for the *Confessions*. Read in one way, the *Confessions* is primarily concerned with a practical and moral purpose. In following this goal, Rousseau may be willing to compromise both the particular and general truthfulness of the work for the sake of its effectiveness. Read in another way, it is a presentation of general truth in an uncommonly perceptible form. Considered in this way, the autobiography is concerned with both effectiveness and general truth. In following this goal, Rousseau is less willing to compromise the general truth of the work. These two goals and ways of reading combine to raise Rousseau's autobiography beyond the level of a purely personal work.[37]

Autobiography as Moral Fable

Rousseau's claim to have written a book of interest to philosophers runs counter to the Aristotelian argument that historical works lack seriousness. Aristotle's argument apparently relegates the *Confessions* to the area of factual truth. But even a modest claim of factual truth is

---

37. Jean Starobinski suggests a division of Rousseau's works into three groups following a roughly chronological order; one identifies the evils of civilized society, a second defines the principles that allow this identification to be made, and the third answers accusations. See Starobinski, "Accuser," p. 42. My interpretation of the *Confessions* would redefine the third group as the account of how someone can gain access to the principles that allow corruption to be seen.

denied by the modern arguments for the inaccessibility of factual truth to an autobiographer. The easiest line of defense against these assaults is to admit that the *Confessions* is not primarily concerned with truth. Although such an admission seems to deny Rousseau's many assertions about his truthfulness, these assertions are more ambiguous than they appear at first glance. Moreover, to deny that the *Confessions* possesses one sort of truth may support its claim to possess another. In order to assess Rousseau's claims of truth for the *Confessions*, it is necessary to see how he understands the relations among philosophic, factual, and other possible sorts of truth.

Rousseau shows that he was well aware of the Aristotelian assessment of the narration of particular facts as unphilosophic. He also anticipates many of the points raised by modern analysts of autobiography. For example, in *Emile* Rousseau uses an implicit comparison with physics to illustrate the defects of history. History is the study of either facts or their causes and effects, just as physics is (*Emile*, 110). It cannot, however, attain the accuracy of physics. First, by "facts" Rousseau means "exterior and purely physical movements." Historical reports of physical movements "are far from being an exact portrayal of the same facts as they happened" (*Emile*, 238). Historians cannot have access to the complete array of events about which they write. Second, the causes and effects of historical facts are less external and physical than they are interior and mental. The physical motions of humans appear random and accidental when unaccompanied by an explanation of motives.

Historians can only speculate about these interior causes and effects. They are forced to construct hypothetical principles of cause and effect, what May calls a posteriori reconstructions of causality. May claims that an autobiographer's reconstruction of causality is likely to bear little resemblance to the real, unknown causes of events, and this is precisely what Rousseau argues with respect to historians. He observes that when historians turn from particular facts to general relations and causes, they almost always become bad historians. Most historians, modern systematic historians in particular, do not understand natural relations of cause and effect (*Emile*, 240). As a result, they produce accounts of events the source of which is in their own imagination. They are like, but perhaps inferior to, bad novelists (*Emile*, 238–39).

Taken in one direction, Rousseau's argument can lead to the conclusion that simple historical narration of facts is impossible. Taken in another direction, his insistence that bad historians are similar to bad novelists opens the possibility that a few good historians are similar to good novelists. Great historians, or autobiographers, could be great novelists. Their sort of history, including autobiography, would ascend to the Aristotelian category of poetry, which narrates what might have happened rather than what did happen. Consequently, like poetry this sort of history would be more serious and philosophic than purely factual history is. Thus the very thing that makes purely factual accounts impossible drives historians toward poetry and philosophy. To provide coherent and complete accounts, they must understand general relations of cause and effect in human affairs.[38]

This sort of poetic history is not merely a hypothetical possibility. In *Emile*, Rousseau refers to Herodotus as the historian who strays farthest from facts in order to serve more important purposes. After discussing Herodotus in particular, Rousseau generalizes his observation:

> The ancient historians are filled with views which one could use even if the facts which present them were false. But we do not know how to get any true advantage from history. Critical erudition absorbs everything, as if it were very important whether a fact is true, provided that a useful teaching can be drawn from it. Sensible men ought to regard history as a tissue of fables whose moral is very appropriate to the human heart.
> (*Emile*, 156)

Thus, according to Rousseau, history can avoid its unphilosophic tendency by abandoning an excessive concern with the accuracy of facts. The description of the value of this sort of history makes it seem appropriate to call any worthwhile history a tissue of fables rather than a factual narrative.[39] According to this argument, no distinction whatsoever can be drawn between good history and good poetry.

Rousseau can defend Herodotus, just as Roy Pascal defends autobiography, only by changing the standard for judging history. As we saw above, Pascal replaces factual truth with the new standard of personal truth. In so doing, he turns from a standard involving "the fact," which is in principle equally accessible to everyone, to one involving "the personal interpretation of a fact," which is directly accessible only to the author. His standard moves from what is simply true to what is true for someone. Rousseau does not suggest anything this personal with his new standard of judgment. He does not refer to Herodotus's

---

38. Thucydides' complex treatment of the causes of the war shows his deep awareness of a similar issue.

39. It has been argued that Thucydides criticizes Herodotus on similar grounds; see Seth Benardete, *Herodotean Inquiries* (The Hague: Martinus Nijhoff, 1969), p. 30.

history as being true of, or for, Herodotus. Instead, he appeals to a universal standard of moral usefulness. This standard is both general and in principle accessible to everyone. It is not immediately clear, however, how it relates to truth.

Rousseau explores the relation of moral utility to both factual truth and philosophic truth in the Fourth Walk of the *Reveries*. His general discussion of the theme begins with a distinction between "general and abstract truth," on the one hand, and "particular and individual truth," on the other.[40] Rousseau claims that the general truth takes precedence and is indeed "the most precious of all goods" (I, 1026). Factual truth, however, is so unimportant that offenses against it need not be considered lies if the matter involved either is useless or has no effect on anyone's interest. Such violations of the truth are not lies, they are fictions. Lies are harmful, fictions are not. The implication is that fiction and lying are more fundamentally opposed than are fiction and truth. Here, as in the discussion of Herodotus, moral utility rather than factual truth is the standard for judging falsehood.

After having discussed these harmless or morally indifferent fictions, Rousseau argues that some fictions can even be morally useful. Such useful fictions, called allegories or fables, make up the category to which Herodotus's history belongs. Far from being lies, these fictions "wrap useful truths in sensible and agreeable forms" (I, 1029). Having already distinguished fictions from lies, Rousseau here links a particular kind of fiction with truth: wrapping the truth makes it more easily "felt." According to this picture, some truths are virtually invisible and hence useless; they must be clothed to be felt.

Rousseau gives an indication of the nature of these useful, or potentially useful, truths when he discusses his own use of fables. In telling fictions, he does not lie; rather, he attempts "to substitute for the truth of facts, at least a moral truth, that is to say, to represent well the affections natural to the human heart and always to make some useful instruction come from them, to make of them, in a word, moral tales or allegories" (I, 1033). Thus an example of the sort of truth that requires wrapping to be felt is a description of "the affections natural to the human heart." These affections are the themes of *Emile*, the *Second Discourse*, and the *Confessions*, although it is not clear how much "wrapping" is provided by each of these works. It may be that the work that

40. The following discussion relies in part on Victor Gourevitch, "Rousseau on Lying: A Provisional Reading of the Fourth Reverie," *Berkshire Review* 15 (1979): 93–107.

supplies the most agreeable wrapping is the most useful portrayal of the truth. In any event, useful fictions, or fables, approach the standard of general and abstract truth which Rousseau calls "the most precious of all goods." According to this understanding, fables can be distinguished from general or philosophic treatises mainly by their more effective or useful portrayal of the truth. Far from being unphilosophic, an autobiography written as a fable could be an example of philosophy made useful.

Rousseau's argument to this point comes close to implying an identity between useful fictions and general truths. At the least, he presents fables as truths that are made useful. His statement that fables "wrap useful truths in sensible and agreeable forms," however, has another implication. Aside from making truths felt, fables also give them agreeable forms. In so far as they can be seen when they are naked, these truths are not agreeable to behold. Moreover, it is difficult to see how the form of a truth can be altered without altering its truthfulness. In fact, Rousseau concedes in the end that fables sometimes disfigure the truth by clothing it (I, 1038). Thus, instead of a complete identity, an uneasy complementarity exists between general truths and fables. In order to become useful, truths must be made more palatable. By taking on a more agreeable form, their truthfulness may be compromised.

Fictions or fables belong in the category of poetry, not philosophy. Rousseau expresses the difference between the two categories in his essay "On Theatrical Imitation." Philosophy allows us to judge the truth of things for ourselves "by successively giving us one dimension and then another" (*Oeuvres*, Geneva 1782–89, XI, 363–64). Poetry judges for us by offering "the whole at once." Poetry is more useful or effective than philosophy because it gives the "appearance" of a thing immediately and in an agreeable form.

Immediately after his general discussion of factual truth, general truth, and fables in the *Reveries*, Rousseau applies his conclusions about truth, fiction, and lies to the *Confessions*. He admits that he was obliged to rely on "imperfect memories" and that he "filled in the gaps" with imaginary details. He concedes that he embellished some events (I, 1035). He evidently puts himself in the same class as the historians he discusses in *Emile* who must invent facts they do not know and conjecture about the causes and effects that connect the facts they do know. In other words, Rousseau describes his own practice exactly in the way that May describes the unconscious practice of all autobiographers. The Fourth Walk even concludes with a final admission that Rousseau has been rather too prone to substitute fables for factual truths (I, 1038). While he admits his failure to live up to the standard of strict factual truth, he denies that he ever "polluted" his views or attributed nonexistent virtues to himself (I, 1036). Thus his departures from factual truth do not belong to the harmful category of lies (except in so far as they may have injured his own reputation), and there is no hint here that Rousseau violates the standard of general and abstract truth.

It is not entirely novel to read the *Confessions* as a moral fable. Sebastien Mercier, one of Rousseau's early champions, defends the *Confessions* precisely by denying its truthfulness. At the end of a lengthy survey of all Rousseau's published words, Mercier finally turns to the *Confessions*:

> Rousseau shows himself there to be the least humble of penitents, and nothing will take the idea away from me that it is a novel that he wished to write, not at the bottom, but in the details; one dismisses in doubt his children put into the hospital; he will have wished to give us an ideal tableau, to paint indigence and misfortune besieging a superior man, and his life falling from the blows of the club of force and despotism. Rousseau will have wished to trace an interesting work, filled with varied particulars; and having set aside its publication to a very distant time, he wished to meet no contradictor and arranged the pleasure of outlining himself in an attitude new among men.[41]

Mercier thus claims that at least in its details the *Confessions* is a work of fiction, a novel. He gives two motives for this fictionalization. One is a peculiar sort of vanity that falsely confesses vices in order to stimulate interest. The other is a desire to dramatize "an ideal tableau" containing a useful lesson. Mercier later refers to these falsifications as parables and fables rather than parts of a novel.[42] The first motive implies a false claim of factual truth of the sort identified by May; the second shows concern for a lesson that is more important than the truth of any particular fact. Thus Rousseau had at least one reader who read him the way he himself read Herodotus.

To see why Rousseau would use his autobiography as a moral fable, it is useful to examine more closely his analysis of the general use of moral fables. Rousseau suggests that some truths become effective only

41. Sebastien Mercier, *De J. J. Rousseau considéré comme l'un des premiers auteurs de la révolution* (Paris: Buisson, 1791), p. 262.

42. Ibid., pp. 267–68. The passages Mercier identifies as parables or fables include Jean-Jacques's false accusation of the young servant Marion (I, 84–86) and his abandonment of his children (I, 356–59). He also argues that *Emile* and *Julie* are parables.

if they are clothed in the form of a fable. He apparently distinguishes between those occasions for which the naked truth is appropriate and those for which suitable dress is required. As his discussion in the *Reveries* makes clear, fables are appropriate in certain sorts of moral contexts. Although his examples of fables in the *Reveries* are mainly from private life, their most important use is political. In fact, it would not be too strong to say that Rousseau sees political life and the appropriate arena for moral fables as coextensive.

The Political Use of Moral Fables

Partisans of open government could well concede the possibility of moral fables without regarding them as the source of political benefit. They could, for example, regard the clothing of the truth that Rousseau views as a part of fables as an invitation to political oppression. Rousseau is aware that rulers can attempt to deceive their subjects. He also admits and even insists that there are circumstances in which any use of fables is simply pernicious. He insists, however, that these circumstances exist only outside political life. He claims that those aspects of the human character that make political life necessary are also the foundation of the effectiveness of fables. The need for fables would disappear only if the need for politics disappeared as well. Because fables can be either useful or pernicious, one must distinguish the different frameworks within which Rousseau discusses them. We can make the necessary distinctions if we first identify the distinctive characteristic of those situations in which fables are useful and then explore the different political contexts described by Rousseau.

The key to understanding the relevance of fables to different political contexts lies in the fable's character as a "clothed" version of the truth and not the truth itself. The essence of a fable is its clothing, or appearance. In "On Theatrical Imitation" Rousseau discusses how appearances win over a large audience. He says that "appearance offers us the whole at once, and under the opinion of a greater capacity of mind, flatters the sense by seducing *amour-propre*" (*Oeuvres*, Geneva, 1782, XI, 363–64). Here Rousseau links the imitative art that produces fictions with the passion of amour-propre. Amour-propre is one of Rousseau's most important technical terms. This passion is the distinctive characteristic of unnatural social humans. It is "only a relative sentiment, artificial and born in society" (*Discourses*, 222). It is characterized by a concern with the intentions and opinions of others and makes one compare oneself to others.[43] Once it has been awakened, this passion is virtually impossible to cure. If amour-propre is at the root of the effectiveness of fables, their effectiveness is restricted to social humans and extends to virtually all of them. In sum, those circumstances in which amour-propre is unavoidable require fables. In those circumstances in which amour-propre is absent, fables are unnecessary or pernicious. The latter circumstances are unpolitical, the former are political.

Several types of behavior are possible for humans: an unpolitical natural amorality that involves no amour-propre; a pure morality based on a rational attachment to virtue independent of amour-propre; a corrupt civilized pseudo-morality based on vanity, a form of amour-propre which degrades the moral; and a civil morality based on the emulation of exemplary figures made possible by a healthier form of amour-propre. Fables can mitigate pseudo-morality and support civil morality. They are absent from both natural amorality and pure morality.

Amour-propre is not present in the condition of natural amorality which Rousseau describes in the *Second Discourse* and the first part of *Emile*. In the pure state of nature, humans neither harm nor help each other because they have virtually no contact with each other. They may learn by observing animals, but they do not imitate each other. The absence of language makes fables not only inappropriate but also impossible in this context. Emile is educated according to the natural standard, although he does learn to speak. Rousseau explicitly banishes both fables and history from the first part of Emile's education (*Emile*, 110–16). In addition to his reservations about the possibility of a factual history, Rousseau also has reservations about the moral effect of the study of any history, however accurate it may be. These reservations apply to poetic fables like those of La Fontaine as well. Rousseau claims that a danger arises from the inability of any young student to understand the adult motives that are the causes and effects of the actions in both histories and fables. He illustrates this danger with the example of a boy who has been studying the life of Alexander the Great. Alexander proves his trust of his friend Philip by drinking wine Philip has been accused of poisoning. The child, however, can understand neither friendship nor risk of life and therefore misses the point of the story. A

---

43. Amour-propre is also "the first and most natural of the passions" (*Emile*, 208). The context of this remark makes it clear that amour-propre is the first of the social passions.

young student cannot help trivializing adult virtues or being infected by vices. Rousseau argues that it is better to prevent such results by postponing the study of history than to attempt in vain to correct the inevitable mistakes that a premature study engenders. At the age of fifteen, the young Emile will have an excellent knowledge of physics, but he will know no history or fables. The *Confessions* could play no part in his early education.

Emile will study history and fables later, when he begins to develop relations with other people and the passions that accompany these relations. As his own feelings develop, he will discover that other people have feelings as well. Because these discoveries draw him into the world of moral relations, he must learn about the corruption and artificial desires of most civilized humans, from whom he has so far been sheltered. The study of history and of lives in particular will allow him to learn about corruption without becoming embittered by direct experience. This period is also "the time of fables" (*Emile*, 247).

These studies are useful now, but they also expose the boy to a new danger. Precisely because he can now understand others and feel what they feel, Emile may begin "to become alien to himself" (*Emile*, 243). Rousseau explains this alienation by saying, "I see from the way young people are made to read history that they are transformed, so to speak, into all the persons they see." Even Emile cannot avoid comparing himself to the people about whom he reads, but Rousseau insists that "if in these parallels he just once prefers to be someone other than himself—were the other Socrates, were it Cato—everything has failed." Everything will have failed because the goal of Emile's education is to preserve natural autonomy, independence, or wholeness. As Rousseau says at the beginning of the book, "natural man is entirely for himself. He is numerical unity, the absolute whole which is relative only to itself or its kind" (*Emile*, 39). To remain a natural independent whole, Emile must not live his life in terms of standards imposed on him by other people.

What makes history dangerous at this stage is the student's emerging amour-propre, which makes him compare himself to other people. These comparisons can lead to a desire to imitate. Imitation is at the ground of the possibility of enslavement to standards alien to oneself. Rousseau emphasizes that Emile must never imitate anyone. In today's language, he must have no role models. "The foundation of imitation among us comes from the desire always to be transported out of ourselves. If I succeed in my enterprise, Emile surely will not have this desire" (*Emile*, 104). Only in the last line of the book, when he expresses a desire to imitate his tutor by educating his own child, does Emile become an imitator. Presumably he wishes to educate his child not to be an imitator.

One can see the importance of Emile's introduction to lives and fables by looking at the *Confessions*, Rousseau's most vivid account of the loss of natural wholeness, or alienation, that can be induced by the desire to imitate characters in books. Jean-Jacques's[44] departure from wholeness illustrates natural wholeness by showing its disruption. Near the beginning of Book I, Rousseau traces his earliest recollections to reading novels: "I remember only my first readings and their effect on me; this is the time from which I date without interruption the consciousness of myself" (I, 8). Not only does Jean-Jacques begin to read at an early age, but Rousseau also describes his reading as the source of, or even the same as, his self-consciousness. One might have expected him to say that his reading was his first consciousness of the world outside himself. In fact, for Emile reading lives and fables will be precisely an extension of his knowledge of people and things outside himself.

How can reading, an apparent opening of oneself to the outside, be the source of self-consciousness? It might be argued that reading, along with many other forms of experience, teaches one how to distinguish oneself from the outside world. Rousseau himself claims precisely the opposite. Other types of experience more natural to childhood may teach the proper relations between oneself and other people and things, but reading, "this dangerous method," obscures the distinctions involved in these relations. In describing his subsequent turn from novels to "the illustrious men of Plutarch" (I, 9), Rousseau says, "I became the personage whose life I read." This experience is presented as a departure from the earlier reading of novels only by virtue of its intensity. He claims that he was so carried away that he once put his hand into the fire of a chafing dish to imitate Mucius Scaevola's display of courage in the Tuscan camp. Both novels and lives encourage Jean-Jacques to identify with characters in books.[45] By linking this experience of identification with the formation of self-consciousness, Rous-

---

44. For clarity, I refer to the narrator of the *Confessions* as Rousseau and the character he describes as Jean-Jacques. This makes it possible to distinguish between Rousseau's descriptions of what he thought or felt while writing the *Confessions* and those of what he thought or felt during the time about which he writes. An absolutely strict separation is not maintained in the movement from proper names to pronouns.

45. For a discussion of this issue, see Jean Roussel, "Le Phénomène de l'identification dans la lecture de Rousseau," *Annales de la Société Jean-Jacques Rousseau* 39 (1972–74): 65–77.

seau indicates that his earliest self-consciousness was his consciousness of being someone other than himself: he was Scaevola or Brutus rather than Jean-Jacques. From the beginning, his self-consciousness is determined by his concern with other people, his amour-propre.

The combination of novels and Plutarch does not only draw Jean-Jacques outside himself; it also puts him in contradiction with himself. In large part, the *Confessions* is the story of Jean-Jacques's attempts to come to terms with these effects of his youthful readings. It warns about the dangers of conflicting or unrealistic objects for imitation. At the same time, by describing the effects of such reading, Rousseau indicates the way he expects his book to affect its reader. We consider the consequences of Jean-Jacques's loss of himself in Chapter 3. For now it is enough to see the dangers that similar readings pose for Emile. To keep him from being alien to himself, he will be introduced to Plutarch (and later to novels) very carefully. Because of some of these potential effects, even an older Emile would not be exposed to a book like the *Confessions*, which encourages this sort of alienation.[46] Thus the educations of Emile and Jean-Jacques illustrate natural wholeness by respectively presenting the advantages of not imitating others and the disadvantages of desiring to imitate them.

Emile's education seems to point to a moral context characterized by a pure rational attachment to morality that depends on no fables or imitation. Rousseau alludes to just such an outcome, even for an education more ordinary than Emile's. He refers to the possibility of a temporary reliance on imitation that will then change:

> I know that all these virtues by imitation are the virtues of apes, and that no good action is morally good except when it is done because it is good and not because others do it. But at an age when the heart feels nothing yet, children just have to be made to imitate the actions whose habit one wants to give them, until the time when they can do them out of disinterest and love of the good. Man is an imitator. (*Emile*, 104)[47]

This implies that imitation can be a temporary stage to be superseded by a more advanced, pure moral motive.[48] However, it is by no means

---

46. Robert Darnton provides an excellent example of Rousseau's success in inspiring this sort of identification in his readers; see "Readers Respond to Rousseau: The Fabrication of Romantic Sensitivity," in *The Great Cat Massacre and Other Episodes in French Cultural History* (New York: Basic Books, 1984), pp. 215–56.

47. Rousseau further qualifies this limited praise of imitation at *Emile*, 110–11.

48. This is Kant's argument in discussing the use of biography for educating young people; see Immanuel Kant, *Critique of Practical Reason and Other Writings in Moral Philosophy*, trans. and ed. Lewis White Beck (Chicago: University of Chicago Press, 1949), pp. 250–52. I am indebted to Joel Schwartz for calling this passage to my attention.

clear that many people are capable of moving from one stage to the other. For most people, the desire to be transported out of themselves, which is rooted in their amour-propre, cannot be overcome.

Among civilized humans who have not received Emile's education, one can safely say "man is an imitator." Even in *Emile*, Rousseau says that in certain circumstances the living outside oneself that comes from reading lives "has certain advantages which I do not discount" (*Emile*, 243). All political life is subject to the influence of the civilized human ability and desire to imitate. The most effective, in fact the only effective, moral fables inspire this desire. The danger of some fables, such as those of La Fontaine, is that they inspire the desire to imitate the wrong things (*Emile*, 115). We can now see the political necessity for moral fables. Civilized humans in general become moral only if they imitate the right objects.

The conclusion that follows from the near inevitability of imitation among civilized humans is that most people are restricted to a sort of morality that takes this desire into account. They have the pseudo-morality of corrupt civilization or the real morality of citizens. Amour-propre can take two forms: corrupt vanity or incorruptible pride (III, 937–38). Most civilized humans, to whom Rousseau refers as "our Harlequins" (*Emile*, 104), are afflicted with vanity and accompanying jealousy. They "imitate the beautiful to degrade it, to make it ridiculous." Pride results in a different form of imitation, which Rousseau calls "emulation." "There is this difference between jealousy and emulation, that emulation tends to elevate us to the level of others and jealousy to reduce the others to our level" (II, 1324). Jealousy is a sort of imitation that expresses hostility. It makes people imitate in order to exploit. Emulation unites citizens by giving them a common aspiration. It is a sort of imitation that can bind people into a social whole after they have lost their natural wholeness.

Thus Rousseau is both a great proponent of emulation of exemplary figures and the most insistent opponent of such emulation. His advocacy of emulation for the majority of civilized humans is derived from his more fundamental position that all forms of imitation are a threat to natural wholeness and independence. Imitation is virtually unavoidable among civilized humans, and once it has arisen "everything has failed" from the natural standpoint. This complete failure means that natural wholeness can no longer serve as a straightforward practical standard. If one instance of emulation means that everything has failed, more instances cannot make the failure more complete.

Thus Rousseau replaces the standard of natural wholeness with one of social wholeness in which a complete and constant emulation takes place. As a result of the introduction of this second standard, he can criticize ordinary civilized humans from two different perspectives. From the standard of natural wholeness, such people are alienated beings who live outside themselves. From the standard of social wholeness, they are selfish beings who exploit others for their own benefit and are torn by the conflicting objects of their imitations.[49] One should always keep in mind that Rousseau treats the issue of emulation from this dual perspective, and that he can do so without contradiction because the two standards exist in a clear hierarchy.

If the vast majority of people, those civilized humans who have not undergone the education of an Emile, are open only to a morality based on imitation or emulation, social life depends absolutely on the cultivation of salutary imitation and the avoidance of corrupting vanity. Rousseau's various discussions of citizenship in his political works frequently refer to the importance of what he calls "examples." Whereas "example" is one of the last lessons in Emile's education, it "is the first lesson" in forming mutually dependent citizens (S.C., 218). Becoming a citizen depends on the ability to live outside oneself in terms of an image shared with fellow citizens. Unlike the natural "numerical unity," a citizen is a "fractional unity," a part of a whole (Emile, 39). Citizens are like the young Jean-Jacques in that they live outside themselves, but they imitate only a single set rather than two contrary sets of exemplary figures, and they live in a republic that supports their emulation rather than a corrupt community that renders virtue useless.

The initial source of proper examples for emulation is the founder or legislator of a community.[50] Once a healthy community has been formed, secondary examples abound. In Considerations on the Government of Poland Rousseau explains at length how to use examples to maintain citizenship. The first examples for inspiring emulation in children are their teachers (instituteurs), all of whom must be distinguished by their moeurs, probity, good sense, and enlightenment (III, 967). By calling the teachers "instituteurs" Rousseau emphasizes their resemblance in function to legislators like Lycurgus, who undertake "to in-

---

49. Allan Bloom characterizes the "bourgeois" in Rousseau's thought as "the man who when dealing with others, thinks only of himself, and on the other hand, in his understanding of himself, thinks only of others" (see Bloom's introduction to Emile, 5).

50. I develop this observation in "'To Persuade without Convincing': The Language of Rousseau's Legislator," American Journal of Political Science 31,2 (1987): 321–35.

stitute [*instituer*] a people" (III, 956). The teachers are themselves examples for emulation and they teach about other examples. By the age
of sixteen, the student should have his heart full of "every fine action
and illustrious man" in Polish history (III, 956).[51] The difference between this education and Emile's is shown by the fact that the Poles'
historical education has ended by the time they reach the age at which
Emile's begins.

Rousseau recommends the extension of examples into adult life as
well. For example, he urges the construction of a monument to the
Confederation of Bar, the confederation of nobles and gentry formed
in 1768 to counter Russian meddling in Polish affairs. This monument
should celebrate more than a particular event alone; it must be in-
scribed with the names of all the confederates (III, 961). Its object is "to
infuse, so to speak, the soul of the confederates into all of the nation"
(III, 959). All the citizens will be "infused" with the soul of the confederates. Like the young Jean-Jacques who reads Plutarch, they will become the characters whose lives they celebrate.

This example of a monument that inspires emulation is an indication that written or spoken lives are not the only genres of significance
to political life. Particularly in the most civilized communities, the arts
determine whether people are channeled into healthy emulation or
unhealthy imitation. It is this consideration that makes Rousseau pay
such careful attention to the place of the arts in public life. The moral
object of the *Confessions* can be determined by seeing how the political
effects of the genre of autobiography compare with those of other arts
that convey moral fables.

Politics, the Imitative Arts, and Autobiography

Rousseau uses the same terms to analyze music, theater, and novels.
He calls each of these "imitative" arts in part because each appeals to
the tendency to imitate found in all civilized humans. Each of these arts
has the potential for conveying moral fables, but each also faces certain
limitations. In particular, different arts, or different genres within an
individual art, are salutary in different social conditions. Rousseau's
judgments about the different arts and their limitations can suggest his
reasons for choosing autobiography. We can follow Rousseau's general
presentation of the political significance of specific arts and then refer
to his own practice of that art.

51. The term "illustrious" is in the title of Plutarch's *Lives*.

Music is the art that makes the purest use of the civilized tendency to imitate, and in principle it can be the most effective for conveying moral fables. Rousseau says that "the art of the musician consists in substituting for the sensible image of the object that of the movement which its presence excites in the heart of the Contemplator" (*D.M.*, 251). In the same context he says that music "will not directly represent things, but will excite in the soul the same movement we feel in seeing them." Music is so effective at channeling people's feelings because it represents them directly. According to Rousseau, sights may elicit feelings, but sounds impose them. Music "submits the whole of Nature to its knowing imitation" (*D.M.*, 308). This imitation, however, is of human feelings, not of nature. Because these feelings are deceptive, it is not surprising that a naturally educated boy like Emile is kept away from passionate, expressive music that would draw him outside himself (*Emile*, 149). He could learn to appreciate music only by becoming an imitative being.[52] Music can be said to be the imitative art par excellence.

It is possible to understand Rousseau's own activity as a music critic and composer as an attempt to restore what he regarded as publicly salutary music. His compositions, most notably *Le Devin du village*, present moral fables that succeeded in forming a popular taste for country life against the corruption of the city. Rousseau did not, like Nietzsche, hope for a rebirth of a healthy culture through music,[53] because he regarded even the most expressive modern music as incapable of the effects of ancient music. Under modern social constraints, music is capable of inducing only marginal improvement in public life.

Rousseau finds a similar split between ancient healthy and corrupt modern practices when he discusses theater. Unlike music, however, theater is intrinsically corrupting and becomes healthy only in exceptional circumstances. Rousseau illustrates this inherent corruption in the *Letter to d'Alembert* by showing the effect that contemporary theater has on amour-propre. The extreme version of this unwholesome effect is seen in the character of the actors, whose own amour-propre makes

---

52. For other assessments of Rousseau's analysis of music, see Marc Eigeldinger, *Jean-Jacques Rousseau et la réalité de l'imaginaire* (Neuchâtel, Switz.: Editions de la Baconnière, 1962), p. 129; Ronald Grimsley, *The Philosophy of Rousseau* (Oxford: Oxford University Press, 1973), pp. 128–29; and Huntington Williams, *Rousseau and Romantic Autobiography* (Oxford: Oxford University Press, 1983), p. 32.

53. On this point, one should consider Rousseau's analysis of the lack of musical potential in the French language; see his *Letter on French Music* (*Oeuvres*, Geneva, 1782–89, XV, 241).

them manipulate the susceptible amour-propre of the audience. In describing the actor's skill, Rousseau repeats in more negative terms his account of the imitative artist's ability to reveal appearances: "What is the talent of the actor? It is the art of counterfeiting himself, of putting on another character than his own, of appearing different than he is, of being passionate in cold blood, of saying what he does not think as naturally as if he really did think it, and finally, of forgetting his own place by dint of taking another" (d'Alembert, 79). The actor's imitation is not an aspiration to become something higher; it is a desire to gain control over an audience. Even when actors do approach internal identification with a character, they do so only temporarily as they move from role to role (d'Alembert, 80). Actors represent the extreme version of civilized vanity moving among conflicting objects of imitation.

The audience does undergo a purer identification with the characters they see on the stage. In fact, Rousseau argues that the passions aroused in the theater "are pure and without mixture of anxiety for ourselves" (d'Alembert, 25). This sort of identification is identical to that inspired in a citizen; its very purity however, prevents it from lasting. People may feel a salutary emotion while in the theater, but reentering their normal lives, which provide no support for this identification, they feel only vanity in being such virtuous and sensitive souls as to be capable of such noble feelings. In the end, this identification is pernicious, because theatergoers become accustomed to regarding such feelings as having their proper place only in the theater. Like certain tyrants, they can be compassionate in the theater and cruel elsewhere.

Rousseau's criticism is directed at a situation in which the theater is the sole or main source of virtuous sentiments. He concedes that in rare circumstances the theater could be of use in reinforcing the sentiments of citizens. For example, in Greece the theater supported patriotism by concentrating exclusively on "national traditions" (d'Alembert, 33). These plays presented "objects capable of inspiring the Greeks with ardent *emulation* and of warming their hearts with sentiments of honor and glory" (d'Alembert, 78, emphasis added). This sort of salutary theater was rare even in antiquity, and Rousseau cites only this example.

In modern times, he argues, the theater is useful only for palliating the ills of an already corrupt society, an argument he used to excuse his own play *Narcisse*.[54] The usefulness of the theater in a corrupt society might suggest that Rousseau's project of presenting a moral fable

54. In the preface to *Narcisse* Rousseau says that his play has the limited goal of distracting corrupt people from bad actions (II, 972).

would have been well served by a career as a dramatist. The intrinsic corruption he identifies in the theater, however, suggests that such entertainment is socially useful only in the worst of times.

In the *Letter to d'Alembert* Rousseau makes a passing reference to one other literary form, which he presents as still more promising for corrupt communities: the novel. The moral effect of the novel, for good or bad, is more limited in scope than that of the theater because novels are read in private. A character in a novel can conceivably be a good object for emulation, but the reading itself runs counter to the public demands of citizenship. As we have seen, Rousseau advises the Poles to teach lives to the young in school. Healthy Polish novels, if such things existed, would imitate Greek drama by being rooted in national traditions. Even so, Rousseau indicates his assessment of both novels and drama in his preface to his novel *Julie*, where he says, "Plays [*spectacles*] are necessary in great cities and Novels for corrupt peoples" (II, 5). In spite of this rather negative description of the novel, Rousseau does manage to make a case for the superiority of the novel to the theater in corrupt times. He discusses novels in the context of a discussion of England, a place less corrupt than France but more corrupt than Geneva. Rousseau praises the English for their "common taste for solitude," from which "arises a taste for the contemplative readings and the novels with which England is inundated" (*d'Alembert*, 82). Such a taste for solitude is incompatible with the conspicuous displays of vanity elicited by the theater. In the *Confessions* Rousseau illustrates the incompatibility of the novel and social vanity with his story of a woman who begins to read *Julie* while dressing for a ball. The novel so absorbs her that she forgoes the ball and reads for the entire night (I, 547). For at least one evening she is distracted from indulging her vanity in social display. The novel is capable of all the limited good of the theater without its dangers. Whereas in England the taste for solitude causes the love of novels, the example from the *Confessions* illustrates that it is possible to use novels to create a salutary taste for solitude. Such a change in public taste is precisely what Rousseau claims to have attempted with *Julie* (II, 22–23). Although the *Confessions* only occasionally adopts the epistolary form of *Julie*, it does have the attributes of a novel which can encourage a taste for solitary reading.[55] It is also an inspiration for an incalculable number of novels written by later authors.

---

55. The *Confessions* adopts an epistolary form in Books IX and X, although not as consistently as *Julie* (I, 476–99). On the variety of literary forms in Rousseau's autobiographical enterprise, see Williams, *Romantic Autobiography*.

From this discussion of Rousseau's analysis of imitative art, it is possible to draw some tentative conclusions about the significance of his choice of this form for his enterprise. Rousseau argues that the novel is distinguishable from other literary forms by its link with a taste for solitude. Autobiography shares this introspective aspect and therefore is equally unsuitable reading for citizens unless this tendency is countered by the material within the autobiography. An autobiography of Moses might be good for citizens, but a work like the *Confessions*, which takes us "inside and under the skin," is likely to make its readers dwell on themselves rather than their communities. Such a tendency is suitable for mitigating corruption. Putting together the limitations imposed by its form with the possibilities open to all imitative art, one can say that Rousseau's choice points to the possibility of a moral reformation, but not to one in the direction of citizenship. The *Confessions* presents its readers with a view of a life directed toward solitary and harmless pleasures that will make them less dangerous to each other.

If the *Confessions* is a work of imitative art which has an effect on its readers' feelings, it is not clear how it can also be a work of philosophy which lays the foundation for a science of human nature. Most of Rousseau's arguments cited to this point stress the incompatibility of imitation and philosophy. In fact, Rousseau generally presents attempts to represent feelings and ideas simultaneously as doomed to failure (see *D.M.*, 39). Such a combination of the imitative and the metaphysical appears impossible; ideas require a careful consideration of the parts of a picture, which is incompatible with the immediate effect of the whole.

Nevertheless, Rousseau believes that this improbable combination is possible. It is precisely this combination that he presents as the mark of genius. According to Rousseau, the genius "renders ideas by feelings . . . and he excites the passions which he expresses in the bottom of hearts (*D.M.*, 227). The genius combines the moral, popular, imitative effect of exciting passions with the philosophic effect of portraying ideas. A reader can become the young Jean-Jacques who imitates Scaevola, but he can also reflect on the importance of this example for showing how the feelings are developed. Frequently in the *Confessions* Rousseau stops his engaging narrative solely in order to demand the reader's reflection on what has just occurred. The *Confessions* fulfills its two goals of fostering imitation and helping philosophers by providing both an immediate effect on the feelings and a delayed effect on the mind.

Although the form of the *Confessions* does not preclude the union of imitation and philosophy in the hands of a genius, the intention of constructing a moral fable can come into tension with the intention of writing philosophy. There is often a difference between the world as it should appear to be and the world as it is. Rousseau can overcome some of this tension by appealing to unreflective readers on the more superficial level of a moral fable and to more reflective ones on the deeper level. In addition, his analysis of the impossibility of undertaking a transformation of contemporary readers into citizens opens another possibility. For an audience of corrupt civilized humans, a fable that is less perfectly moral and more directly connected with the truth may be both possible and more effective than a fable of perfect citizenship. Chapter 2 will pursue this matter with an examination of the relation between the exemplary life presented in the *Confessions* and other exemplary lives that Rousseau wishes to replace. Now it is necessary to consider the suitability of an autobiography for conveying a philosophic teaching.

The Possibility of Philosophic Autobiography

By arguing that histories can be read as moral fables, Rousseau disposes of the need to judge these works by the standard of factual truth. By claiming that moral fables are presentations of useful general truths in a persuasive form, he shows that an autobiography that is also a fable can express more than a merely personal truth. It remains to be seen how a historical work can present general truths unaccompanied by the distortions contained in a fable. As we see in this section, Rousseau gives examples of such historical works; he discusses the advantages of presenting general principles in the form of particular examples; he asserts that the *Confessions* itself makes this sort of presentation of general principles; and finally, he gives an extensive treatment of how particular facts, hypotheses, and general truths can be blended in a single work.

To illustrate the possibility of history as a moral fable, Rousseau chooses the example of Herodotus. To illustrate the possibility of a history that leads to the consideration of general principles, he points to Thucydides. According to Rousseau, Thucydides' greatness does not consist simply in his ability to write useful fictions in the guise of history; rather, he "reports the facts without judging them, but he omits none of the circumstances proper to make us judge them ourselves"

(*Emile*, 239). By making his readers judge, Thucydides forces them to discover the general causes and effects of the particular facts. In Thucydides' hands, historical study turns into philosophy rather than into a novel.

Thucydides confirms Rousseau's characterization of him at the beginning of his work. His account of the war between the Peloponnesians and the Athenians begins with the claim that this war is more worthy of examination than all others. He calls it "the greatest motion that ever happened among the Greeks."[56] The investigation of a motion and its causes, effects, and relations is the sort of inquiry that can turn factual history into a philosophic discipline. Thus both Thucydides and Rousseau use particular facts to lead to a concern for general principles. Perfect knowledge of the facts alone is simply impossible according to Rousseau, but an a posteriori reconstruction of causality can be accurate if it is based on true general principles.

Rousseau's description of Thucydides in *Emile* reflects what he says of his own method in the *Confessions*. In the latter work, he says of his reader, "It is for him to assemble the elements and to determine the being they compose; the result ought to be his work, and if he then fools himself, all the error will be of his doing. Now for this end it is not sufficient that my recitals be faithful it is also necessary that they be exact. It is not for me to judge the importance of facts. I should say all of them, and leave to him the trouble of choosing" (I, 175). Here, as in his remarks about Thucydides, Rousseau argues that the reader is forced to undertake a burden, to "judge the importance of facts" in order to assemble a proper picture of Jean-Jacques. The reader who does this well will have not only an accurate portrait of Rousseau but also the understanding of the principles of human nature necessary for arriving at the portrait. Such an understanding is possible even if Rousseau does not fulfill the goal stated here of setting forth all the facts. Those he omits can be hypothetically reconstructed on the basis of the general understanding derived from those facts he does present.

The complexity of the relation between particular facts and general truths in historical works such as Thucydides' history or the *Confessions* seems to carry a disadvantage for the presentation of truth. Straightforward philosophic treatises seem much more capable of conveying a philosophic teaching. Against these appearances, Rousseau argues that

56. Thucydides, *The Peloponnesian War*, I, i.

it is the systematic character of the treatise which carries the real danger. As we see in the next section, when developing his own system Rousseau encourages a profound mistrust of philosophic systems in general. Rather than fit the system to things, philosophers characteristically fit things into their systems. This flaw of systematic treatises is one of Rousseau's reasons for adopting the intermediate form of a mixture of treatise and novel for *Emile*. He says, "Instead of yielding to the systematic spirit, I grant as little as possible to reasoning and I trust only to observation" (*Emile*, 254). While he proceeds in an orderly way through the course of the book, he relies on the particular example of his fictional student to test his general principles. He justifies this procedure, by saying, "I know that in undertakings like this one, an author—always comfortable with systems that he is not responsible for putting into practice—may insouciantly offer very fine precepts which are impossible to follow. And in the absence of details and examples even the feasible things he says, if he has not shown their application, remain ineffectual" (*Emile*, 50). Rousseau pushes this antisystematic method two steps farther in the *Confessions*. He uses a real rather than an imaginary example and he refuses to spell out the general conclusions revealed by the example. He urges readers, not merely to test someone else's conclusions, but to draw their own.

It must be conceded that not all lives lend themselves to the illustration of general principles of human nature equally well. The same is true for historical events that are filled with accidental occurrences or have causes buried too deeply to be discernible by any means. To allow the reader to make an accurate consideration of causes and relations, the author must choose particularly revealing events or a particularly revealing life. Rousseau does not underestimate this difficulty. He insists that even great historians such as Thucydides are all too likely to become fascinated by the superficial significance of wars. Historical causes and effects of such conspicuous events are so hidden that they are virtually impossible to determine. In the end, Rousseau seems to believe that even Thucydides may be as misleading as a fabulist like Herodotus.

Because the general significance of events reported by historians is so hard to discern accurately, Rousseau turns to individual lives as an object of study for Emile's education. Of course, accidents happen in lives as well as in battles, but the effects of accidental occurrences on an individual reveal things that are not accidental. Accordingly, in *Emile*

Rousseau employs Plutarch's *Lives* to give his student knowledge of human nature (*Emile*, 240).[57] Nevertheless, in the Neuchâtel preface to the *Confessions* Rousseau indicates that lives also have their defects as sources of accurate knowledge. Although lives are superior to histories, focusing less on superficial actions and more on the internal causes and effects of actions, the authors of lives lack direct access to the "internal model" (I, 1149). Biographers such as Jesus's disciples or Socrates' followers can be accurate about externally observable events such as speeches and deeds.[58] In fact, these writers make few attempts to conjecture about the interior lives of their subjects. They consider actions, and particularly speeches, as the most important parts of their subjects' lives. Rousseau dismisses these exterior manifestations of character as meaningless unless they are explained by their interior causes, namely, the speakers' thoughts and, above all, feelings. To be sure, descriptions of speeches and deeds are necessary to the revelation of feelings because "feelings are described well only by their effects" (I, 104). Without some confirmation in action, feelings can be easily misunderstood. Yet this admission of the need to look at the external manifestations of feelings reveals that the goal is the portrayal of feelings. In sum, biographies are superior to histories because they are more capable of focusing on the internal life, the springs of human actions, but even biographers are ultimately reduced to mere conjecture about this internal life.

Rousseau's reservations about biographies lead him to adopt autobiography. Autobiography is superior to both history and biography because the autobiographer has direct access to the interior model. It is this direct access to feelings which makes possible an accurate knowledge of human nature. In the end, Rousseau can conclude that the *Confessions* will always be a precious book for philosophers because he can claim that it is the first autobiography to be completely frank in its presentation of the internal causes of human behavior.

The objection can be made that, however complete his account may be, Rousseau makes it impossible for his reader to formulate an independent appraisal of that life. In other words, one can grant the need for a completely frank autobiography without admitting that the *Confessions* is the appropriate autobiography. One might claim that Rousseau distorts the account of his life to fit the theoretical principles

---

57. In less perfect educations it is possible for lives to give misleading information (*Emile*, 110).

58. For example, Xenophon claims that he reports Socrates' words and deeds at *Memorabilia*, I, 20.

expressed in his earlier works. Thus, although Rousseau says of the reader, "It is for him to assemble the elements and to determine the being they comprise" (I, 175), he himself may have unfairly shaped the mold into which the elements can be assembled. Even if Rousseau does not make his interpretation of himself explicit, he still appears to be caught in May's dilemma of an implicit a posteriori construction of causality.[59]

Rousseau provides two answers to this charge. He argues that the *Confessions* is only a first step. His work is only the "first piece of comparison for the study of man" (I, 3).[60] Our knowledge of Jean-Jacques may be flawed, but this flaw can be overcome by other comparisons, the first of which is our knowledge of ourselves. Rousseau also asserts that the complexity of his method offers an internal check on his picture. He presents both his memories and his act of remembering, his recollections and his reaction to his recollections. He offers the reader a picture, not only of his development, but also of what he is now (I, 1154). Even if his picture of the past is (intentionally or unintentionally) distorted, the reader has a second chance to grasp the truth by comparing the Rousseau of the present with what he says about the Jean-Jacques of the past.

The possibility of comparing Jean-Jacques to Rousseau and both to oneself answers one objection, but the need to undertake such comparisons also raises a question about how much one can expect to learn from the *Confessions*.[61] Starobinski argues that, although making these comparisons may save Rousseau's readers from his errors and deceptions, if the *Confessions* is the first frank autobiography, such comparisons cannot have been made by Rousseau himself. Others need to know Jean-Jacques in order to learn about themselves and human nature in general. Yet Rousseau acts as if he has no reciprocal need to know others. The conclusion that follows from Rousseau's own argument is that a reader can confirm, supplement, or refute Rousseau's account of human nature, but Rousseau himself cannot prove, he can only assert his own veracity. Starobinski insists that Rousseau has caught himself in a trap of his own making.

A full answer to Starobinski's objection can emerge only from the interpretation of the *Confessions*, after Rousseau's account of his self-

59. May, *L'Autobiographie*, p. 77.
60. Rousseau also insists on the importance of parallels for the study of history in general (III, 539).
61. Starobinski, *Transparence*, p. 225.

knowledge has been elaborated. But a preliminary answer to Starobinski's objection lies in the very passage he cites to make his argument (I, 1150). First, Rousseau argues that, in fact, he has been able to
make comparisons, if not with other autobiographers, at least with a
wide range of people. He says, "Counting experience and observation
for something, in that regard I am possibly in the most advantageous
position in which a mortal has ever found himself." He supports this
claim by pointing to his life in a wide variety of social conditions: "Without having any station myself, I have known all stations. I have lived in
all from the lowest to the highest except the throne." Second, Rousseau
points to the range of his internal experience. Even a king, whose
station is beyond Rousseau's experience, cannot match the range of his
ideas and feelings. Thus Rousseau claims that the range of his ideas,
feelings, and experiences is as close to universal as is humanly possible.
His internal and external lives are varied and deep enough to provide
comparisons unavailable to other people. While a critic may describe
the events of Rousseau's life as a series of spectacular accidents that
fascinate but teach very little about human nature, Rousseau claims
that his uniqueness is crucial for providing the sort of knowledge he
requires. Contrary to Starobinski's claims, Rousseau does not exempt
himself from the requirements he imposes on others; rather, he accepts
these requirements and argues that he is the only one, or virtually the
only one, who can fulfill them without assistance from a piece of comparison like the *Confessions*. Elsewhere he says, "You can know to the
bottom Pierre or Jacques and have made very little progress in the
knowledge of man" (III, 53). In the *Confessions* he insists that knowledge
of one very unusual person, Jean-Jacques, allows such progress. In
making this claim he is at least as concerned with the requirements of
his argument as he is with his assertions of uniqueness.

Once it is seen that Rousseau's project in the *Confessions* is to provide
a case study that illuminates general principles of human nature, his
admissions of fabrications and omissions from gaps in memory can be
viewed in a new light. Instead of explaining these departures from fact
as parts of fables, as Mercier would, or as inevitable flaws of an autobiography, as modern critics might, we can explain these departures as
guided by the standard of the general truths about human nature.

That the reconciliation of such general truths with particular facts is
not a purely personal or autobiographical issue is indicated by Rousseau's treatment of the same theme in the theoretical context of the
Second Discourse. At the end of the first part of the *Second Discourse* he

describes how he will move from his description of the general truths about human nature in the pure state of nature to an account of the present condition of society. He says that "when two facts given as real are to be connected by a series of intermediate facts which are unknown or considered as such, it is up to history, when it exists, to present the facts that connect them; while it is up to philosophy, when history is lacking, to determine similar facts that might connect them" (*Discourses*, 141). In the *Second Discourse* Rousseau uses a historical account to make a theoretical argument; he also uses philosophy to construct his historical account. The fabrications and omissions of the *Confessions* are not lies or mistakes; they are philosophically derived "facts that might connect" the remembered facts.[62]

The method is the same in both works. The difference between them lies only in the greater number of facts available to the autobiographer. The *Second Discourse* presents, first, the general features of the state of nature that are inaccessible to experience and historical evidence; second, the observable particular facts of the present social condition; and third, the hypothetical history that may have led from one to the other. In Rousseau's own case in the *Confessions* he has direct recollection of the origin of his self-consciousness, if not of his earliest existence.[63] He also has knowledge of the particular facts of his present condition. Both the original facts and the concluding facts are particular, historical circumstances. But Rousseau lacks knowledge of some of the connections between the past and the present. To give an account of these connecting events, he must resort to hypothetical, or philosophic, history; that is, he must present what may have happened rather than what did happen. He cannot substitute things that could not have happened. The narratives of both works are equally dependent on knowledge of the general truth about human nature.

In both the *Second Discourse* and the *Confessions*, history (or autobiography) and philosophy complement each other. Philosophy fills the gaps of history and history serves as the raw material for philosophic reflection. It hardly needs to be said that this is a delicate complementarity. There is always the risk that philosophers will consciously or unconsciously distort facts and the relations between them so that they

---

62. On the question of whether the account of the state of nature in the *Second Discourse* is hypothetical or historical, see Goldschmidt, *Anthropologie*, pp. 108–53, and Masters, *Political Philosophy*, p. 118.

63. In the "Letters to Malesherbes" Rousseau describes an attempt at autobiography with language that directly echoes that language of the *Second Discourse* (I, 1134).

can prove their own systems. This possibility of distortion raises a further question about the relation between the *Confessions* and Rousseau's more obviously theoretical works. We have seen Rousseau's evidence for the possibility of a philosophic autobiography in which knowledge of human nature allows the author to fill gaps and in which particular events are illustrations of general principles. It is still necessary to consider why and how his theoretical concerns lead him to believe in the necessity or desirability of writing a philosophic autobiography.

The Necessity of Philosophic Autobiography

The two preceding sections arrive at different conclusions about the possibilities open to an autobiographer, but they begin from the same premise. Rousseau's denial of the possibility of a history guided by the standard of factual truth leads him to two notions of history guided by either the imitative standard of moral utility or the philosophic standard of general principles of human nature. How the *Confessions* manages to combine these two very different possibilities, how it manages to put the truth in an agreeable and useful form without distorting it, can be determined only in the course of the interpretation of the work. The somewhat different question of why Rousseau would wish to write a philosophic autobiography can be addressed prior to that interpretation. The possibility of an enterprise does not prove its desirability. Rousseau himself wrote numerous works, both poetic and philosophic, in which he follows more traditional modes of presentation. What the *Confessions* adds to these works can be considered in two ways. First, it gives fuller treatment to themes that are touched on in other works. Viewed in this light the *Confessions* complements Rousseau's other works by filling in gaps in his philosophic system. Second, it directly addresses one question of crucial importance for Rousseau's system, or indeed any philosophic system. Viewed in this way the *Confessions* can be said to be necessary for the justification of Rousseau's entire system.

The first approach points to the complementarity of the *Confessions* with *Emile* and the *Second Discourse*, the most complete expressions of Rousseau's system.[64] Each of these three works is concerned with the same fundamental theme, the development of artificial passions out of natural desires,[65] but each considers this theme from a different per-

---

64. On the importance of the *Second Discourse*, see I, 388; on that of *Emile*, see I, 566.
65. In the Neuchâtel preface Rousseau identifies the conditions necessary for com-

spective. The *Second Discourse* portrays this development in the human species as a whole. *Emile* portrays an alternative healthy development within a single, ordinary person (*Emile*, 52) whose education proceeds on the basis of an adequate understanding of nature. Particularly in Part One, the *Confessions* shows the unhealthy development of the passions in an individual who is given a defective education; in Part Two it shows how an extraordinary person (I, 62, 174) comes to terms with, or even overcomes, his civilized corruption. By focusing on an extraordinary individual the *Confessions* adds an important dimension to the picture provided by *Emile* and the *Second Discourse*. A reading of these earlier works may give the impression that a continually worsening corruption is inevitable once it has begun, in both species and individual. The *Confessions* opens the possibility that such a development of artificial sentiments is not entirely irreversible.

Not only do these three works consider a common theme, they also follow a similar method. Each begins by identifying, explicitly or implicitly, primitive characteristics of human nature and proceeds by presenting what Rousseau calls in the *Confessions* the "chain of feelings" (I, 18, 104, 175, 277, 413), "the history of my soul" (I, 278). In the *Second Discourse* he declares to humanity as a whole, "Here is your history as I believed it to read, not in the books of your fellow-men which are lies, but in nature which never lies" (*Discourses*, 103–4). He says of *Emile*, "This ought to be the history of my species" (*Emile*, 416).[66] Each of these "histories" is concerned with the causes of artificial sentiments. Each is equally a philosophic account and a chronological narrative. That the *Confessions* gives a history of an individual character and that it chooses an extraordinary individual as its subject indicates its complementarity generally with Rousseau's major theoretical writings. In drawing out these aspects of the major themes of the other works, the *Confessions* fills certain gaps in the system. The ability of the *Confessions* to shed new light on the predominant features of Rousseau's thought is an adequate justification for a treatment of its theoretical importance.

The second approach to the philosophic importance of the *Confessions* goes even further. This approach is based on Rousseau's indica-

---

plete knowledge of a human character. He says, "It would be necessary to distinguish the acquired from the nature, to see how it was formed, what occasions developed it, what secret chain of affections rendered it so, and how it was modified to produce sometimes the most contradictory and unexpected effects" (I, 1149).

66. That both the *Second Discourse* and *Emile* are histories has been noted by Allan Bloom, at *Emile*, 3.

tions that the *Confessions* provides a necessary underpinning for his entire system. From the beginning to the end of his literary career, explorations of various aspects of the relation between a thinker's life and his claim to knowledge are implicit or explicit in Rousseau's works. In the *First Discourse* Rousseau discusses in detail the conflicting motives that lead people to seek wisdom or the reputation of wisdom. The *Dialogues*, one of Rousseau's last works, is concerned in large part with the relations among the doctrines found in Rousseau's books, his public reputation, and his true character. In addition, a consideration of the arguments of the *Second Discourse* shows that what appear to be unphilosophic intrusions of personality into an argument are in fact important indications of a serious philosophic issue.

Rousseau poses the epistemological problem confronting his investigation of human nature in the Preface of the *Second Discourse*: "And how will man manage to see himself as nature formed him, through all the changes that the sequence of time and things must have produced in his original constitution, and to separate what he gets from his own stock from what circumstances and his progress have added to or changed in his primitive state?" (*Discourses*, 91). With this statement Rousseau reveals a profound difficulty for the project of separating what is natural from what is conventional in humans. The passage continues by suggesting that an answer to Rousseau's question "would need even more philosophy than is generally thought" (*Discourses*, 93). With this Rousseau indicates a radical rethinking of the requirements for an understanding of human nature. He next argues that even the "experiments necessary to achieve knowledge of natural man" have not yet been thought of and would be virtually impossible to perform under existing social conditions. While he is very cautious with anthropological evidence, Rousseau makes his disagreement with his predecessors abundantly clear (*Discourses*, 203–13). He cites Buffon on several points (*Discourses*, 82, 183, 187, 191), but he agrees more with Buffon's statements of the problems of knowing human nature than with his proposed solution.

On Rousseau's analysis, the difficulty of knowing human nature worsens by stages. First, humans have no natural desire to know anything, least of all themselves. Second, the character of their eventual motivation to learn severely limits the sort of knowledge they can acquire. Finally, the development of reason denatures the human character beyond recognition. In this argument Rousseau lays the foundation for his own system by exposing the obstacles that have caused the failure of other philosophic systems.

Rousseau first attempts to establish that nature provides no need or desire for knowledge. He does claim that the requirements of survival force natural humans to acquire strength and agility and to develop acute senses of sight, hearing, and smell (*Discourses*, 106, 113). He argues, however, that the development of the senses and the natural fertility of the earth make the acquisition of much knowledge unnecessary in the pure state of nature. Natural humans can satisfy all their needs without reason. In his "Moral Letters" Rousseau spells out the consequences of this for knowledge: "Our senses are given to us to preserve us not to instruct us, to warn us about what is useful to us or the opposite and not about what is true or false. Their destination is not at all to be employed for research about nature" (IV, 1092).[67] Natural humans, whose experience of the world is restricted to the immediate exercise of their senses, do not acquire anything that could be properly called knowledge. The ease with which they preserve themselves allows them to enjoy a sort of self-absorption, but this self-absorption should in no way be confused with self-knowledge. About a man in the state of nature who has fulfilled his immediate needs Rousseau says, "His soul, agitated by nothing, is given over to the sole sentiment of its present existence" (*Discourses*, 117). Sensing, or feeling, one's existence is not the same as knowing oneself. There is no natural motive that could inspire an attempt to acquire this knowledge. Natural needs and desires, then, provide no motive for learning.

Rousseau argues next that, because the desire to know comes from an unnatural passion such as greed or vanity, we are more likely to desire useful knowledge than pure knowledge. The motive for learning can be supplied only by the derivative artificial passions, whose own origins are obscure (*Discourses*, 115–16). In addition, once knowledge is acquired, it can modify these passions further. Thus the acquisition of knowledge is both the symptom of a departure from nature and the cause of a further departure. The unnatural passions demand an ability to gain greater control over nature or over our fellows. The power that useful knowledge brings enables us to satisfy these passions. Driven by either an artificially inflamed fear of death or artificial passions such as vanity, humans are likely to recognize only what gratifies these passions rather than what is simply true. As Rousseau says in the *First Discourse*, there is no criterion independent of these distorting passions by which the truth can be judged (*Discourses*, 49). A scientist whose desire to know stems from his distorting artificial passions is unable to distinguish what

67. These letters were written to Sophie d'Houdetot in 1757 and 1758.

is natural from what is powerful or gratifying to his vanity. In the "Moral Letters" Rousseau makes the same point: "Perceiving no object, each of us makes for himself a fantastic image of everything which he then takes for the rule of truth." That humans lack a pure desire to know, a desire untainted by concerns of utility and distorting passions, means that they judge things by "a fantastic image" rather than an accurate rule of the truth. In so far as the "knowledge" acquired from these notions is useful, it transforms rather than preserves the natural world. This transformation makes nature inaccessible even to someone who miraculously acquires a pure desire to know: "Man has denatured many things the better to convert them for his use; in that he is not at all to be blamed. But it is nonetheless true that he has often disfigured them and when in the works of his hands he believes that he truly studies nature he fools himself" (IV, 1188).[68] In short, the only knowledge available to civilized humans is a knowledge of their own products.

Rousseau now concludes that the interplay of knowledge and passions makes civilized humans themselves into just another set of disfigured artifacts. Anyone who attempts to understand them will focus attention only on their acquired, modified, or denatured passions. Thus reasoning humans are able to distinguish between the natural and the artificial in each other even less than in external objects (see S.C., 158–59). The problem of understanding other people extends equally to knowing oneself. The self one seeks to know is as denatured as other people are. As Rousseau says in the "Moral Letters,"

> unfortunately, what is precisely the least known to us is what is most important for us to know namely man. We see neither the soul of another, because it is hidden, nor our own, because we have no intellectual mirror whatsoever. We are at every point blind men, but born blind men who do not imagine what sight is. Not believing any faculty to be missing we wish to measure the extremities of the world while our short sight like our hand reaches only two feet from us. (IV, 1092)

Rousseau compares "us" to blind or extraordinarily nearsighted men who can see nothing beyond their reach and are unable to reflect on themselves. The intellectual nearsightedness of natural humans is no barrier to their preservation and happiness, and it leads to no attempt to "measure the extremities of the world." It is we civilized humans

---

68. In this context Rousseau refers to the disfiguring of plants which makes knowledge of their nature impossible.

whose blindness leads to distorting judgments of the world, others, and ourselves.

Generally, the more so-called knowledge we acquire, the more artificial our passions become (*Discourses*, 92, 115–16). All civilized humans are guilty of judging themselves and the world around them according to a fantastic image rather than an accurate rule of truth, but philosophers are the worst offenders. They are the ones who most rigorously and systematically apply their fantastic images to the world. Even Descartes, who began with radical doubt and proceeded with the greatest care, "believed he went toward the truth and found only falsehood" (IV, 1095). Thus Rousseau describes human knowledge as trapped in a circle. It seeks to overcome false judgment, but it is inextricably rooted in the distorting passions that cause false judgments.

Rousseau uses this reasoning to show the flaws in the analyses of human nature developed by his predecessors. His argument is a potent weapon against his rivals, but if it is true it must also be applied to his own systematic understanding. He argues that the rigorous application of a systematic spirit leads philosophers to error, but he also claims that he himself has discovered a "true but afflicting System" (III, 106). In fact, such claims occur in his works throughout his career as a writer.[69] By insisting on the systematic character of his own thought, Rousseau raises the issue of the relation between his system and the illusory systems of previous philosophers.[70] This appears to be another illustration of Starobinski's claim that Rousseau sets up rules for others which he then feels free to violate.

That Rousseau regarded his system as different from those of other philosophers is clear. It is equally clear that his claim is not unselfconscious. His works are filled with invitations to the reader to exercise the same skepticism with which Rousseau approaches other thinkers.[71] Rousseau is not blind to the significance of his claim that systematic thought is caught in a circle. But on what grounds does he exclude himself from this circle? How did he find the standard of truth that eludes others?

The potential role of the *Confessions* in solving this dilemma is indicated by Rousseau's remarks in the Neuchâtel preface about his goal in

69. On the systematic character of Rousseau's works, see I, 933–35.
70. Rousseau says that others are likely to regard the systematic part of *Emile* as "a visionary's dreams" (*Emile*, 34).
71. Rousseau indicates the need to examine his examples and details at *Emile*, 50–51. He expresses his distrust of books at *Emile*, 184.

the *Confessions*. There he refers to the barriers that stand in the way of
knowledge of human nature. In doing so, he repeats some of the arguments that he used against other philosophers in the "Moral Letters":

> One makes oneself the rule for everything and this is precisely where
> the double illusion of amour-propre awaits us. Either we falsely lend to
> those we judge the motives which would have made us act as they did in
> their place, or in this very supposition we deceive ourselves about our
> own motives, by not knowing how to transpose ourselves sufficiently
> into a situation other than the one in which we are. (I, 1149)

As he says, in the "Moral Letters," we are blind to others and lack an
intellectual mirror to see ourselves. Here he focuses on amour-propre
as the source of the problem. We interpret others in the light of our
self-understanding, but we also fail to understand ourselves. This double illusion is the culmination of all the barriers to the knowledge of
human nature Rousseau describes in the *Second Discourse*, and this is
what the *Confessions* is meant to overcome. If the *Confessions* can demonstrate Rousseau's own ability to overcome this illusion, that is, to overcome the effects of his artificial passions and compel others to do so, it
will serve as the foundation for his system as a whole.

If the *Confessions* can do what it sets out to do, Rousseau will have
been able to confront the problem of the basis for his understanding of
his system. For this system to be persuasive, it must account for Rousseau himself as its discoverer. Natural humans with no distorting artificial passions know virtually nothing. Civilized humans may be able to
know how to manipulate things for their own preservation and advantage, but they cannot know their own nature or those of anyone or
anything else. Rousseau must show an alternative to these two positions. In short, he must be able to demonstrate how he became a philosopher. This is a difficult task for autobiography. In an autobiographical sketch that predates the *Confessions*, Rousseau gives an indication of
the sort of knowledge he hopes to convey by writing about himself: "I
am an observer and not a moralist. I am the botanist who describes the
plant. It is for the doctor to regulate its use" (I, 1120).[72] This image of
botany describes a sort of knowledge not guided and distorted by considerations of utility or any artificial passions. To be done properly, it
requires an object that has not been disfigured by human manipulation.

72. On Rousseau's understanding of botany, see Chapter 6.

The *Confessions* promises to be the story of how such knowledge can be attained.

How Rousseau's autobiography can serve as an adequate account of the discovery of the true system of nature can be seen in relation to another attempt to account for the development of understanding, the one given by Hegel in the *Phenomenology of Mind*. In his preface to the *Phenomenology*, Hegel describes the relation between his book and complete knowledge or science. He says that the *Phenomenology* is not a description of the science itself; rather it sets forth the "process by which science in general comes about, this gradual development of knowing."[73] Hegel distinguishes his account, which begins at the most primitive stage of consciousnesss and moves through progressive steps to science, from the accounts of other philosophers which are characterized by "the sort of ecstatic enthusiasm which starts straight off with absolute knowledge as if shot out of a pistol."[74] What Hegel proposes is to conduct "the individual mind from its unscientific standpoint to that of science." This focus on an individual mind might be considered autobiographical,[75] but Hegel chooses to follow a universal or general individual because to focus on a particular would mean looking at one predominant characteristic and seeing others only "in blurred outline." Thus the *Phenomenology* is a sort of philosophic biography, an account of knowledge's self-consciousness about its own origin.

The *Confessions* similarly shows the process by which Jean-Jacques's system comes to be known, combining a gradual development of consciousness and a dramatic inspiration. By showing this process, the *Confessions* attempts to free Rousseau's system from a charge of being "shot out of a pistol." Unlike the *Phenomenology*, the *Confessions* focuses on a particular individual and his predominant characteristics. Rousseau is acutely conscious of the inherent dangers of an account derived from the examination of a single case (III, 53; *Emile*, 451–52); nevertheless, as we saw in the preceding section, he claims that the unique range of his own experiences helps to overcome these dangers. Thus he can say that "in the space of fifty years I have been able to live several centuries if I have been able to profit from myself" (I, 1151). Rousseau claims to be the singular case of a particular individual who is at the

---

73. G. W. F. Hegel, *Phenomenology of Mind*, trans. J. B. Baillie (New York: Harper & Row, 1967), p. 88.

74. Ibid., p. 89. On the interpretation of this passage, see Emil Fackenheim, *The Religious Dimension in Hegel's Thought* (Boston: Beacon Press, 1967), p. 29.

75. See Hegel, *Phenomenology*, pp. 89–90.

same time a general or universal individual. The *Confessions* is a sort of phenomenology of mind.[76]

This parallel between Rousseau and Hegel reveals two important differences between their enterprises. The more obvious is Rousseau's bold claim to be a universal individual. The difference is significant, but it should not be overestimated. There is ample evidence that the Jean-Jacques of the *Confessions* is not simply an exact copy of the particular Jean-Jacques Rousseau whose life he appears to represent. Rousseau modifies events, reports them in a revealing order, and portrays them in a way calculated to bring out their general significance.[77] The particular Jean-Jacques represents the general principles of Rousseau's system as much as he represents himself. He is almost a universal individual given a particular name.[78]

The second difference is harder to discern. The process Hegel promises to reveal is a gradual development, a systematic movement from stage to stage. The process of Jean-Jacques's life is an alternation between one passion and another, with a more fitful development of these passions. The crucial stage in his acquisition turns out to be a "sudden inspiration," not a straightforward or even dialectical culmination of a development from stage to stage. The acquisition of knowledge is simply a fateful accident—and that it is an accident is an essential consequence of Rousseau's account of the barriers to understanding human nature.

Rousseau's Intention in the *Confessions*

The importance of the particularity and the accidental character of Jean-Jacques's acquisition of knowledge remains to be seen. For now it is sufficient to summarize the three aspects of, or ways of considering, Rousseau's *Confessions* identified so far. First, Rousseau suggests that

76. On a parallel between the *Phenomenology* and *Emile*, see Bloom's introduction to *Emile*, p. 3.

77. See Olivier Marty, *Rousseau de l'enfance à quarante ans* (Paris: Nouvelles Editions Débrisse, 1975), p. 113.

78. For the relation between Hegel himself and his system, consider the remark of Alexandre Kojève: "Hegel presupposes the existence of the *Philosopher*: for the dialectical movement of the *Phenomenology* to come to its end, marked by the idea—and the realization—of Wisdom, of absolute Knowledge, at each dialectical turning point there must be a *Philosopher* who is ready to become *conscious* of the newly constituted reality"; in *Introduction to the Reading of Hegel*, trans. James H. Nichols, Jr. (New York: Basic Books, 1969), p. 85.

historical accounts of particular events can be read as moral fables. Viewed in this way the *Confessions* is intended to persuade the ordinary reader of certain morally useful views. How the *Confessions* does this is considered in Chapter 2 in the context of an examination of Rousseau's understanding of past exemplary lives. Second, Rousseau suggests that an autobiography can be a proper medium for presenting an understanding of human nature. Viewed in this way the *Confessions* is intended for philosophers. How the *Confessions* shows human nature and its alteration in society is considered in Chapters 3 and 4 in the context of a discussion of the relation between Rousseau's account of himself and his account of more obviously natural men. Third, Rousseau's system requires that he explain how it is possible for him to arrive at his understanding of human nature in spite of the obstacles between any civilized human and the recovery of nature. How the *Confessions* provides an account of Rousseau's own recovery of naturalness is shown in Chapters 5 and 6 in the context of an examination of his attempt to work through and overcome the denaturing caused by civilization.

In following this outline, I primarily address three questions. First, why is it necessary to present a new salutary teaching or moral fable in the *Confessions*? Second, what is the philosophic understanding of human nature presented in the *Confessions*? Third, is Rousseau able to present a criterion for judging the adequacy of his own system?

[2]

The Need for a
New Exemplary Life

Traditional Exemplary Lives

Rousseau's arguments for the usefulness of exemplary lives are based on acknowledgment of a difference between the demands of philosophic argumentation and those of political speech. Philosophy is concerned primarily with general and abstract truth, whereas politics is concerned with both particular facts and the application of useful general truths. This difference in ends determines the difference in means. Because Rousseau is pessimistic about the effectiveness of public appeals to reason, he regards the political alternatives as either persuasion or force. Although he is aware of the possibilities of fraud and fanaticism inherent in political rhetoric, he insists that the alternative to such rhetoric is a despotism that uses neither reason nor nonrational persuasion. Each participant in a philosophic discussion can be the judge of each part of the argument, but public rhetoric must engage the audience's unreflective assent to a picture of the whole truth. Philosophy proceeds by slow reasoning; politics proceeds by immediate appearances. Exemplary lives provide the most important pictures of the whole truth in the best political communities.

It is clear that Rousseau attributes an important political and moral function to the literary genre of exemplary lives. To consider the political moral function of the *Confessions*, we should understand why Rousseau considered it desirable to add to the number of exemplary lives. An analysis of those lives he considered to be greatest and most influential and an account of what those lives fail to do may help us to understand why he chose to write his own.

The exemplary lives Rousseau considers most important are those of Socrates, Cato, and Jesus. As we have seen, when exposing the dangers that lives pose to Emile, Rousseau says that "if in these parallels he just once prefers to be someone other than himself—were the other Socrates, were it Cato—everything has failed" (*Emile*, 243).[1] Time and again Rousseau returns to these two men in his works, both separately and together. Their only rival is Jesus, whom Rousseau also frequently treats in conjunction with Socrates. Cato is "the greatest of humans" (*d'Alembert*, 29). Socrates is the "wisest of men according to the judgment of the gods" (*Discourses*, 45). Jesus shows the life and death "of a god" (*Emile*, 308). Although Rousseau refers to other exemplary figures, such as Moses and Lucretia, these three are his highest examples of objects of emulation. Each of the three represents a very different claim for what the best human life is, and people who imitate any one of them will lead very different lives. Those who try to imitate all three will find themselves plagued by irreconcilable internal tensions. Rousseau's analysis of these three figures reveals his opinion about the most serious contenders for the understanding of the best human life. His account of their defects reveals his understanding of the defects of the tradition of exemplary lives. It is against the background of this understanding that we can begin to grasp the purpose of the *Confessions*.

Rousseau makes use of Cato, Socrates, and Jesus as vivid illustrations of some of his major concerns. He uses Cato to portray the perfect denatured citizen who is whole only by participating in his community. He uses Socrates to portray the preservation within a corrupt community of something approaching natural independence accompanied by the civilized characteristic of wisdom. He uses Jesus to portray the attempt to combine social concerns with something resembling Socratic wisdom. Because Rousseau alternately holds up each of these figures as the highest human possibility, he is able to accomplish several purposes. The image he paints of each is a moral fable meant to inspire emulation. The different moral fables represented by each serve different goals in different circumstances. In large part the apparent contradiction in praising citizenship in one place, independence in another, and a combination of the two in a third can be resolved by

---

1. Rousseau also has high praise for Cato the Elder (*Discourses*, 45), but his frequent references to Cato the Younger make it clear that the latter is meant here.

examining context and detail. Rousseau is characteristically precise in the terms of his praise and in the identification of his different criteria for judgment.

The Citizen: The Case for Cato

The figure of Cato has a special place in Rousseau's writings for a number of reasons. As an example of citizen virtue he illustrates the standard Rousseau sets for himself when he adopts the persona of the "Citizen of Geneva" in many of his writings. Cato can be understood as one of the exemplary figures whom Rousseau himself imitates. Rousseau specifically identifies Cato as "the greatest of humans" (*d'Alembert*, 29). This praise seems to leave little doubt about Cato's rank. As one commentator has said, "here is a model to imitate, a model superior to Socrates, . . . but who remains on this side of Christ."[2] Only Jesus, who is more than human according to the Savoyard vicar (*Emile*, 308), appears to be able to stand a comparison. But what makes Cato the greatest of humans?

Rousseau adds specificity to his claim of Cato's greatness in a recently discovered collection of fragments. In an isolated sentence he says, "There is no death in the world more beautiful than that of Socrates, but there is no life as beautiful as that of Cato" (*J.J.*, 54). Because this fragment comes without context, its significance is hard to judge. Nevertheless, its precision makes it a useful guide for further investigation. It establishes Cato's greatness through a specific comparison with Socrates; yet, by referring on the one hand to Socrates' death and on the other hand to Cato's life, it avoids a direct comparison.

Both of these features occur frequently in a variety of contexts in Rousseau's works. Socrates and Cato are often compared, but the comparison is always indirect. The best example of this curious practice occurs in "On Political Economy." Rousseau declares, "Let us dare to compare Socrates himself to Cato" (*S.C.*, 219). His comparison begins by adopting virtue as the standard for judging the two: "Socrates' virtue is that of the wisest of men. But compared to Caesar and Pompey, Cato seems like a God among mortals." That this statement conveys a sense of Cato's superiority cannot be denied, but Cato's godlike appearance does not occur in a comparison with Socrates. Rousseau also gives no

2. Denise Leduc-Fayette, *J. J. Rousseau et le mythe de l'antiquité* (Paris: J. Vrin, 1974), p. 57.

indication of how Socrates would appear if he were compared to Caesar or Pompey. The promised comparison has not been made.

The supposed comparison proceeds with still more indirection. Rousseau continues, "A worthy student of Socrates would be the most virtuous of his contemporaries; a worthy emulator of Cato would be the greatest. The former's own virtue would constitute his happiness; the latter would seek his happiness in that of all others. We would be taught by one, but ruled by the other, and that alone would determine our preference." Once again Cato is given high praise, but once again there is no direct comparison with Socrates. Nor is there even a direct comparison between students of each. Rousseau compares a student of one to an emulator of the other. Furthermore, he implies only that we would rather be ruled by the emulator than taught by the student. He does not tell us which of the two we would rather be. There is much of the moral fable in this and other comparisons between Socrates and Cato. Like an imitative artist, Rousseau gives the general impression of Cato's superiority, but like a philosopher he also gives details that provide a somewhat different account. Both the general impression and the details can guide us to Rousseau's considered judgment.

Rousseau comments on Socrates' death throughout his works (II, 525; III, 15, 73; d'Alembert, 121). In these remarks he usually emphasizes Socrates' attachment to virtue, more than his wisdom, as the source of the poignancy of his execution (cf. S.C., 219). On the whole, Rousseau presents the beauty of Socrates' death in terms of his intransigent attachment to virtue in the face of the corruption around him. This picture presents a strong case for the superiority of Socrates to Cato when one recalls that Cato self-consciously imitated Socrates' behavior at his death (II, 380). The imitator is inferior to what he imitates.

A somewhat less exalted picture of Socrates' death appears in the "Profession of Faith of the Savoyard Vicar" in *Emile*. The vicar first argues that it is only Socrates' death that proves that he was not a mere sophist; his life alone would not prove this. This criticism is consistent with the fragment's reference to Socrates' death and its silence about the rest of his life. Next the vicar emphasizes the ease of this death (*Emile*, 307). He concludes, "The death of Socrates, philosophizing tranquilly with his friends, is the sweetest one could desire" (*Emile*, 308). Although Rousseau does not agree with the vicar on every issue, he does repeat this judgment in his own name elsewhere.[3] In his own

---

3. Rousseau says that when he heard the vicar's account of natural religion, he "saw a multitude of objections to make to him" (*Emile*, 294).

statement he qualifies the vicar's harshness against Socrates only by
calling Socrates' death both "beautiful and sweet" (IV, 1146; II, 1274).
In sum, Socrates' death is beautiful or noble, but no uniquely so. It is its
sweetness or gentleness (*douceur*) that distinguishes it most.

Rousseau makes a somewhat better case for the rest of Socrates' life
in other contexts. He does this, however, by emphasizing Socrates' virtue; that is, he makes Socrates compete on Cato's ground. In the *First
Discourse*, for example, he modifies the argument of Plato's *Apology of
Socrates* to make it more compatible with his own argument.[4] The "Citizen of Geneva" presents Socrates as the "Citizen of Athens" (*Discourses*,
43–44; see also III, 73). Rousseau's culminating praise of Socrates in
this context is that he set a good example. According to Rousseau, if
Socrates were alive today, "he would leave behind to his disciples and
our posterity no other moral precept than the example and memory of
his virtue" (*Discourses*, 45). Socrates here is made to appear as much like
an exemplary citizen as possible. Rousseau praises him, however, more
for resisting the general trend toward vice than for influencing others.
He praises Socrates so that he can point out the inability of a wise man
to make society as a whole combine virtue and pursuit of the arts
(*Discourses*, 43; III, 64–65, 970–71). Socrates' independence from the
community is coupled here with his inability to serve as a generally
effective example. Although Socrates' life can be made to appear virtuous in comparison to those of other philosophers, it cannot match
that of Cato. While Socrates' life may have been virtuous (IV, 1142), he
was not the most virtuous of men, as Cato was (IV, 1142; II, 1268; cf.
II, 87). The beauty of Cato's life is its unrivaled virtue. This is the
standard according to which Cato is the greatest of men. We do not yet
know if this is the highest possible standard.

Rousseau sets out to identify the highest standard by which to judge
Cato and Socrates in his "Discourse on the Question: 'What Is the Most
Necessary Virtue for a Hero and Who Are the Heroes in Whom This
Virtue Was Lacking?'" In this essay Rousseau contrasts heroes, among
whom he numbers Caesar, Pompey, and Cato (II, 1267–68), with wise
men, among whom he numbers Socrates (II, 1263). He begins the
discourse by referring to the difficulty of deciding which of the two

---

4. Raymond Trousson demonstrates conclusively that Rousseau's paraphrase of the
Apology, in which he makes Socrates attack artists rather than artisans, is taken from
Diderot; see *Socrate devant Voltaire, Diderot et Rousseau* (Paris: Lettres Modernes Minard,
1967), appendix. That this view of Socrates may have originated with Diderot does not
mean that Rousseau accepted it without reflection.

categories is superior. He resolves the difficulty by saying, "To place the true hero in his rank, I have recourse only to this incontestible principle: that among men it is he who renders himself most useful to others who should be the first of all. I do not fear at all that the wise will appeal a decision founded on this maxim" (II, 1264). This maxim allows Rousseau to find in favor of the hero. One might say that the wise would have to become heroes to satisfy this standard of judgment. The virtue of a hero like Cato deserves the highest rank because it is most useful to others. This accords with the judgment in "On Political Economy" that we prefer the emulator of Cato to the student of Socrates because he would be a better ruler. Social utility is the standard according to which Cato is the greatest of men.

One might be tempted to deny Cato's greatness in terms of this standard. His failure in opposing Caesar's tyranny and his ultimate suicide appear to show the futility of Cato's efforts. Rousseau admits that Cato's deeds lack the superficial attractiveness of military victories: "This man did not become at all illustrious in combat and did not at all fill the world with the noise of his exploits" (II, 1268). He did have one accomplishment, however, which is too often forgotten because of his final defeat by Caesar: he "formed out of a body of men of war a society of wise, equitable, and modest men." According to Rousseau, this enterprise was "the most difficult which had ever been undertaken and the only one which will never be imitated." Cato's one accomplishment during his life is comparable to the task of a political founder, although on a smaller scale. He formed a society. His founding is more impressive than those of Lycurgus and Solon, who are mentioned in this context, because it is a reformation. Cato performed the almost impossible feat of beginning with corrupt men and curing their corruption.[5]

Plutarch, Rousseau's source for this story, attributes Cato's success to his persuasion and instruction of the soldiers. His account concludes by emphasizing the role of emulation in this instruction. Plutarch indicates that most people come to love virtue only when they see it embodied in someone like Cato.[6] They love the person first and emulate his

5. In his analyses of legislators, Rousseau concedes that a few, such as Lycurgus, Numa, and Moses, did legislate for partially corrupt communities (III, 499, 952). Their success depended, in part, on "clearing the area and setting aside all the old material" (*Discourses*, 163). Because of the apparent impossibility of a repetition, Cato's success is still more impressive, coming as it does after those of Numa and Brutus (S.C., 71; *Discourses*, 80; III, 506–7). For more on this question, see Kelly, "To Persuade without Convincing."

6. Plutarch, *Life of Cato*, XV. For an account that claims that it is virtue itself we love rather than the man who incorporates it, see *Life of Pericles*, I.

virtue because it is his. Similarly, in the "Discourse on the Virtue for a Hero" Rousseau calls Cato "this model of citizens" (II, 1268). It is his ability to serve as a model inspiring emulation that makes Cato so great.[7] Thanks to Plutarch and other historians, Cato's ability to be a model for citizens did not end with his life. In his "Last Response" to the critics of the *First Discourse* Rousseau continues Plutarch's work by defending Cato against modern philosophers who ridicule his virtue: "I do not know if he did nothing for his country as the critics claim; but I do know that he has done much for the human race, by giving it the spectacle and the model of the purest virtue which could ever have existed (III, 87). Cato's example is an effective one in those places where corruption is not irremediable, places like Poland and Corsica. Rousseau's resuscitation and defense of Cato's example can help perpetuate its influence.

In sum, Cato's superiority to Socrates, or to the wise in general, comes from his capacity to inspire others to imitate him: "The philosopher can give some salutary instruction to the universe; but his lessons will never correct the great who despise them, nor the people who do not hear them" (II, 1263). At most, philosophers can have an effect on heroes who in turn have a more general effect. The "abstract views" of the philosophers simply do not have the direct effect of concrete images. Abstractions may convince the few who are wise, but they are unable to persuade the many. Socrates was a far better citizen than most philosophers, but in many respects even he was a useless citizen in comparison to a Cato (III, 55, 72).

The model of Cato as the greatest of humans is the perfect example of a life that serves as a moral fable. Cato's life presents virtue in an easily felt and agreeable form. Rousseau uses the story of Cato in one of his most passionate defenses of morality: The Savoyard vicar says,

> If there is nothing moral in the heart of man, what is the source of these transports of admiration for heroic actions, these raptures of love for great souls? What relation does this enthusiasm for virtue have to our private interest? Why would I want to be Cato who disemboweled himself, rather than Caesar triumphant? Take this love of the beautiful from our hearts, and you take all the charm from life. (*Emile*, 287)

---

7. In *Julie*, Saint Preux refers to Cato "whose august and sacred image animated the Romans with a holy zeal" (II, 381). In the community at Clarens, Julie has a similar influence. It is described in general terms: "Souls of a certain sort . . . transform so to speak the others into themselves; they have a sphere of activity in which nothing resists them: you cannot know them without wishing to imitate them, and from their sublime elevation they attract to themselves everything that surrounds them" (II, 204).

By giving charm to the lives of other citizens, Cato's life inspires exactly the sort of emulation required of them. That Cato's greatness consists in being a model for emulation, however, also raises a possible qualification to his rank as the greatest of humans. As we have seen, emulation or imitation is regarded favorably on only one of Rousseau's standards, that of civil dependence or social utility. Socrates may fare better in the comparison under one of the other categories.

The Philosopher: The Case for Socrates

From the standpoint of moral utility, Rousseau's comparison between Cato and Socrates grants Cato's superiority. Before drawing a final conclusion, however, one should note the contexts of the arguments for Cato's preeminence. The most unqualified praise of Cato occurs in the *Letter to d'Alembert* and the "Last Response" to the critics of the *First Discourse*. In each, Rousseau identifies himself as "Citizen of Geneva." These are works in which he explicitly adopts the standards of citizenship. An explanation of why he varies his identification is found in the second preface to *Julie*. There Rousseau says that he will not identify himself as a citizen of Geneva at the head of this novel because to do so might "profane" the name of his fatherland (II, 27). This book, unlike the *Letter to d'Alembert*, is directed to relatively uncorrupt French provincials (II, 20), not to virtuous citizens. Thus, generally speaking, the works in which Rousseau explicitly identifies himself as a citizen are works appropriate to citizenship. These works consider the issue at hand predominantly from the standpoint of what is good for a healthy community. The works not designated in this way are intended for another audience. Works in this latter category never condemn Cato, but they do not contain the most unqualified praise either.[8]

The "Discourse on the Virtue for a Hero" gives some indication of how to evaluate the different perspectives by which Cato is judged. It explicitly gives the highest place to heroes, and therefore to Cato, by adopting social utility as its measure. Rousseau considers the two categories, wise man and hero, "in their relations with the interest of society" (II, 1263). If the two types of men were to be considered "in themselves," rather than in relation to society, the conclusion would be

---

8. One explanation of this silence is that, when he discusses his own citizenship in these works, Rousseau does not wish to draw attention to the highest example of citizenship.

different. In this case, Rousseau says that the preference would go to the wise man and therefore to Socrates over Cato.

This reversal of ranking is confirmed in Rousseau's works that do not explicitly adopt the perspective of the citizen. In a fragment, Rousseau compares Socrates and Cato by saying, "Socrates was able to live under the Tyrants because he was very certain of conserving his freedom everywhere. Cato abhorred Tyranny, because it was not enough for him to be free, he wished that all citizens be so" (*J.J.*, 54). This comment confirms Cato's superiority from the standpoint of social utility, but it raises a question about whether Cato was as capable as Socrates of being free everywhere. This reverses the judgment we have seen before in which Socrates' independence is regarded as inferior to Cato's virtue. This difference is made even sharper by another fragment in which Rousseau says, "If you are a philosopher, live as Socrates, if you are only a statesman, live as Cato" (*J.J.*, 53). Without qualification, Cato is accorded a lower status than Socrates. The political life ranks lower than the nonpolitical life. It is worth nothing that here Rousseau is discussing who one is rather than by whom one would prefer to be ruled. As the context of the remark makes clear, the consideration of freedom is the source of this relative ranking.[9] Thus, while the standard of social utility teaches the superiority of Cato, the standard of freedom or independence teaches the superiority of Socrates.

Rousseau's most comprehensive consideration of the standard of freedom independent of social utility occurs in the *Second Discourse*.[10] He argues that, in a condition of natural freedom, people are completely independent of each other because they have almost nothing to do with each other. While social utility necessarily involves one's relations with others, liberty involves only oneself. From the standpoint of social utility, people in the pure state of nature are clearly inferior to Cato; from that of freedom, they are inferior to no one. Both Socrates and a natural human are given their greatest praise when judged according to the standard of freedom. Because freedom and independence from others are the natural standards, Socrates must ultimately be judged superior to Cato.

To conclude the comparison, we can return to the emulator of Cato and the student of Socrates. Emulation applies to the citizen and study

---

9. The fragment begins "Both of them were born free" (*J.J.*, 53).

10. The *Second Discourse* appears to be a partial exception to Rousseau's general practice in writings in which he identifies himself as "Citizen of Geneva." It is only in the dedicatory letter that the citizen perspective takes primacy.

to the philosopher. Rousseau stresses the political or moral effect of the example of Cato. Because citizens, unlike philosophers, are essentially emulators, Cato remains the superior object of emulation or role model. Nevertheless, Socrates is superior to Cato according to the standard of nature. The student of Socrates finds his happiness in his own virtue, which is "the virtue of the wisest of men," rather than in an imitation of Socrates. He learns from Socrates; he does not emulate him. Furthermore, he apparently has no effect on others. Happiness that depends on independence and freedom is a natural standard that illuminates Socrates' superiority to Cato.

We are now in a position to explain the remark with which this chapter began. At least two different sets of reasons lead to Rousseau's conclusion that Emile should not wish to be either Cato or Socrates. To imitate Socrates would be to parody a philosopher;[11] to imitate Cato would be to give oneself up to a community. Emile, who is educated according to nature, is to avoid both alternatives. Since the goal of natural education is natural independence or freedom, and the superiority of Socrates to Cato is his greater independence, it is tempting to say that Socrates, like Emile, represents the highest human possibility. He is the model of someone free of the bounds of role models. Socrates appears as a sort of natural man in civil society.

This is a rather surprising conclusion in the light of Rousseau's frequent denials that the development of reason is natural. One response to questions about Socrates raised on this issue would be to point out that Emile maintains his natural independence in social conditions only by developing his reason. Furthermore, Rousseau stresses the exceptional character of Socrates. He is virtually the sole example of a noncorrupt philosopher. Finally, however, we must be prepared for Rousseau to call into question Socrates' approximation of the natural standard. He does this in his comparison of Socrates with Jesus.

A Revolution in the Universe: The Case for Jesus

In his most thorough comparison between Socrates and Cato, Rousseau avoids a direct confrontation of the two. In this way he maintains

11. One might say that Emile does imitate Socrates in certain respects even though, or precisely because, he is unaware that Socrates ever existed. Rousseau says that a child who has been brought up properly "interrogates like Socrates" (*Emile*, 179). He does so, not because he has studied Platonic dialogues, but because he is interested only in what is truly useful rather than in other people's opinions about him.

the salutary impression of the superiority of the citizen while leaving
open the case for the superiority of the philosopher. This complicated
procedure is an excellent example of how Rousseau combines salutary
moral fables with more complicated philosophic teachings. The persuasive superficial image in his account gives one impression and the
convincing argument underneath the surface gives another. In turning
away from Cato to the comparison between Jesus and Socrates, Rousseau undertakes a more direct confrontation that at first appears to
leave little doubt about Jesus's superiority. In his depreciation of the
death of Socrates, the Savoyard vicar concludes that "if the life and
death of Socrates are those of a wise man, the life and death of Jesus are
those of a God" (*Emile*, 308).[12] While the wise man or philosopher may
ultimately be superior to the statesman, a god is obviously superior to
both.

The terms of this comparison are much more direct than those of
the comparisons between Socrates and Cato. Cato appears to be a god
only in relation to Caesar and Pompey; Jesus does so in relation to
Socrates. Nevertheless, we should keep in mind that this comparison is
made by the vicar, not by Rousseau. When Rousseau undertakes the
comparison in his own name, he softens it somewhat. After referring to
the "beautiful and sweet" death of Socrates, he says, "As for Jesus, the
sublime flight taken by his great soul always elevated it above all
mortals" (IV, 1146). The comparison still supports Jesus's superiority,
but without the straightforward attribution of divinity. Like Rousseau's
statement praising Cato as the greatest of humans, this one is vague
about the criteria used to reach this judgment. This vagueness is a
token of the complexity of Rousseau's understanding of the differences
between Jesus and Socrates.

Aside from the "Profession of Faith," the major contexts for this
comparison are the "Fiction or Allegorical Piece on Revelation" and the
"Letter to M. Franquières."[13] The "Letter" contains remarks on the
death of Socrates that parallel and qualify the statements of the Savoyard vicar. The "Fiction" is an extended presentation of Socrates and
Jesus in the form of an image or dream. This image reveals some
reservations about Socrates that do not emerge from Rousseau's comparisons between Socrates and Cato. Specifically, while in comparison

---

12. I have capitalized "God" to conform with the French (IV, 626).

13. The "Fiction" has been attributed to a series of dates ranging from 1750 to 1777
(IV, 1766–67). The "Letter" was written in 1769 eight months before Rousseau started
Part Two of the *Confessions*.

to Cato Socrates looks like a model of natural independence preserved in a civilized human, in the "Fiction" the extent and foundation of Socrates' independence is called into question.

In the "Fiction" an old man whose appearance and life clearly resemble those of Socrates is presented as attempting to free humans from the delusions of fanaticism.[14] He publicly strips the veil off a statue that represents the false gods people worship, but he is unable to lessen their attachment to their enslaving prejudices and for his efforts is put to death. To this point the picture of Socrates corresponds to the one in the comparison with Cato outlined above. Considered in terms of his ability to influence others, Socrates is a failure; but considered in terms of his own freedom and independence, he is unexcelled. The first troubling addition to the picture here is that Rousseau insists that Socrates is not content with his own freedom; like Cato, he attempts to secure that of others. He no longer represents complete independence.

To this can be added a certain confusion about the old man stemming from the events surrounding his death. Rousseau narrates the events reported in Plato's *Crito* and *Phaedo*, including Socrates' refusal to leave Athens, his exhortation to his followers to respect the law, and his death. Rousseau expresses "doubt and confusion" concerning this behavior (IV, 1053). He is clearly impressed with the old man's apparent freedom from enslaving prejudice and his boldness at exposing fanaticism in others. However, Socrates' willingness to obey the law and his submission to the public cult on his deathbed give the appearance of an act of homage to the very prejudice he has unveiled.[15] This combination of boldness and caution, desire to free others and to be independent of them, is a sign of contradiction in his character which Rousseau admits he is unable to resolve satisfactorily. With his expression of doubt and confusion, Rousseau concedes that there is something unfathomable about Socrates.

Rousseau offers a very tentative explanation of Socrates' behavior as he proceeds to a comparison of the old man to another figure. This new figure is a young man identified as "the son of man" (IV, 1053).[16] He has an "imposing and gentle aspect." The one direct comparison made of him to the old man is that his bearing is "even less affected than that

14. My interpretation of the symbols in the myth follows those of Starobinski in *Transparence*, pp. 79–85, and Henri Gouhier, *Les Méditations métaphysiques de Jean-Jacques Rousseau* (Paris: Libraire Philosophique J. Vrin, 1970), pp. 194–208.
15. The reference is to Socrates' dying words; see Plato, *Phaedo*, 118a.
16. See Gouhier, *Méditations*, pp. 202–3, for a discussion of the "son of man."

of his predecessor." The one visible flaw in Socrates is a barely perceptible degree of affectation, which does not show up in the comparison with Cato. Rousseau's picture of Jesus reveals a flaw in Socrates' independence with respect to his concern for reputation.[17] We return to this question at the end of this chapter. For the moment it is sufficient to note that Rousseau indicates a failing of Socrates, one invisible in the comparison with Cato, which emerges in the comparison with Jesus.

A second difference between Socrates and Jesus is implied by the latter's methods and success in overcoming fanaticism. Socrates unveils the true nature of fanaticism, but this exposure does not cure more than a few people of their prejudices. Unlike Socrates, the son of man replaces the image of fanaticism. He not only urges the people to "know what is," he also seizes the statue they worship and "reverse[s] it effortlessly." "Mounting the pedestal with very little agitation, he seemed to take back his own place rather than to usurp that of another." Whereas Socrates attempts to remove all images for emulation, Jesus replaces a harmful image with a good one. Unlike Rousseau's Socrates, his Jesus shows an awareness of the public need for exemplary figures.

Rousseau describes the effect of this toppling of the old image and its replacement with a new one as a "revolution" (IV, 1053–54). He says, "His air, his tone, his gestures caused an extraordinary fermentation in the assembly; the people were seized by them to the point of enthusiasm." Jesus is able to inspire this enthusiasm, not by the force of his argument, but by the tangible signs of his greatness of soul. It is true that "the language of the truth cost him nothing because it had its source in him." Nevertheless, this language of truth is not rational demonstration. Rousseau says that "his instructions were fables and allegories, common conversation but full of justness and profundity." He both uses fables and enacts one in the example of his life. In Rousseau's interpretation, Jesus is the master of the salutary use of moral fables.

Jesus seems to represent a combination of the specific excellence of Socrates and the very different excellence of Cato. He is even freer of dependence on convention than Socrates and even more effective as a

17. In the *First Discourse* Rousseau traces the origin of "moral philosophy" to pride (*Discourses*, 48).

model for emulation than Cato. He seems to satisfy both the standard of nature and that of social utility. That Rousseau regarded the superiority of Jesus to Socrates mainly in terms of the standard of emulation or social utility is confirmed by his other extended comparison in the "Letter to Franquières." This comparison also provides more information about the difference between the "revolution" effected by Jesus and those caused by legislators like Lycurgus, Numa, and Moses. Following the pattern set in the comparisons between Cato and Socrates, this one occurs in the context of a discussion of the insufficiency of philosophy as a support for morality (IV, 1137). Philosophy forms only the "abstract image of virtue" (IV, 1143), which is incapable of resisting any concrete object of an immoral desire. Reason provides no motive for being just. Following this argument, Rousseau begins the comparison between Socrates and Jesus with a similarity. They are both wise and therefore can be judged according to a shared standard. A discussion of their relative consistency of character is the closest Rousseau comes to comparing their wisdom. He praises Jesus's unwavering behavior and condemns Socrates' lapses into the sophistic practices he claims to oppose. Consistency takes the place of wisdom in the comparison, and on this score Jesus wins.

After making this preliminary judgment in favor of Jesus, Rousseau drops Socrates from the discussion altogether and continues his argument with a description in political terms of Jesus's "noble project." His assertions about Jesus's wisdom, consistency, and independence quickly move to the background. Rousseau says that his project was "to raise up his people, to make them once more a people free and worthy of being so." This project is the most difficult one that a legislator can undertake, namely, to reform a corrupt people. It is comparable on a larger scale to Cato's reformation of his soldiers.

This project of reforming a people faced two obstacles the combination of which rendered it impossible. First, according to Rousseau, Jesus's people had become too corrupt to be influenced by "his genius and his virtue" alone (IV, 1146). In this case, harshness like that of Brutus or Moses would have been a necessary supplement to emulation. Second, Jesus was incapable of the necessary harshness because of "the too great gentleness of his own character." After realizing the impossibility of executing his project of purely political reform, Jesus "extended it in his head and . . . not being able to make a revolution among his people by himself, he wished to make one in the universe by his disciples." Just as he had in the "Fiction," Rousseau here presents this revolution as being outside the realm of normal political activity.[18] The extension of this revolution to "the universe" cannot but make it appear a grander project than a political revolution in one people. Rousseau's judgment about this revolution concerns, first, how or to what extent the revolution succeeded and, second, what the substance of the revolution was.

In the "Letter to Franquières" Rousseau gives several indications of Jesus's method. Aside from extending the revolution from his people to the universe, Jesus also extended his means from himself to his disciples. One of the tokens of his divinity is that he, "out of such shabby disciples, nevertheless made with their coarse but proud enthusiasm, eloquent and courageous men" (IV, 1147). This ability to inspire enthusiasm is the essence of useful moral fables (IV, 1053). Rousseau insists that Jesus's disciples were not convinced by reason because they did not understand his arguments (IV, 1146). In Rousseau's language about fables, Jesus had to clothe the truth to make it felt by his humble followers.

Rousseau denies that Jesus made any use of miracles whatsoever in his revolution. This deemphasis of miracles is consistent with Rousseau's other treatments of Jesus. In the *Letters Written from the Mountain* Rousseau discusses the place of reason, miracles, and exemplary lives in the success of Christianity.[19] Miracles are the least important of the three. While in this context Rousseau does not deny that Jesus performed miracles, he does claim that his miracles were unrelated to his mission. Miracles are inadequate proofs because they impress only those who are "incapable of coherent reason, of slow and sure observation, and slave of the senses in everything" (III, 729). Furthermore, false miracles are as effective as true ones for persuading such an audience.

The effective proofs of Christianity are then reason and exemplary lives. Reason is the more certain of the two. Christian doctrine is proven by "its utility, its sanctity, its truth, and its profundity" (III, 727–28). The importance of this proof is reduced somewhat by the fact that so few people are capable of grasping it. For those who lack sufficient

18. In the "Fiction" Rousseau shows the unpolitical character of this revolution by comparing Jesus's activity to the activity of philosophers and by showing the opponents as "Ministers of the Temple."

19. The *Letters Written from the Mountain* were written in 1764. Shortly after finishing them Rousseau began work on the *Confessions*.

wisdom, but who are not simply the slaves of their senses, another proof is needed. This proof is found in the character of

> the men chosen by God to announce his word; their sanctity, their veracity, their justice, their mores pure and without stain, their virtues inaccessible to human passions are along with the qualities of under-standing, reason, mind, knowledge, prudence, as many respectable in-dices, the combination of which, if nothing belies them, forms a com-plete proof in their favor, and say that they are more than men. (III, 728)

For most decent people, the proof of a doctrine is to be found in the example of the teacher, not in the argument. Jesus himself is the pri-mary exemplary figure who "proves" Christian doctrine to "the good and upright people" who trust good character more than arguments.

By inspiring an *imitatio Christi*,[20] Jesus is like a political founder, although the sort of emulation he inspires is not political. The enthusi-asm formed in people by a Lycurgus or Brutus is connected with their harshness. It is Jesus's gentleness "which causes torrents of tears to be shed by whoever knows how to read his life as is necessary" (IV, 1146). The harshness of ordinary political emulation entails a revulsion to-ward people outside one's own community. "Every patriot is harsh to foreigners. They are only men. They are nothing in his eyes" (*Emile*, 39). Jesus's gentleness, which is unsuited for the narrowness of patrio-tism, is appropriate for a universal, transpolitical revolution.

In his earliest account of Jesus, Rousseau describes the progress of the Christian revolution in the universe after Jesus's death:[21] "Of all the miracles with which God honored the apostles' faith, the most striking was the sanctity of their life; the disciples followed this example and their success was prodigious" (III, 45). Thus the apostles imitated the example set by Jesus and in turn inspired the imitation of larger groups of disciples. Again, humility and gentleness in the face of persecution are the distinctive features of Christianity. "All the Christians ran to martyrdom, all the peoples ran to baptism." Thus Christianity began with the example of one life and grew and preserved itself through the examples of imitations of Christ. Christianity is the example par excel-lence of the power of exemplary lives.

---

20. When Rousseau began writing the *Confessions*, he was engaged in a careful study of the *Imitatio Christi* along with his customary nightly reading of the Bible; see Ronald Grimsley, *Rousseau and the Religious Quest* (Oxford: Clarendon Press, 1968), p. 30.

21. The work is his "Observations" on a response to the *First Discourse*.

Rousseau's comparisons between Socrates and Cato are conducted according to two sorts of criteria: each is considered first in his relations with others and then in himself. Cato wins according to the first of these criteria, Socrates wins according to the second. In the comparison between Socrates and Jesus, Jesus wins according to both criteria. His victory according to the first is clear. He is much more influential than Socrates as an exemplary figure. Rousseau's judgment according to the second criterion is less decisive, but his references to Jesus's consistency and complete lack of affectation compared to Socrates are compatible with a case for Jesus's superiority when considered in himself.

While Rousseau is willing to make direct or indirect comparisons of Socrates to Cato and Socrates to Jesus, he makes no direct comparison between Cato and Jesus. A comparison between these two would be on the grounds of their relations to others. It would entail weighing the respective goals of the revolution in the universe and a revolution in a single city. To see Rousseau's final judgment about the Christian revolution, one must consider its substance in more detail. This consideration can form a part of the analysis of Rousseau's account of the need for a completely new exemplary life.

Jean-Jacques: The Case against Jesus, Socrates, and Cato

Rousseau uses Cato, Socrates, and Jesus to exemplify his concerns with politics, philosophy, and religion. As convenient embodiments of different characteristics, they allow Rousseau to make both broad and precise comparisons. There is one further dimension to his frequent recourse to these figures. He induces a series of comparisons not only among the three, but also of each of these three with himself. Rousseau's designation of himself as "Citizen of Geneva" in several works identifies him with the standard of moral utility set by Cato. This identification earned Rousseau the nickname Citizen among his Parisian friends (I, 395).[22] Similarly, his use of Socrates to support his arguments in the *First Discourse* involved Rousseau in a series of disputes in which he became identified as a great defender of Socrates (III, 55, 65, 94–95). This identification became so well fixed that, when Rousseau suffered persecution, comparisons between him and Socrates became commonplace in both public discussion and private correspondence.[23]

22. On Rousseau as the Citizen, see Leduc-Fayette, *Mythe*, pp. 66–67.
23. See Burgelin, *Philosophie*, p. 189.

Rousseau himself did much to encourage and nothing to discourage such a parallel. Finally, Rousseau's portrait of Jesus also bears a close resemblance to his presentation of himself. Both find themselves surrounded by corrupt contemporaries.[24] Both present a picture of virtue that leads to persecution.[25] Further, both are rendered unfit for conventional politics because of gentleness of character.[26] These implicit parallels have been noted by modern scholars[27] and by Rousseau's contemporaries.[28] His description of Jesus in the "Letter to Franquières" lends credence to this evaluation, but with important qualifications. In highlighting similarities between himself and Jesus, Rousseau does not claim divinity for himself; rather, he presents Jesus as a human comparable to others like Socrates and Cato.[29] This presentation is a shocking departure from ordinary piety and leads to a revised view of Jesus's final achievement. In short, Rousseau ceaselessly invites his audience to measure him against the highest standards.

It would be easy to interpret Rousseau's attempts to link himself with each of these three figures as examples of his vanity, his inconsistency, or both. This identification, however, also establishes a series of moral fables about Rousseau's personality that adds to the effectiveness of his works. His analysis of the success of political founders and of Christianity proves his understanding of the importance of the use of good character as a proof of a teaching. Furthermore, his identifications with these characters are far from complete. He draws distinctions between himself and the others which are as subtle and precise as the ones he draws among them. These distinctions reveal what he judges to be the defects in these exemplary figures. Both by using the pictures of Cato, Socrates, and Jesus and by setting himself against them, Rousseau gives a picture of a new exemplary life or moral fable to rival the old ones.

We have already seen the substance of Rousseau's reservations about the unnaturalness of Cato's citizenship and the affectation in Socrates' wisdom; we return to his criticisms of these figures at the end of this section. Rousseau's presentation of Jesus is the hardest of the

24. Consider the epigraph to the *First Discourse* (*Discourses*, 31): "*Barbarus hic ego sum quia non intelligor illis*" (Here I am the barbarian, because no one understands me).
25. On Jean-Jacques as an unappreciated example of virtue, see I, 362.
26. On Rousseau's judgment of his lack of fitness to be a legislator, see I, 648–51.
27. See Gouhier, *Méditations*, pp. 185–220; Starobinski, *Transparence*, pp. 87–90; and Grimsley, *Rousseau and the Religious Quest*, p. 30.
28. For general discussions of the identifications made of Rousseau, see Gouhier, *Méditations*, and Trousson, *Socrate*.
29. See Leduc-Fayette, *Mythe*, p. 46, and Starobinski, *Transparence*, p. 88.

three to judge. Part of the difficulty stems from his unconventional approach to Jesus, one token of which is the enmity with which his views were received by both the religious authorities and the anti-religious partisans of the Enlightenment (I, 435–36). Another part of the difficulty comes from Rousseau's insistence that much of Christian tradition, the thought of Augustine for example,[30] is a corrupt departure from Jesus's true message. To establish Rousseau's final judgment of Jesus, one must establish his understanding of the true message of Christianity.

We can begin by recalling that, according to Rousseau, Jesus began his revolution in the universe out of a conviction that a restoration of civic virtue was impossible (IV, 1146). In the "Letter to Franquières" neither Socrates nor Jesus but the elder Brutus is the model of civic virtue: "Brutus putting his children to death might have been only just. But Brutus was a tender father; it tore his entrails to do his duty, so Brutus was virtuous" (IV, 1143). Because virtue implies the strength of soul that can overcome one's attachment to one's children, it is more impressive than mere justice. This sort of action is precluded by Jesus's gentleness. Christianity embraces self-sacrifice, but it leaves sacrifices of sons to God the Father. In a fragment Rousseau shows anger at Augustine for his disparagement of Brutus's virtue and accuses the fathers of the church of teaching Christians to be cowards (III, 506). He is careful to place responsibility for this depreciation of courage on the church fathers rather than on Jesus. Jesus's original political project is an indication that he would take Brutus seriously. Nevertheless, the emphasis on Jesus's gentleness tends from the beginning toward a depreciation of civic virtue. The revolution that began by regarding the harshness of civic virtue as an impossibly high goal quickly came to regard this goal as undesirable. The virtue of a Brutus becomes a splendid vice.

The example of the martyrs shows that a depreciation of all forms of courage is by no means essential to Christianity, but a depreciation of civic courage is unavoidable. While Brutus's actions aim at inspiring an active spirit of sacrifice for the community, the martyrs' self-sacrifices are not directed to such political purposes. Rousseau's famous criticism

---

30. See IV, 938. He also blames Augustine for the doctrine of the Trinity (IV, 1000). On the strength of Rousseau's condemnation of the doctrine of original sin, see Karl Barth, *Protestant Thought: From Rousseau to Ritschl* (New York: Harper and Brothers, 1959), p. 108. For a more complete treatment of the relation between Rousseau and Augustine, see Hartle, *Modern Self.*

of Christianity as a poor civil religion in the *Social Contract* makes the same point as his attack on the fathers of the church. After he charges Roman Catholicism with the destruction of political life by dividing citizens' loyalties between church and state, Rousseau turns his attention to the pure religion of the gospel. He includes the primitive Christianity of Jesus in his attack because it forms citizens who "know how to die rather than to win" in a war (*S.C.*, 129). Even if Christianity does preserve courage, it does so by giving it an apolitical form.[31] According to Rousseau, this result is, not a corruption of Jesus's message, but a direct consequence of the revolution in the universe.

In Rousseau's view the most salutary aspect of the Christian revolution is the superiority of Christian gentleness, not to republican virtue, but to the vices of corrupt civilized humans. As an alternative to this corruption, Christianity does serve the goals of moral utility. But the success of the Christian revolution carries a grave danger. Jesus's transformation of the standard by which human excellence is judged places severe obstacles in the way of any future Brutus or Cato. A new Brutus in a Christian country would seem to be a monster rather than a hero. Rather than being a sign of his virtue, the civic pride that would make him execute his sons would be taken as a sign of "vainglory" (III, 507). Thus, civic virtue takes on the appearance of vice. The Christian teaching, wittingly or unwittingly, abets the debunking of ancient virtue and therefore indirectly helps the vicious.

One may well observe that the Jean-Jacques of the *Confessions* is, with a few important exceptions, almost as apolitical as Jesus. Rousseau shows the difference between the two forms of rejection of politics in the *Dialogues*, in which he indicates an important affinity between Christianity and the corruption of ordinary civilized humans. This passage is one of the very few in his works in which he distinguishes his own views from those of Jesus on a specific issue. The context of the passage is the account given by the character "Rousseau" of his visit to "Jean-Jacques."[32] In a lengthy discussion of the latter's character, "Rousseau" says, "He thinks about his interest, that is to say about the future, only in an absolute calm; but then he falls into such a numbness that he might as well not have thought about it at all. He can well say,

---

31. Compare Rousseau's letter to Usteri, 18 July, 1763. *Correspondance complète de Jean-Jacques Rousseau*, Edition critique établie et annotée par R. A. Leigh (Geneva: Institut et musée Voltaire, 1965–), XVII, 62–65.

32. "Jean-Jacques" is the author of Rousseau's books. "Rousseau" is Rousseau himself as he would be if he had not written the books (I, 661–66).

contrary to the people of the gospel and those of our days, that where
one's heart is there also is one's treasure" (I, 818). The allusion here is
to the Sermon on the Mount, in which Jesus says,

> Lay not up for yourselves treasure upon earth, where moths and rust
> doth corrupt, and where thieves break through and steal:
> But lay up for yourselves treasure in heaven, where neither moth
> nor rust doth corrupt and where thieves do not break through nor steal:
> For where your treasure is, there will your heart be also.[33]

Jesus's statement is an attack on the vices of corrupt humans similar to
attacks frequently made by Rousseau. Jesus criticizes the pursuit of
treasure on earth as the pursuit of the transient and corruptible. His
concluding statement, however, "For where your treasure is, there will
your heart be also," applies to lovers of money and Christians alike.
Both have desires that draw them out of themselves toward a future
enjoyment. The form of the desires of both, a longing for future enjoyment, is the same. It is the object of these desires that differs. Jesus seeks
to replace one object of desire with another. By reversing the terms to
"where one's heart is there also is one's treasure," "Jean-Jacques" attacks both the object of the desire and its form; that is, he attacks any
desire that takes one outside oneself, whether the object is on earth or
in heaven. Viewed in this light, the distinction between Christians and
those who pursue wealth or fame is secondary to a more fundamental
agreement. Both live in hope of some future enjoyment that they distinguish from their present condition of misery and insecurity. Jesus's
revolution can affect corrupt civilized humans because it indulges,
rather than attempting to uproot, one of the sources of their corruption. This revolution gives a new object for foresight which is more
salutary than money or fame because it suggests that injustice will be
punished in the end, but it makes no attempt to eliminate personal
hopes for future enjoyment.

The discussion of Christianity in the *Social Contract* is directed particularly at this aspect of the Christian revolution. Rousseau claims that
the support for justice found in Christian beliefs is insufficient for
political purposes because, "far from attaching the citizens' hearts to
the State, it detaches them from it as from all worldly things. I know of
nothing more contrary to the social spirit" (*S.C.*, 128). Civilized corrup-

33. Matthew, 6:19–21.

tion detaches humans from their communities and begins to destroy their social spirit. Christianity makes this corruption less harmful, but it does so only by completing the destruction of the social spirit.

In sum, the particular genius of the Christian revolution in the universe is its ability to redirect without abolishing those qualities that make corrupt humans unsuited for citizenship. Its success stems from its ability to turn softness and selfishness into gentleness and desire for "treasure in heaven." Because it is less radical than that required for political reformation, this revolution can be successful in circumstances in which a political reformation must fail. The Christian revolution makes corrupt people less vicious, but it destroys any possible ground for citizenship by completing the destruction of the social spirit.

Because Rousseau recognizes both that Christianity mitigates the consequences of civilized corruption and that it simultaneously undermines the possibility of citizen virtue, his response is quite complicated. On one hand, he supports Christianity in the face of more pernicious alternatives by attempting to restore the exemplary status of Jesus; on the other, he attempts to weaken those aspects of Christianity that he regards as most hostile to political life. The two goals of mitigating civilized corruption and restoring some possibility for healthy politics must to some extent remain in tension with each other.

In the *Confessions*, Rousseau attempts to present a new exemplary life that can support an earthly alternative to perverse civilized pleasures without a radical rejection of politics. The image of Jean-Jacques in the *Confessions* is one of a man who enjoys harmless pleasures found in this world. It is even the image of someone intermittently overcome by enthusiasm for civic virtue. It offers an alternative to both pursuit of future worldly pleasures and longing for salvation and it does so without demanding the denaturing required of a citizen. It by no means restores civic virtue, but it offers a view of worldly happiness at the fringes of political life rather than in direct opposition to it.

The emphasis both on pleasures of the heart and on a life that is possible for someone who has lost natural goodness without acquiring civic virtue is reflected in Rousseau's epigraph for the *Confessions*, "*Intus et in cute*." As mentioned in Chapter 1, this epigraph focuses attention on internal life, the life "inside and under the skin." By doing so it turns attention away from those pleasures that exist outside oneself. Less obviously, it calls attention to civilized corruption. The phrase is taken from Persius's *Satires*, where it is applied to a man of republican heritage who has descended to vice.[34] By choosing this epigraph Rousseau indicates his own character as a less than virtuous man. He is an exemplary figure within the reach of other corrupt civilized humans.

It is the failure of Jesus's synthesis of Socratic independence and Catonic public spirit that shows the need for a new exemplary life, especially for the corrupt modern age. Before turning to the detailed analysis of this new image of human life, we can summarize Rousseau's general reservations about the two irreconcilable alternatives represented by Socrates and Cato.

Rousseau's depiction of Socrates as a man who preserves his independence in the face of civilized corruption and who lives a life of some virtue while not being a perfect citizen may well seem a model suitable for corrupt times. Part of Rousseau's hesitation to use Socrates as *the* exemplary figure can be explained by the fact that Socrates' greatness is precisely that he is not an exemplary figure. He imitates no one and inspires no true imitation. He has students, not emulators. His character as a model of independence makes him ineffective at influencing others.

Rousseau's hesitation about Socrates as a representative of the highest human type is also found in his reference to Socrates' affectation. The issue posed by this affectation can be phrased as follows. Socrates' obvious independence from the prejudices of his contemporaries is grounded in his activity as a philosopher, but Rousseau does not admit that philosophy can lead to such independence. Although he frequently refers to Socrates as an almost unique example, Rousseau does not discuss in a thematic way the precise nature of Socrates' ability to overcome civilized corruption. He is normally content to contrast Socrates' relatively good citizenship with the corruption of modern philosophers.

Rousseau never refers explicitly to Socrates in his discussions of the motives that lead people to philosophy. The most approximate reference to Socrates in such a discussion occurs in the preface to *Narcisse*, where Rousseau refers to the "taste for letters which is born from the desire to distinguish oneself" (II, 965). From this statement it is unclear whether one can distinguish a different sort of taste for letters which is born from another source. In the same context, Rousseau asserts that "the first philosophers made a great reputation for themselves by teaching men the practice of their duties and the principle of virtue." He

34. Persius, *Satires*, III, 30.

does not identify these first philosophers by name; he merely distinguishes them from Leucippus, Diogenes, Pyrrho, Protagoras, and Lucretius. These latter, according to Rousseau, attacked justice because they desired to distinguish themselves. The first philosophers did, in fact, distinguish themselves also, although Rousseau's formulation makes it possible to believe that reputation was only an unintended consequence of their publicspirited teaching. At any rate "true philosophers," whatever else their desires may be, do not praise vice simply to make names for themselves. This argument implies at least that true philosophers do not seek reputation at any cost. At most, it does not exclude the possibility that true philosophers are uninterested in the great reputations they acquire. If the former is the correct interpretation of Rousseau's view, philosophers are similar, but inferior, to citizens like Cato, and they deservedly acquire lesser reputations because they are less successful teachers of virtue. If the latter is correct, it remains necessary to determine what does interest these true philosophers who are not interested in reputation.

The question of the motives that lead to true philosophy is one of the most complex themes in the *Confessions* in which Rousseau describes his own development as a thinker. In his other works, the most elaborately developed character who appears to be both philosophic (unlike a natural man) and uninterested in public distinction (like a natural man) is Wolmar, Julie's husband in *Julie*. Wolmar, an atheist, is meant to demonstrate the merits and virtues of philosophy to the partisans of religion, just as Julie is meant to demonstrate the merits and virtues of religion to the partisans of philosophy (I, 436). Wolmar argues that his dominant passion is love of observation, and he expresses his wish to be a "living eye" who can look at men without acting on them in any way (II, 491).[35] This is a remarkable image of disinterested philosophy or contemplation, and it makes Wolmar seem similar to the Socratic presentation of a philosopher.[36] His role as the representative of philosophy suggests that Wolmar can present Rousseau's most favorable account of the motives for true philosophy.

Wolmar himself presents an account of these motives. He emphasizes his love of order, but this love of order makes him study, not

35. For a discussion of Wolmar, see Joel Schwartz, *The Sexual Politics of Jean-Jacques Rousseau* (Chicago: University of Chicago Press, 1984), pp. 118–21. Schwartz points out that Wolmar is unable to maintain a perfect independence.

36. Whereas Wolmar is a sort of "living eye," Socrates is shown in Platonic dialogues to be more of a living ear and mouth.

nature, but "the play of fortune and the actions of men." Rather than attributing his love of contemplation solely to his love of order, Wolmar admits that there is a "recompense for amour-propre" in judging people correctly as they play their roles. Here is an important respect in which a philosophic life differs from a natural life. At least a part of the pleasure Wolmar receives from his contemplation is the comparison he can make between his own independence and wisdom and the folly of others. Natural humans are incapable of such pleasure because they are incapable of making the comparison. Wolmar is independent because of his quasi-natural absence of passions, but he also prides himself on his role as an observer. He does not imitate anyone, but he does compare. The difference between Wolmar's amour-propre and that of corrupt civilized humans is that the latter feel pride in appearing to be different from others. They wish others to observe and praise them. As a result, they are extremely dependent on recognition and go to great lengths to achieve it. Wolmar, to the contrary, has no desire whatsoever to be admired. He prides himself on his real rather than apparent independence from human folly.

Thus Rousseau's account of philosophy does not imply that philosophers are exempt from the amour-propre that characterizes civilized humans. In fact, they represent the most refined version of this passion. A citizen's amour-propre causes an identification with one's fellow citizens or community (cf. S.C., 219); a corrupt human's amour-propre causes a desire to appear to be unlike one's fellow citizens; a true philosopher's amour-propre causes a pride in being independent of the illusions of others. A true philosopher, such as Wolmar or Socrates, is much more independent than either a false philosopher or a citizen. Nevertheless, this independence is intimately connected with an artificial, unnatural passion.[37] It is a questionable, or affected, independence.

Rousseau connects philosophy or thinking and amour-propre at several points in the Confessions. In a relatively minor reference he argues that the pleasure in a theoretical activity, such as solving a difficult problem in mathematics, is a feeling of amour-propre at doing something difficult that others cannot do (I, 179). He does not suggest that the contemplation of order contributes to this pleasure. Contemplation, or thinking, is painful rather than pleasurable in itself. Furthermore, when he discusses his moral reform after the publication

---

37. Unlike Rousseau, Wolmar believes that amour-propre is natural (II, 491).

of his first philosophic work, the *First Discourse*, he consistently emphasizes his pride at being independent of public opinion (I, 362, 388). Philosophic activity is intimately connected with a desire to approach something resembling natural independence, but this desire comes from unnatural amour-propre.

The single reference to the affectation of Socrates is the closest Rousseau comes to making a direct connection between specifically Socratic philosophy and amour-propre. In the final analysis, as we have seen, he admits that there is something about Socrates for which he cannot account. Nevertheless, the possibility, or likelihood, that Socrates' independence is based on a refined version of amour-propre makes him unacceptable to Rousseau as the model of the highest human type. Although the Socratic approximation of the life of natural independence is ultimately preferable to the life of a citizen, it is an imperfect approximation of the simply natural life because it is based on the unnatural desire to compare oneself to others. If this desire could be overcome altogether, a closer approximation to the life according to nature would be possible. It is this possibility that Rousseau explores in the *Confessions* and the *Reveries*. In this exploration he paints a picture of himself as a dreamer rather than a thinker. He shows a life that simultaneously is a product of civilization and meets the natural standard. This way of life, like that of Socrates, cannot be a simple object of imitation in every respect. Even so, it is a standard that can be taught and in the light of which all other civilized ways of life can be judged.

Although Cato is called the greatest of humans, he is inferior to Socrates and Jesus in crucial respects. Because Cato is perfectly denatured, he cannot meet the natural standard of independence. Even his perfection as a model for emulation has one flaw: Cato can inspire emulation only in relatively uncorrupt people who are capable of becoming citizens, or in a body of corrupt soldiers over whom he has personal command; for others, his life is only a reproachful reminder of the heights to which human virtue can aspire or an object of jealous mockery and derision. In corrupt times Cato's life is useful as a reminder, but lesser models are necessary for a broad practical effect.

Although extended comparisons may reveal Cato's weakness, Rousseau never says a single bad word about him. He openly expresses reservations about Socrates' citizenship and affectation and about the antipolitical consequences of Jesus's revolution, but he is silent about any defects in Cato. This marks an important distinction. Rousseau's reservations about Jesus and Socrates concern their failure to measure up to the highest standard, the standard of natural independence. Cato makes no pretense of meeting this standard. He is the perfectly denatured citizen who lives only in and for his community. His standard is that of his relations to others. He measures up to this standard to the point of complete identification with it. He is the standard. There is consequently no need to replace him as the model of civic virtue, and Rousseau makes no effort to do so in the *Confessions*.

These reservations about Cato, Socrates, and Jesus are objections to them as models of the peak of human nature. Aside from his reservations about the substance of each of these models, Rousseau also has some criticism of the means used to establish each as a model. We know about each because they were written about by others; none of them wrote about himself. In Chapter 1 we saw Rousseau's account of the impossibility of accurate biography. He discusses another aspect of the problem of biography in one of his discussions of Jesus. On the whole, Rousseau insists on the effectiveness of the chain of emulation that established Christianity. The impressiveness of Jesus's example is increased by its ability to transform such humble followers. Furthermore, the ignorance of the first disciples helped to preserve Christian doctrine from the contaminating influence of sophisticated learning. Nevertheless, Rousseau sees one flaw in the relation between Jesus and the disciples. It was imprudent to entrust authorship of the Gospels, the life of Jesus, to such followers. Rousseau says that these "poor people" disfigured Jesus's "life" with rubbish. He implies that they misrepresented the significance of Jesus's actions and, in particular, the miracles. With the speeches they were somewhat more faithful: "Fortunately they respected and faithfully transcribed his discourses which they did not understand; remove several oriental or badly rendered turns, not a word which would not be worthy of him is seen there" (IV, 1146). According to Rousseau, the apostle's defects as authors of lives are the source of Jesus's inferior reputation among the learned who revere Socrates. Rousseau writes to one of these educated champions of Socrates: "If Jesus were born at Athens and Socrates at Jerusalem, so that Plato, Xenophon had written the life of the former, Luke and Matthew that of the latter, you would change your language very much" (IV, 1146). Socrates was more prudent or lucky in his followers, as was Cato in having Plutarch. Because the choice of one's biographers depends to some degree on fortune, the use of written lives to preserve one's example is extremely risky unless one takes matters into one's own hands by writing an autobiography. Rousseau chose not to run this risk and therefore became his own Plato, Plutarch, or Matthew.

In sum, Rousseau's presentation of those people he regards as the three most important exemplary figures indicates the direction of his construction of a new exemplary figure. Considered as a moral fable meant to inspire emulation, the *Confessions* does not aim at the standard of the greatest citizenship. Instead, it shows a life that can be attractive to corrupt civilized humans who cannot be turned into citizens. In its philosophic function, the *Confessions* presents an account of how civilized humans are denatured and how they can overcome this denaturing. Rousseau is unwilling to entrust either of these projects to anyone but himself.

[3]

The Awakening of the Imagination and the Departure from Nature (Book I)

The Structure of Part One of the *Confessions*

Rousseau's analyses of Cato, Socrates, and Jesus reveal his regard for them as the most powerful examples of human excellence. Each represents a distinct image of what human nature is and what an individual human should aspire to be. Because of the failings he identifies in these three lives, Rousseau is compelled to provide a new image that can serve both as a more adequate description of human nature and as a moral fable suitable for corrupt times. He chooses to put this new image in an autobiography for both philosophic and practical reasons. He claims that only an autobiographer has access to the hidden feelings that most clearly reveal human nature, and he learned from Jesus's reliance on his disciples that depending on biographers entails unnecessary risks. For careful reading of the *Confessions*, we must be guided by Rousseau's philosophic purpose, but without losing sight of his practical purpose.

That the *Confessions* is meant to lay the foundation for the study of human nature means that it shares much with Rousseau's other works, primarily *Emile* and the *Second Discourse*. In fact, some scholars have noticed structural and thematic similarities between the *Confessions* and these works. In particular, they note parallels between *Emile* and Book I of the *Confessions*, both of which present the education of a young boy.[1] Perhaps the most complete argument for this similarity is made by

1. See Raymond, *Quête*, pp. 81–83.

Philippe Lejeune, whose case is based on the structure Rousseau orig-
inally planned for *Emile*. In his notes for the first draft, Rousseau divided his fictional student's life into thematic "ages" that correspond to
chronological ages: four ages for his education and another to describe
his life after his education. The first four ages presumably were to be
the substance of the book *Emile*. Rousseau's note reads as follows:

1. The age of nature   12
2. The age of reason   15
3. The age of force   20
4. The age of wisdom   25
5. The age of happiness   all the rest of life (IV, 60)

Lejeune notes that Rousseau divides his account of his own education
in Book I of the *Confessions* into four parts: with his father, with his
uncle's family, with the Lamberciers, and with a master engraver (I,
31).[2]

Lejeune stresses the formal similarity of the two works, but he argues
that the substance of the *Confessions* simply contradicts the theories about
human nature found in *Emile*.[3] He explains the apparent discrepancy by
praising Rousseau's honesty about himself which compelled him to
speak the truth even when it conflicted with his philosophic understanding. In this view, the personal success of the *Confessions* entails the
acknowledgment of the philosophic failure of *Emile*. Lejeune's conclusion is based on accurate observations about the differences in the
development of the feelings of Emile and Jean-Jacques. What Lejeune
does not notice is that these differences are required by Rousseau's
account of human nature. If Jean-Jacques's feelings developed in the
same way as Emile's feelings, this would prove that people who are given
a bad education are not denatured by it. Such a result would strike at the
heart of Rousseau's teaching about human nature and society. As the
remainder of this chapter shows, an analysis of the differences between
Emile and Jean-Jacques explains and confirms the theoretical teaching
of *Emile*.

Lejeune's insistence on the similarity between the structure of *Emile*
and Book I of the *Confessions* is one of the major sources of his mistake.
In particular, he overestimates the importance of the formal similarity
of the number of parts. Rousseau's lack of commitment to this particu-

2. See Lejeune, *Pacte*, pp. 90–96.
3. Ibid., pp. 109, 147, 153.

lar structure is shown by his final version of *Emile*, which has five books instead of four ages. Furthermore, Lejeune neglects the fact that, even in Rousseau's note, the four stages of Emile's education correspond to specific chronological ages. At the end of the "age of nature," Emile is said to be twelve; at the end of the "age of reason," fifteen; at the end of the "age of force," twenty; and at the end of the "age of wisdom," twenty-five. At the end of Book I of the *Confessions*, Jean-Jacques has just reached the age of sixteen (I, 41). Therefore, if the parallel between the two works is taken strictly, Book I of the *Confessions* corresponds to the first two ages in Emile's education, which include Books I–III in the final version of *Emile*. Following the division into years strictly, Jean-Jacques reaches the end of Emile's third age at the end of Book IV of the *Confessions*, and the end of the fourth age at the conclusion of Book V. One indication that these chronological ages can serve as a basis for comparison between the two books is indicated by Rousseau's remark near the beginning of Book VI of the *Confessions* that "here begins the short happiness of my life" (I, 225). This book, at least, corresponds to Emile's "age of happiness."[4] Thus Lejeune's construction of a formal parallel between *Emile* as a whole and Book I of the *Confessions* is misleading. If the substance of the books is considered as well as the formal elements stressed by Lejeune, the parallel is between *Emile* and all of Part One of the *Confessions*.

In this chapter and the following one I use the structure of "ages" (and the books in the final version of *Emile*) as a tentative guide. In this chapter I examine Book I of the *Confessions*; Chapter 4 has three sections corresponding to Books II–IV, V, and VI. One note of caution is in order. The similarities between *Emile* and the *Confessions* can be useful as long as the differences between Emile and Jean-Jacques are carefully noted. For example, if Jean-Jacques is the recipient of a defective education, one should not expect him to be the incarnation of reason at age fifteen, the culmination of Emile's "age of reason." The proper use of the parallels requires the use of Emile's development as the representative of the natural standard of independence and self-sufficiency from which Jean-Jacques departs. Jean-Jacques undergoes experiences analogous to the important incidents in Emile's education, but he undergoes them in a different sequence, at different ages, and in different ways. Each of these differences helps to mark either a fresh departure from nature or the exacerbation of a previous departure.

---

4. Emile's "age of happiness" is for the remainder of his life after his wedding (IV, 60). The sequel to *Emile* raises questions about this but does not decisively settle them.

Imagination and Living outside Oneself

The *Confessions* begins with a brief description of Rousseau's inimitable project of showing "a man in all the truth of nature" (I, 5). It turns to a short account of his parents' courtship and marriage. In the first paragraph devoted to himself Rousseau describes the circumstances of his birth and his precarious first days. These are events he knows only by report or from their consequences.

After this brief introduction, he turns to impressions based on his memory of direct experiences. It is to his first reading that Rousseau traces the beginning of his self-consciousness. He begins this account by referring to what he shares with everyone: "I felt before thinking; this is the common lot of humanity" (I, 8). It is the form that these first conscious feelings take that distinguishes him from others and particularly from a natural child like Emile. His first feelings come from the reading of novels and Plutarch, which we discussed briefly in Chapter 1. There we used Rousseau's account of this early reading as his clearest example of the tendency of civilized humans to live outside themselves or to become imitators of other people. As was noted in that context, this tendency, rooted in amour-propre, distinguishes civilized from natural humans. Through his identification with the characters in the books, Jean-Jacques becomes conscious of himself as being someone else. His first conscious feeling is one of living outside himself.[5] That Jean-Jacques's very first conscious feelings cause him to depart from nature is of immense significance. This moment of departure must be examined with care.

The account of reading in *Emile* is a useful basis for this examination. Emile is almost fifteen when he is given his first book. This is perhaps the first important instance of Emile being allowed or encouraged to form an unnatural characteristic.[6] It is only after the lengthy "age of nature" that Emile puts himself into the place of another person for the first time. Emile reads *Robinson Crusoe* to learn to judge the real utility of things. He even thinks "that he is Robinson himself" (*Emile*, 185). This identification does not violate Rousseau's claim that Emile must never wish to be someone else, because Emile never emulates the fictional character and is more attentive to Robinson's position of self-sufficiency on a desert island than to Robinson's feelings. Unlike Jean-

5. See Starobinski, *Transparence*, p. 17.
6. This is the age by which young Poles should be completely acquainted with the lives of the illustrious Poles of the past. Citizens are completely denatured before the age at which Emile begins to acquire unnatural characteristics.

Jacques's reading, Emile's first step toward living outside himself is undertaken with the greatest possible care. Rousseau signals the importance of even this very tentative identification by saying that it is by this reading "that the first exercise must be given to his imagination" (*Emile*, 184). Here Rousseau stresses the connection between imagination and living outside oneself.

Imagination makes an important contribution to amour-propre. When we identify with someone else, we in fact identify with an image we have of them rather than with them directly. When in the Neuchâtel preface Rousseau refers to the "double illusion of amour-propre" that keeps us from understanding both ourselves and other people (I, 1148), he says that we interpret the behavior of others in terms of our own feelings. From our feelings we construct an image of their feelings. Thus we acquire a false image of them. Amour-propre depends on imagination. Without the ability to form images of other people's feelings we could not become concerned with their intentions and opinions; we would regard them as inanimate beings. Furthermore, imagination is directed by amour-propre when we attribute our own motives to other people. It is the development of the set of faculties embracing amour-propre, imitation, and imagination that distinguishes civilized life from life in the state of nature.

In Chapter 1 I explain the difference between civilized and natural humans in terms of amour-propre and imitation. A comparable explanation can be given in terms of imagination. Because the development of this faculty determines much of the organization of the *Confessions*, an outline of the natural status of imagination is particularly necessary. I undertake a brief overview here and return to the more technical aspects of Rousseau's view of the imagination at the conclusion of this chapter.

In the first part of the *Second Discourse* Rousseau portrays natural humans in the natural environment. He characterizes them essentially by their self-sufficiency or independence, which is limited only by their need to satisfy seldom-felt sexual desire.[7] Any modifications in original characteristics, such as toughening skin or developing a keener sense of smell (*Discourses*, 113), serve the sole function of maintaining independence and self-sufficiency. This physical independence is reflected in psychological independence, which is shown most clearly by the calm of imagination. When Rousseau discusses how unlikely it is that anyone

7. On the significance of this qualification, see Schwartz, *Sexual Politics*, p. 76.

would ever leave the pure state of nature, the first reason he gives is that "his imagination suggests nothing to him; his heart asks nothing of him" (*Discourses*, 117).[8] It is imagination that turns a purely natural need into a civilized passion.[9] The undeveloped imagination of a natural human leads to nothing beyond purely physical needs.

Emile will find himself in unnatural circumstances that tend to stimulate the imagination, but his education is guided by the natural standard of self-sufficiency, independence, and wholeness. Because of the different requirements of his circumstances, Emile will be in some respects very different from a savage, even in the way his senses develop (*Emile*, 138, 157). Rousseau explains the necessary differences by saying, "One must not confound what is natural in the savage state with what is natural in the civil state" (*Emile*, 406).

After the age of twelve, however, Emile begins to acquire characteristics that are not merely adaptations of natural faculties but positively unnatural characteristics from the standpoint of self-sufficiency. Most of these characteristics, such as compassion, religion, taste, and love, are directly derived from imagination. In *Emile*, Rousseau distinguishes the natural from the artificial condition by appealing even more directly to imagination than he does in the *Second Discourse*: "Only in this original state are power and desire in equilibrium and man is not unhappy. As soon as his potential faculties are put in action, imagination, the most active of all, is awakened and outstrips them. It is imagination which extends for us the measure of the possible, whether for good or bad, and which consequently excites and nourishes the desires by the hope of satisfying them" (*Emile*, 80–81). Here Rousseau concedes that imagination is only one of the potential faculties, but he argues that it is the predominant source of the malleability of humans. The imagination forms desires for change by opening a potentially limitless horizon of possibilities for change. One instance of this extension of the "measure of the possible" is the desire to be someone else that comes from imitation. In this context Rousseau adds foresight as another example. Both imitation and foresight take humans outside themselves and destroy naturalness. Thus, once Emile's senses have

---

8. Only a few scholars have insisted on the centrality of the imagination to Rousseau's thought. Among the exceptions are Benjamin Barber, "Rousseau and the Paradoxes of the Dramatic Imagination," *Daedalus*, 107,3 (1978): 79–92; Allan Bloom in introduction to *Emile*; Eigeldinger, *Réalité*; and Schwartz, *Sexual Politics*.

9. Rousseau's distinction between natural and moral love should be compared to his distinction between natural and imitative music.

been toughened or exercised, the rest of his education is almost exclusively concerned with first retarding and then directing the development of his imagination.[10] Even the education of the senses is guided by how each sense can affect or be affected by the imagination. The power of the imagination to modify all other aspects of human life is the reason Emile's imagination is kept from awakening as long as possible. Because Jean-Jacques's imagination has awakened prematurely, his subsequent experiences are subject to its influence.

The differences between Emile's experience and Jean-Jacques's show that Rousseau has good reason to label this crucial early step in his education "this dangerous method."[11] The very first step in Jean-Jacques's education entails the disruption of natural wholeness. This beginning of an education could well be appropriate for a citizen who learns to alienate himself to his community by identifying with its heroes, but Jean-Jacques's early reading differs decisively from that of a young citizen. To be sure, he does develop a "free and republican spirit" by reading Plutarch (I, 9). But unlike a citizen, he also reads romantic novels, which give him "an intelligence unique for [his] age on the passions." Only one paragraph after stressing his participation in the common lot of humanity, Rousseau emphasizes his uniqueness. He differs from others because his early reading stimulates a premature development of passions; he departs from the natural condition of quiescent passion earlier than they do. Thus he begins his life with "bizarre and romantic notions of human life."

These "romantic" notions, unrelated to anything real, coexist uneasily with Jean-Jacques's more "Roman" republicanism. Because of this combination he is alienated not only from himself, like a citizen, but also in contradiction within himself (I, 12). If a natural man like Emile is an integer or whole and a citizen is a complementary part or fraction, Jean-Jacques is a fractional being made up of incompatible parts. The supposedly "natural" Rousseau begins the *Confessions* by showing himself as being radically unnatural.[12] While *Emile* gives the natural psychology as it can develop in society, the *Confessions* gives an unnatural psychology of civilized corruption.

Another sign of this unnaturalness occurs in this same introductory section. While speaking about the aunt who brought him up, Rousseau

10. This distinction between the two parts of the education is signaled near the beginning of Book IV (*Emile*, 215).
11. See Raymond, *Quête*, p. 96.
12. This has been shown by Lejeune, *Pacte*, p. 106.

says, "I am persuaded that I owe to her the taste or still more the passion for music which developed completely in me only later" (I, 11). Although Emile's exposure to music is limited to a few very simple tunes, Jean-Jacques learns "a prodigious quantity" of songs, including love songs. These songs further inflame his passions without directing them toward any real object. The opening pages of the *Confessions* go a long way toward establishing Jean-Jacques as a completely social being. Both his reading and his exposure to music transform him into an imitative being. To be sure, he does not immediately depart from nature in every respect. Rousseau says that "never did they have to repress or satisfy in me any of those fantastic humors which are imputed to nature, and which are all born from education alone" (I, 10). His failings hardly extend beyond a harmless gluttony and he has no whims (see *Emile*, 48).[13] At this point Jean-Jacques's imagination has been awakened, but the very variety of things influencing it keep it from taking any fixed direction. He is unnatural, but he has not yet become vicious. The early development of the imagination apparently does not result in a complete departure from nature.

The first awakening of Jean-Jacques's imagination radically distinguishes him both from someone in the pure state of nature and from Emile. His very first conscious feeling is that of being someone else. Not only does he begin by living outside himself, he also is torn by two different types of artificial feeling. He is prevented from achieving a citizen's identification with his community because he has "romantic" feelings that conflict with his Roman pride. This division in him is compounded by the bizarre character of his romantic notions. Thus he has desires that are both contradictory and incapable of satisfaction. Aside from his lack of vices, Jean-Jacques is almost the perfect picture of a denatured corrupt human who lives outside himself, has contradictory opinions and desires, and longs for things that cannot exist. It remains to be seen how long his remaining natural characteristics can persist as his developing imagination causes the formation of more and more artificial characteristics.

Although the early development of Jean-Jacques's imagination is indispensable for the development of his other artificial characteristics, it does not determine absolutely the form that each takes. A series of decisive events occurs during his stay at the village of Bossey under the tutelage of M. Lambercier and his sister. Each experience builds on the

---

13. For Rousseau's toleration of gluttony, see *Emile*, p. 152.

denaturing that began in Geneva; the imagination plays an important role in them all. These events are the first experiences of sexual desire, anger, and vanity. Each is connected with relations among people. Because of their social character, these passions are of particular importance for understanding the departure from natural independence.

Far from excluding the possibility of variations in the formation of artificial sentiments, an active imagination is the ground of human malleability. This possibility for wide variation in development makes it necessary to follow the details of Rousseau's presentation with care. First, one must consider the general background that leads to the possibility of further denaturing; second, one must see how Jean-Jacques's teachers' methods differ from those used in Emile's education; third, one must pay attention to the particular events, or occasional causes, that precipitate the unnatural development; finally, one must observe the peculiar form taken by Jean-Jacques's passions as a consequence of these other factors.

Imagination and Sexuality

Rousseau's discussion of the emergence of sexual desire takes place in a calm pastoral setting, a setting as far removed as possible from both political life and civilized corruption. Nevertheless, this most private of passions emerges in the context of punishment, an overtly political theme. Furthermore, Rousseau shows that the premature arousal of sexual desire can lead to far-ranging consequences for one's relations with other people and the world. These consequences even have the potential to shape one's future capacity for citizenship.

Rousseau begins this new section of Book I almost as if his departure from natural wholeness has been reversed.[14] The section opens, "Two years passed in the village softened a little my Roman harshness, and led me back to the state of a child" (I, 12). Rousseau emphasizes his remaining natural characteristics and deemphasizes his imagination, but his silence about any easing of his romantic, as distinguished from Roman, sentiments indicates that his aroused imagination is present. His romantic imagination is temporarily held in check only because reading, which is now forced on him, has lost its power to enchant. In short, Jean-Jacques has almost, but not quite, returned to naturalness.

In addition to restoring Jean-Jacques to a more natural condition

14. He does the same thing at *Emile*, 212.

for a child, this move to the country puts his civilized development on a more normal track. Instead of continuing to acquire "elevated but imaginary feelings" (I, 13), he forms a more prosaic but also more real friendship with his cousin and fellow student, Bernard. Although even this feeling is premature from the standpoint of Emile's education, it is less unnatural than Jean-Jacques's earlier feelings in that it is directed toward a real object. In a sense, he continues to live outside himself, but the "outside" is limited to a very small number of people rather than open to an unlimited and contradictory imaginary world. Rousseau says that his life at Bossey suited him so well that only time was necessary for it to fix his character absolutely (I, 14). A "fixed" character would share the natural characteristics of stability or wholeness while accommodating a partial development of some unnatural tendencies. Rousseau is suggesting, then, that he could have become an approximation of Emile, a natural man in civil society.

Unfortunately, misguided educational methods prevent his character from becoming fixed in this way. Instead it becomes simultaneously fixed and unlimited—fixed in that it acquires a specific bent or set of bents, but unlimited in that its new form opens a much greater horizon for departure from nature. The cause of this distortion is a mismanagement of punishments for his childish misdeeds.[15] Rousseau shows the importance of this theme by referring to its general importance for all educations, not merely his own. He says, "How one would change one's method with youth if one saw better the distant effects of that which one employs always indistinctly and often indiscretely!" (I, 14). He holds up his own case as an example from which one can draw general conclusions about the wrong way to educate a child.

The correct way is shown in *Emile*. Emile is never punished beyond suffering the natural consequence of his actions; that is, no punishment is imposed on him by another person (*Emile*, 121–24). Jean-Jacques's punishments are imposed from outside and they lack any direct connection with his actions. As a result he turns his attention to the person inflicting the punishment. His focus on the punisher prematurely elicits his first experiences of sexuality. Here, just as is the case in the

15. Rousseau's practice of treating each incident in his early life as decisive for his development has given birth to disputes among scholars over which incident is truly decisive. Starobinski argues for the false accusation (*Transparence*, pp. 17–22). Lejeune argues for the earlier punishment by Mlle Lambercier (*Pacte*, p. 52). The present study progresses beyond Lejeune by directing attention back to the beginning of Jean-Jacques's self-consciousness in his reading. It should be recognized, however, that Rousseau deliberately presents each of these events as decisive in its own way.

first exercise of his imagination, Jean-Jacques is in complete contrast to Emile.[16]

One can begin to see the unnaturalness of Jean-Jacques's introduction to sexuality and the relative naturalness of Emile's by comparing them to that of someone in the pure state of nature. In the *Second Discourse* Rousseau distinguishes between natural or physical sexual desire and moral or civilized sexual desire. Physical sexual desire "is that general desire which inclines one sex to unite with the other" (*Discourses*, 134), whereas moral sexual desire fixes desire on a particular object and is "an artificial sentiment born of the usages of society" (*Discourses*, 135). The former leads to no feelings of jealousy and is felt very seldom.[17] Because individual preference is of no concern to natural men and women, satisfaction of this sexual desire causes little or no disruption of natural independence.[18]

Emile's sexual desire or sentiment of love clearly falls into the category of moral or civilized love. Its development follows the awakening of his imagination and is conditioned by this unnatural faculty. It awakens during the "age of force" and is directed during the "age of wisdom." He is attached to a particular woman and feels both strong desires and jealousy. By forming this attachment, he has certainly compromised his independence. Sophie even exercises authority over him (*Emile*, 424). This submission to authority plays two equally important parts in Emile's education. First, his attachment to Sophie proves to be the major link between Emile and civil society. He becomes interested in the broader community so that he can care for his family. In this respect Emile clearly departs from naturalness. Nevertheless, the attachment to Sophie is not the cause of this departure, it is only a consequence. Because the development of imagination in civil society and consequent arousal of sexual desire beyond the merely natural level are inevitable, Emile's departure from the simple standard of nature is independent of his fixation on Sophie. Were he not to fall in love with Sophie, his artificially aroused sexuality would lead him to pursue many women. Thus, while Sophie completes the civilizing of

16. The issue of punishment is also connected with Rousseau's attack on original sin. He claims that punishments inflicted to repress a supposedly innate sinfulness are more likely to cause bad results than to prevent them. The mistakes in the punishment of Jean-Jacques are meant to show the unintended consequences that follow from the Christian understanding. It should be noted that the punishments are administered by a clergyman and his sister.

17. Rousseau does not mention sex in his first list of natural needs (*Discourses*, 105).

18. On this point see Schwartz, *Sexual Politics*, pp. 16–40.

Emile, she also controls and limits an artificial passion. Therefore the second part she plays in his education is to prevent him from turning into a corrupt civilized man. Sophie can serve these two purposes because Emile's imagination has been so carefully held in check and is so well directed. His unnatural attachment to one woman makes him moderate with respect to others. This is as close to an approximation of natural independence as is possible in civil society. After the awakening of his imagination in Book III, Emile is doomed to some form of personal dependence, but his dependence can be modeled as closely as possible on the natural life.

Emile's sexuality is that of a natural man in society. Jean-Jacques's imagination has already made him somewhat unnatural. Because Jean-Jacques's imagination is awakened earlier and increases in power much more rapidly, it cannot be surprising that his first experience of sexuality is much more intense and difficult to contain. That it occurs as the result of a mistake by his tutors compounds the problem.

Rousseau reveals the importance of the specific experience that aroused his sexuality by calling it "the first and most painful step in the obscure and miry labyrinth of my confessions" (I, 18).[19] The difficulty in making this first step derives from the "ridiculous and shameful" nature of the confession. As Rousseau has already indicated, shame is one of his most powerful passions, exceeded only by the desire to be loved (I, 14). In fact, both shame and the desire to be loved profoundly affect the experience. Rousseau argues that his good behavior came in part from his desire not to displease the Lamberciers. Nevertheless, it happened that he did occasionally deserve punishment. His first punishment, a spanking administered by Mlle Lambercier, carries with it an unintended consequence: "I had found in the pain, even in the shame, a mixture of sensuality" (I, 15). Thus, while Jean-Jacques has a precocious imagination, he also has a "precocious instinct for sex." As Rousseau argues in both *Emile* and the *Second Discourse*, it is the imagination that gives sexuality whatever force it possesses beyond the natural physical desire. Here Rousseau shows the artificial or moral side of love in both its intensity and its fixation on a specific object.[20]

This first punishment is given an absolute causative status: "Who would believe that the punishment a child received at eight years by the

19. This is one of Rousseau's rare uses of the term "confess" in his book. For a general discussion of confession, see Chapter 1.

20. This is one of the places Lejeune sees a difference between Jean-Jacques and Emile and mistakenly asserts a contradiction between the two books; see *Pacte*, p. 153.

hand of a girl of thirty has decided my tastes, my desires, my passions, for me for the rest of my life, and this precisely in the sense contrary to that which ought to follow naturally" (I, 15). These acquired desires are unnatural both because they are premature and because they are fixed contrary to the natural direction. This "bizarre taste" for being spanked directs his sexual desire away from its natural aim. The result of the doubly unnatural stimulation and diversion of sexual desires strangely brings about a quasi-natural result. As he says, "what should have lost me, saved me" (I, 17). The strange direction taken by his desires means that they can be satisfied only by passivity. Because his desires are mingled with shame, Jean-Jacques cannot make advances. As a result, he is unable to act on these desires "up to the age at which the coldest and latest temperaments are developed." The peculiar bent of Jean-Jacques's imagination leaves him in a condition similar to that of the Emile before his imagination has developed. The young Emile is chaste because he has no desires; Jean-Jacques is chaste because he cannot act on his desires. Thus in certain conditions an unusually strong imagination can have the same effect as a weak imagination.[21] At this point Rousseau may seem unjust in blaming the Lamberciers for making a mistake in his education. This consequence of the punishment was surely unintended, and it can appear to be only ridiculous and shameful. At the same time, it has been shown to be desirable. Rousseau admits that it saved him.

The truly negative consequence of this method can be seen in the role the imagination plays in this event and the way it is affected by this new taste. Rousseau repeatedly refers to his imagination in explaining the way this fixing of his tastes prevents him from acting: "Tormented for a long time, without knowing by what, I devoured with an ardent eye beautiful women; my imagination recalled them to me ceaselessly"; "In my foolish whims, in my erotic furors, in the extravagant acts to which they sometimes carried me, I borrowed imaginatively the help of the other sex"; "I have possessed few, but I have not failed to enjoy many in my manner; that is to say, with the imagination" (I, 17). As these remarks and others in the same context make clear, this premature development of sexuality is not only the result of the premature awakening of the imagination, but also the cause of a further stimulus to the imagination. Now Jean-Jacques's imagination does not merely

---

21. Yet another example of how extreme measures can correct the precocious development of sexual passion is given at *Emile*, 231.

feed on the material given to it by books; it also "ceaselessly recalls" images. Before, Jean-Jacques became what he imagined. Now he enters into relations with the objects he imagines. He now remains himself, but his self is constantly tormented by imaginary objects and insatiable desires. Although his external life is very similar to Emile's, his internal life moves farther and farther away from nature.

The passivity and flights into the imagination developed in this first experience of sexuality have political as well as personal significance. Rousseau here describes the origin of submissiveness and the reaction to it of withdrawal from active life. In the right circumstances, the first of these could well turn into a willingness to be politically enslaved. The second represents one possible servile reaction to political enslavement. Rousseau thus indicates the political consequences that can follow from an early experience of punishment.[22]

In the second half of Book I, Rousseau shows a more advanced consequence of the form of sexual passion he acquired from Mlle Lambercier. In his first experience, three important things happen: a natural passion is stimulated prematurely, the unnatural direction given to the passion keeps Jean-Jacques in a quasi-natural condition by forcing him to remain passive, and an additional stimulus is given to his imagination because of his inability to find satisfaction. Each of these features plays a part in the continued development of his sexuality.

The premature stimulation of the passions makes it possible for Jean-Jacques to fall in love at an early age. At eleven he falls in love with two girls at once, Mlle Goton and Mlle de Vulson. He argues that these are genuine cases of two different types of love, "very distinct, very real, and which have almost nothing in common" (I, 27). In the Neuchâtel manuscript of the Confessions, Rousseau distinguishes the types quite precisely by categorizing them as "one sensual, or of temperament, and the other platonic, or of opinion" (I, 1247). The first corresponds to the initial impetus and direction given to his sexuality. This is the more natural of the two types. Here it is represented by Mlle Goton, with whom Rousseau emphasizes both the ferocity of his passion and his passivity. With Mlle de Vulson he emphasizes the lack of sensuality in his feelings (I, 27). This sort of love must be derived from opinion or the imagination alone. Rousseau says that in this case, unlike the case of

22. On this point see Judith Shklar, "Rousseau's Images of Authority," in Hobbes and Rousseau: A Collection of Critical Essays, ed. Maurice Cranston and Richard S. Peters (Garden City, N.Y.: Anchor Books, 1972), p. 337.

Mlle Goton, his "relationship" with his beloved existed only in his fantasy. Distinguishing among the senses, the heart, and the head, he argues that his love for Mlle de Vulson partook of the latter two, while that for Mlle Goton partook of the former two. The heart or imagination is an element of both cases. Neither form of love is strictly natural, but that for Mlle de Vulson leaves out the natural element of the senses altogether.

The peculiar direction given to Jean-Jacques's sexuality in his early experience is thus shown to be susceptible to a split that puts him into contradiction with himself. He has both extreme sensual desires and an imagination stimulated by, but not wholly in accord with, his senses. As a result he is open to two different types of love, neither one of which can satisfy him. Emile's love for Sophie, on the other hand, unites all three elements. This combination is possible because his senses, heart, and head are not at war with each other, and none of them is particularly inflamed. Jean-Jacques's very different development makes this impossible. His senses demand overtures from Mlle Goton which are incompatible with his elevated image of Mlle de Vulson.[23]

Jean-Jacques's apparent fickleness may seem to resemble the trait of a natural man, who also is not restricted to one member of the opposite sex. However, it is not true that all women are the same for Jean-Jacques. Like Emile, he has an imagination that demands women with specific attributes. Unlike Emile, he desires attributes that cannot be combined in a single woman. His senses drive him in one direction, his opinions in another. Emile's senses and imagination give him a quasi-natural moderation in mind and body. Jean-Jacques is chaste in body, but only at the expense of much torment in his soul.

In sum, by their peculiar nature, Jean-Jacques's first experiences of sexual passion throw into relief the natural sexuality of the pure state of nature, the modified naturalness of Emile, and ordinary civilized sexuality. For someone in the pure state of nature, the senses and the imagination combine to preserve independence; desire is seldom felt and easily satisfied with any member of the opposite sex. For Emile the senses and imagination combine to produce a modified independence; desire is stronger but is satisfied by Sophie. In a corrupt civilized human, the senses and imagination combine to produce dependence; desires are intense and frequent, yet highly selective and promiscuous. Jean-Jacques's case is by far the most complicated. His desire is extremely intense, but in a form that makes it difficult to satisfy. He is

23. Cf. Lejeune, *Pacte*, pp. 132–33.

saved from an extreme, dependent promiscuity, but he continues to be tormented by intense, conflicting desires. He is at the same time less dependent on sexual activity than many corrupt people and more dependent on his imagination. On the whole he presents a singular picture of civilized dependency and dividedness, although he escapes some of its consequences. Even with this partial escape, the particular form of his sexual desire is unlikely to lead toward good citizenship. Emile is ultimately a good citizen out of concern for his family. Someone whose desires lead to passivity and flights into the imagination lack this motive for involvement in the community.

Imagination and Anger: On the Naturalness of the Sentiment of the Just and Unjust

Rousseau's discussion of the origin of anger is linked with his discussion of sexuality by the issue of punishment. This new passion is of even greater political significance than the submissiveness derived from the first experience of sexuality. Anger is an extremely explosive political passion. In the right circumstances it can turn into the pride and the hatred of injustice characteristic of the good citizen. In other cases it can find expression as the resentment of punishment, no matter how just. In the worst case, anger is the characteristic of those who wish that not only other people, but also the world itself respond to their whims. Such angry people are capable of regarding themselves as justly entitled to domination over the universe. Rousseau has already dealt with the origin of submissiveness; now he turns to the origins of both revolution and tyranny.

For both Jean-Jacques and Emile, the first experience of anger is conditioned by earlier experiences. The stimulus given to his imagination by reading and his first experience of sexuality laid the foundation for the rest of Jean-Jacques's education. These developments precede his introduction to anger. In contrast, the themes of imagination and sexuality are late developments in Emile's education—elements that can be controlled with relative ease because his earlier education has laid the proper foundation for them. These themes show Emile at his least natural, but because they have been carefully controlled they lead to no bad consequences. Most important, Emile experiences anger before either imagination or sexuality has arisen in his education. Again, the importance of these differences can be seen in a comparison of the details of the two accounts and the form the passion takes in each.

The prevention of anger is of great importance for the entire project of Emile's education. It is the first artificial sentiment to which Emile is exposed. (The epigraph for *Emile* is from Seneca's *On Anger*.) While it may seem contrary to the goal of preserving naturalness to arouse this passion early, in fact it is this step that allows the tutor to inoculate Emile against anger. The imagination provides little fuel for this artificial passion, and since Emile's first experience of anger occurs before his imagination has received any stimulus whatsoever, it is less dangerous than it might have been.

In the *Second Discourse* Rousseau refers to "the calm of passions" (*Discourses*, 130) of men in the state of nature and insists that they lack hate, desire for revenge, and insolence (*Discourses*, 222). He allows no place for anger in the natural psyche. The potential for anger begins with some of the first social institutions. Because of his need to live in civil society, Emile must be taught the notion of private property. This social institution, absent in the pure state of nature, gives the first impetus to anger. Once he has acquired this notion, through planting and tending a garden, he is susceptible to a feeling of injury. Emile's first feeling of anger follows the destruction of his garden. This "first sentiment of injustice" is quickly calmed, however, and he learns how to make an advantageous contract in which he keeps his own produce and acquires melons in addition. At this early stage of his education, then, Emile runs the risk of acquiring an artificial sentiment. But the feeling is aroused only to be calmed. Emile does not feel anger on his own account again until the final stage of his education (*Emile*, 426). The initial calming of Emile's indignation leaves him in a mental condition very close to natural even when he is exposed to unnatural prods to anger.

Because he is in control of the events that arouse the anger, Emile's tutor is able to calm the boy immediately. Throughout the incident he stands as Emile's ally; he never opposes him. This role of the tutor is reversed in the case of Jean-Jacques. Rather than being his allies, his tutors are the objects of his anger. This difference has fateful consequences.

For both Emile and Jean-Jacques the first experience of anger is connected with an experience of injustice.[24] Emile's anger is quickly calmed because the apparent affront is quickly revealed to be no affront at all. For Jean-Jacques no such easy resolution is possible. Jean-Jacques's first experience of anger, like his first experience of sexuality,

24. On the absence of injustice in the state of nature, see *Discourses*, 128.

is caused by a misguided punishment. Like the earlier punishment, this one is the source of "one of the most vigorous springs of my soul" (I, 18). Rousseau emphasizes the importance of the experience of punishment by pointing to the radically different consequences of apparently slight variations of punishments. He thereby demonstrates that the attempt to repress supposedly natural evil is in fact the cause of evil. The first punishment, inflicted by Mlle Lambercier, affects the romantic side of his character brought out by his first reading. The later punishment, inflicted by M. Lambercier, affects his Roman side. Instead of revealing the servility of the slave, this example gives birth to the resentment of the slave revolt. Rather than leading to a flight from the world, this experience leads to an active rebellion against the world. In each case the earlier bent given to his imagination by reading is intensified and acquires a more specific direction. The clearest distinction between the two punishments is that the earlier one is deserved whereas the second is not.

In this second case, Jean-Jacques is falsely accused of breaking a comb. The particular importance of the incident stems from two factors. First, appearances implicate him absolutely. The comb is broken when he is the sole person with access to it. Second, Jean-Jacques himself is unable to see the overwhelming character of the case against him. Rousseau says, "I did not yet have enough reason to feel how much the appearances condemned me, and to put myself into the place of the others" (I, 19). Since Rousseau earlier has insisted his ability to transform himself into another person, this assertion requires explanation.

We have already seen two different types of identification with others, Jean-Jacques's complete transformation and Emile's more detached identification. Emile does imagine himself to be Robinson Crusoe, but he is aware of differences between himself and the character in the book. Robinson has fears that Emile would never have and makes mistakes that Emile would never make. Emile identifies with Robinson's situation rather than with the man. Accordingly, it is appropriate to say that Emile puts himself in Robinson's place. This sort of identification allows him to see things as Robinson sees them while maintaining a degree of detachment from Robinson's feelings. Jean-Jacques's identification is much stronger and more clearly allied with feelings. For example, he identifies with Scaevola's firmness and then seeks circumstances that allow him to demonstrate firmness. Rousseau remarks on the childishness of his imitation of the Roman: he imitates Scaevola's firmness in circumstances not requiring firmness; so complete is his identification with the feelings of Scaevola that he is incapable of seeing things as they are (I, 9). In the case of the false accusation, he attributes feelings to his accusers, but he has no idea of their perspective on the matter. Because he does not know their feelings and cannot put himself in their place, he must infer these feelings from their actions. In making this inference, he can understand only his own innocence and so must account for a punishment inflicted by his previously gentle tutors. He describes the predicament: "What a reversal of ideas! what disorder of feelings! what an overturning in his heart, in his brain, in all his small intelligent and moral being! I say, imagine all that, if it is possible; as for me, I do not feel myself capable of unraveling, of following the least trace of what occurred in me then" (I, 19). This extraordinary confusion leads the young Jean-Jacques to the conclusion that he is being willfully tortured by people who are aware of his innocence. Because he cannot put himself in the Lamberciers' place, he incorrectly attributes their behavior to a desire to harm him.

This incident has been accorded a decisive importance in the *Confessions* and, indeed, Rousseau's work as a whole by Jean Starobinski. While several points in the interpretation given above are in agreement with Starobinski's discussion, there are two differences of some importance. First, Starobinski underestimates the importance of earlier events in the *Confessions*, particularly the emergence of Jean-Jacques's self-consciousness through reading. Second, he overemphasizes the discovery of the separation between appearance and reality in the account of the punishment.[25] In stressing this admittedly important theme, Starobinski does not preserve the split between Rousseau's later understanding of the circumstances and Jean-Jacques's youthful experience of them. Accordingly, he attributes the fateful impasse to the Lamberciers' inability to see beyond the incriminating appearances rather than to Jean-Jacques's inability to see the appearances that incriminate him. Contrary to what Starobinski claims, Jean-Jacques feels no split between appearance and truth. He feels a split between the Lamberciers' past gentleness and their present injustice. Treachery is added to the punishment itself as the source of indignation. The contradiction felt by Jean-Jacques is between two sets of facts rather than between appearances and reality.[26]

Starobinski's interpretation is based most firmly on Rousseau's state-

---

25. Starobinski, *Transparence*, p. 20.
26. Jean-Jacques has learned to distinguish between words and deeds more than he has learned to distinguish between appearance and reality; see IV, 966.

ment that, after the unjust punishment, he and his cousin "no longer regarded them as Gods who read in our hearts." This does confirm that subsequent reflection on his experience made Jean-Jacques aware of his lack of transparency. Nonetheless, different circumstances would have allowed him to discover this lack without the accompanying experience of injustice. The primary importance of this episode is the feeling of being deliberately mistreated. In effect, Jean-Jacques's misunderstanding of the tutors' intention is more important to this event than his discovery of his lack of transparency.

Because of his misguided identification, Jean-Jacques imagines that his tutors share his own knowledge of his innocence. One might say that Jean-Jacques believes that the tutors can be completely successful in identifying with him and therefore must know his innocence as well as he does. Therefore they must be lying when they claim that they are punishing him out of a concern for justice. He can only regard their mistreatment of him as arising from a malicious intention. The tutors are transformed in his eyes into willful torturers because in identifying himself with them he is unable to distinguish between what he knows and what the external evidence tells them. Here Rousseau shows as clearly as possible the disastrous consequence of a disproportion between the strength of imagination and the ability to reason.

It is only after the stirring of moral indignation that Jean-Jacques takes the final step of realizing his lack of transparency. This realization comes too late to undo the effects of his anger. One might think, according to Starobinski's interpretation, that learning to dissemble, or to manipulate false appearances, is the only result of the "fall." Rousseau says that, after this false accusation and the similar experience of his cousin, "we were less ashamed to do wrong, and more afraid of being accused: we began to hide ourselves, to mutiny, to lie." In fact, this tendency to dissimulate only begins here and does not fully develop until Jean-Jacques's apprenticeship, of which Rousseau says, "so it was that I learned to covet in silence, to conceal, to dissimulate, to lie, and finally to steal" (I, 32).[27] Jean-Jacques apparently perfects dissimulation only years after leaving Bossey. The most important lesson of the "fall" at the time is that Jean-Jacques acquires an overwhelming anger at injustice. This anger is caused by his failure to realize that there is a split between appearance and reality.

In the case of the premature development of unnatural sexual pas-

---

27. This discovery would be the second stage in Jean-Jacques's understanding; see IV, 966.

sions, the consequences of Jean-Jacques's miseducation are ambiguous. On one hand, the form taken by his desire prevents him from succumbing to some forms of dependence to which civilized humans are prone. He is unable to indulge his desires in action. On the other hand, the stimulus given to his imagination indicates a further departure from nature. The consequences of the development of anger are ambiguous in other ways. This experience cannot be construed as a preservation of naturalness. The experience of anger coincides with a full-blown development of amour-propre. For a citizen, such an experience would be compatible with an identification with the community. For Jean-Jacques the ambiguity arises from the fact that his anger is directed at the fellow members of his community. His ability to identify with them, but not to put himself in their place accurately, separates him from them rather than uniting him to them. He regards his benevolent tutors as oppressive tyrants.

The positive and negative aspects of this experience can be seen in its long-term consequences. Rousseau presents this event as the source of his hatred of "every unjust action" (I, 20) and specifically of violence inflicted on the weak by the strong. He says that whenever he hears of or observes such injustice, his "first sentiment of violence and injustice" returns with all its original force. He is keenly aware of the feelings of all vicitims of unjust violence. Even his adult awareness of his misjudgment of the Lamberciers does not lessen the force of this identification. Understanding alone does little to counter the force of strong artificial passions once they appear.

That adult hatred of injustice arises from a childhood experience that need not have occurred, and not even from the experience itself but from a childish misinterpretation of it, raises the question of the natural attachment of humans to justice. Jean-Jacques's general hatred of injustice stems from this childish anger—anger based on his unnatural and mistaken attribution of motives to other people. Thus hatred of injustice, if not love of justice, comes only from living outside oneself. In this context Rousseau himself draws an ambiguous conclusion: "This movement may be natural to me, and I believe that it is; but the profound memory of the first injustice that I suffered has been tied to it for too long and too strongly, not to have reinforced it very much" (I, 32). With this formulation, he claims both that hatred of injustice is natural and that it is reinforced by specific experiences. How it would develop with different experiences and how this natural movement might manifest itself in natural circumstances are left unclear.

In the *Second Discourse* Rousseau argues that the specific manifestation he attributes in the *Confessions* to a natural sense of justice is simply unnatural. He says of a natural man in the state of nature that he

> could have neither hate nor desire for revenge, passions that can arise only from the opinion that some affront has been received; and as it is scorn or intention to hurt and not the harm that constitutes the offense, men who know neither how to evaluate themselves nor compare themselves can do each other a great deal of mutual violence when they derive some advantage from it, without ever offending one another. (*Discourses*, 222)

After the punishment from the Lamberciers, Jean-Jacques, unlike a natural man, is mortally affronted. His feeling of offense is also derived from his focus on the intention of the Lamberciers to torture him rather than on the actual physical harm he receives.

In *Emile*, Rousseau does refer to "the sentiment of the just and unjust" that is innate in humans (*Emile*, 66). To illustrate this innate sentiment, he tells the story of the rage of an infant who is struck by his nurse. At first glance it may be difficult to see why an infant feels rage at a blow whereas a natural man feels only pain. In the case of the infant, Rousseau insists that it is not the pain but "the manifest intention of offending" that inspires rage. In the state of nature, the intention behind fights is always protection or advantage, never offense. Thus what distinguishes the infant from the natural man is the situation. The infant sees a manifest intention directed against himself, just as Jean-Jacques does with the Lamberciers. If there were no manifest intention to offend, offense would not be taken. Thus the natural sentiment of the just and unjust has its origin in the capacity to attribute the intention of offense to others. Rousseau portrays this capacity as innate but shows that it can remain quiescent unless circumstances cause it to be exercised. It is even possible that some practice is required before this ability begins to show itself; that is, the baby may not be angry the first time he is struck. After a first feeling of anger, he may imagine intentions to offend where none exist.

This capacity can draw incorrect conclusions, as it does in Jean-Jacques's case. A natural man could draw the opposite wrong conclusion, for example, when attacked by someone (presumably a civilized human) intent on enslaving him. He might think that the desire behind the attack was merely for his food rather than for domination. A natural man requires some time to recognize civilized intentions; on learning to recognize them, he becomes less natural. In *Emile*, Rousseau insists both that a child can learn very quickly to attribute intentions to others and that with care this tendency can be postponed indefinitely. In short, while it is natural for humans to feel anger at intentions to harm them, as opposed to accidental injuries, they must learn to recognize such intentions; in the pure state of nature they are very unlikely to do so.[28] The sentiment of the just and unjust, then, is in some sense a derivative of social experience, no matter how natural its root is.

Imagination and Vanity: Pride versus Vanity

The last of the artificial sentiments to arise in Jean-Jacques is vanity. This is the passion that Rousseau most identifies with corrupt political communities. In his "Project for a Constitution for Corsica" he compares the unhealthiness of vanity with the pride characteristic of good citizens (III, 938). The pride of citizens comes from sharing objects of emulation with their fellows; it points to an estimable standard beyond itself.[29] The vanity characteristic of corrupt civilized humans comes from their desire to aggrandize themselves in the opinion of others; it comes from opinion alone and points to no estimable object.

Vanity is the most complicated of the artificial sentiments in that it depends on the most complex operation of the imagination. Both pride and anger are based on an immediate identification with someone else, and sexuality is, at base, a natural passion, whatever modification it may undergo because of the imagination. Vanity presupposes the ability to move outside oneself and therefore has a common root with pride and anger. It is distinguished from these passions in being less immediate and more calculating and manipulative. It is distinguished from sexuality in having no natural root whatsoever. The vain wish for others to think highly of them for any reason at all so that they can exploit them or merely enjoy their flattery. Thus, while pride can be a shared social passion, "vanity by its nature is individual."[30] It is individual, not because it is consistent with natural independence, but because it sets people against each other and keeps them out of a social whole

In the pure state of nature there is neither vanity nor pride (*Dis-*

28. Later in *Emile* Rousseau says that "the first sentiment of justice does not come to us from the justice we owe but from that which is owed us" (*Emile*, 97).

29. See the discussion of imitation in Chapter 1.

30. This discussion is Rousseau's most complete treatment of the relation between pride and vanity.

course, 137). Pride begins to stir in a natural man with "the first glance he directs upon himself," an occurrence that Rousseau claims immediately precedes the simplest social relations (*Discourses*, 144). Vanity begins later, when each "begins to look at the other and to want to be looked at himself" (*Discourses*, 149). The essence of vanity is this concern with how one is looked at by others. It depends on the developed imaginative ability of thinking about other people's opinions and oneself at the same time. This artificial sentiment distinguishes corrupt civilized humans from both citizens and natural humans, just as pride distinguishes citizens from natural humans.

Both Emile and Jean-Jacques have their first movements of vanity after their first encounters with injustice (*Emile*, 175). As in the case with anger, Emile's experience comes before his imagination has been stimulated by reading. As a result, his vanity like his anger can be repressed with relative ease. The difference in treatment of the two passions in Emile is in the harshness with which vanity is repressed. While Emile's anger is first elicited and then calmed, his vanity is brutally crushed after it is aroused. Jean-Jacques's vanity, like his anger, is neither calmed nor crushed.

The discussion in *Emile* shows that the danger of vanity arises with the acquisition of knowledge. Unlike someone in the pure state of nature, Emile acquires a large stock of scientific knowledge. This knowledge clearly improves his ability to survive in all conditions; at the same time, it increases his ability to make comparisons and exposes him to the ignorance of other people. When he first takes pleasure in displaying his superiority, he undergoes "the first movement of vanity." It is impossible simply to calm this new sentiment by offering Emile a melon. The pleasure of vanity is much more intense than a desire for food (*Emile*, 173). As a result of its relative power, Emile's vanity must be uprooted by a humiliating public exposure of the limits of his knowledge. In spite of the greater harshness with which Emile is treated in this case, the pattern of instruction is the same as that of his first experience of indignation: his education exposes him to the risk of acquiring an artificial passion, he is given a small dose of the passion, and after the inoculation he is cured. His remaining vanity is later transformed into compassion (*Emile*, 221).

From the beginning of his treatment of his own experience of vanity, Rousseau depreciates the importance of this sentiment in his own development. In describing his lack of corruption on his arrival at Bossey, he asserts, "I believe that never has an individual of our species had less vanity than I" (I, 14). Because all members of the species naturally lack vanity altogether, Jean-Jacques's uniqueness must consist in his lack of susceptibility to this artificial passion. In spite of this relative immunity, Jean-Jacques contracts vanity at Bossey (I, 24). Coming as it does after his imagination has been aroused, this first experience is not the last. Even relative immunity from a passion does not preclude the possibility of its development.[31]

Rousseau's treatment of this first movement is much more playful than his corresponding treatments of sexuality and anger. He describes a very comic adventure using a mock heroic style complete with a Latin motto.[32] He and his cousin are allowed to participate in the ceremonial planting of a walnut tree by M. Lambercier. They decide to imitate and dupe their tutor by diverting the supply of water from the walnut to a willow they have planted by themselves. It is the pleasure at having duped his tutor that gives Jean-Jacques what he calls his "first well-marked movement of vanity." Although this scheme is quickly detected, Jean-Jacques receives no public humiliation. Consequently his vanity is not uprooted along with the willow.[33] This passion is not yet as strong as his pride, anger, or sexual desire, but it has begun an unchecked growth.[34] The playful incident has a serious result. Rather than being inoculated against vanity, Jean-Jacques is infected with it. As it develops, it will undermine his ability to be a good citizen by encouraging him to take advantage of others rather than to cooperate with them.

The Development of the Imagination and the Origin of Crime

The civilized acquisitions discussed so far, sexual desire, anger, and vanity, have gone a long way toward destroying natural psychological independence in Jean-Jacques. To this point, however, he has been relatively independent of the whims of others. His family and teachers may have seemed tyrannical, but in fact they have left him relatively

31. For a somewhat different view, see Hartle, *Modern Self*, p. 90.

32. The motto, *"Omnia vincit labor improbus,"* connects this story to Emile's labor in his garden (*Emile*, 98).

33. In *Emile* Rousseau says that the growth of vanity must be prevented at its birth. He then says, "The sole folly of which one cannot disabuse a man who is not mad is vanity. For this there is no other cure than experience—if, indeed, anything can cure it" (*Emile*, 245).

34. On Jean-Jacques's vanity, see Chapter 5.

free from compulsion. As a result, the passions he has experienced are only potential sources of full-blown political passions like slavishness, pride, resentment, or manipulativeness. These latter passions begin to emerge at the end of Book I as Jean-Jacques experiences a real dependence based on an unjust social hierarchy.

At the end of his stay at Bossey, Jean-Jacques is roughly the same age as Emile at the end of Book II. At this age Emile has experienced only anger among the artificial sentiments. Emile experiences vanity and a stimulus to his imagination in Book III, between the ages of twelve and fifteen, and emerging sexual desires only in Book IV, between fifteen and twenty. At the corresponding point in his own education, Jean-Jacques has experienced each of these artificial sentiments to a very high degree. Rather than being a natural man, the young Jean-Jacques is the model of the product of a bad, unnatural education.

The difference between Emile and Jean-Jacques at the age of twelve is marked by the number of artificial passions avoided by the former and acquired by the latter. Emile's education up to this age is largely negative. Because it consists in avoiding dangers more than in learning, one might be tempted to call this period lost time (*Emile*, 93). Rousseau argues, however, that a negative education that retards the development of artificial sentiments is the necessary foundation for a later positive education. The alternative is a falsely positive education that complicates all further developments by prematurely stimulating these sentiments. At the age of twelve Emile has no artificial passions. He is prepared to acquire useful learning that will preserve his self-sufficiency and lead to virtue rather than vice.

These differences are even more apparent during the next stage of education, from ages twelve through sixteen. Emile begins his positive learning by acquiring a wide variety of skills of self-sufficiency. As part of this positive education, he is apprenticed to a carpenter. This career is chosen according to the natural standard of utility. Whereas the early part of his education prevents him from acquiring passions that would make him psychologically dependent on others, this part secures those skills that make him physically independent. In Book III Emile learns to make his way in the world through a practical knowledge of science. In effect he learns his own place in nature.

Instead of learning his own place in nature, at the same age Jean-Jacques begins to learn his lack of a place in society. In this phase, the remainder of Book I of the *Confessions*, Jean-Jacques develops no radically new artificial passions. Instead he reveals the consequences of those he has already developed. Rousseau begins the account of this new phase just as he did the earlier move to Bossey and the Lamberciers. Once again he belittles the importance of the decisive events of the previous stage, this time the events at Bossey, as he moves to the next stage of his education. Although his account leaves no question about the denaturing errors made by his father and tutors, Rousseau describes his condition after leaving Bossey as if he were the recipient of Emile's education. He again emphasizes his friendship with his cousin and says that "it must be that our first education had been well directed so that, masters of almost all our time and at such a tender age, we were so little tempted to abuse it" (I, 26). It is as if, once removed from the Lamberciers, the disastrous effects of their miseducation disappear. His first assertion of a reversion to a quasi-natural condition allowed Rousseau to emphasize the impact of the events that disrupted the restored harmony without concealing the importance of earlier events for conditioning this response to the new ones. Similarly, in this new context the form of the new disruption depends on the artificial sentiments acquired earlier. These sentiments both influence and are influenced by Jean-Jacques's reception into the social order.

Jean-Jacques's entry into the world in an effort to find a career sets the context for his renewed departure from nature. Instead of securing his self-sufficiency, these efforts increase his dependence. After a brief trial at "the useful profession of pettifogger" (I, 30), Jean-Jacques is apprenticed to an engraver. He is given an occupation that owes its value only to convention. Rather than making him self-sufficient, his occupation makes him incapable of taking care of himself in circumstances in which merely decorative skills are not in demand (I, 73). As a result Jean-Jacques is forced into the servile position of a lackey. Even more significant than this dependence on convention is the more tangible dependence on his violent master, M. Ducommun, who Rousseau says brutalized his character (I, 30). Rather than returning him to something resembling a natural condition, M. Ducommun brings him to a degenerated position by his harshness (I, 31).

Rousseau attributes the origin of his vices to the tyranny of his master: "I was bold at my father's, free at M. Lambercier's, discreet at my uncle's; I became fearful at my master's, and from then on I was a lost child" (I, 31). Even though he has earlier said that at the Lambercier's home he and his cousin learned to hide themselves, to mutiny, and to lie (I, 21), he now says that under his master he began "to covet in silence, to conceal, to dissimulate, to lie, and finally to steal" (I, 32). The two lists are very similar, and the second must therefore represent an exacerbation of the qualities mentioned in the first. The difference between the lists concerns the acquisition of covetousness, which leads to theft. Theft was impossible before, largely because his domestic setting allowed Jean-Jacques to satisfy his material desires without stealing. In the broader social order, this ceases to be the case.

The vice introduced and developed in this part of Book I involves Jean-Jacques's relations with private property, the conventional institution that introduces Emile to the experience of anger. Because private property is so closely related to the question of conventional inequality, it necessarily raises complex issues of justice and injustice. Emile's first feeling of indignation is at the destruction of the garden he carefully planted (*Emile*, 98–100). Because his first experience of injustice is related to property external to himself rather than to an accusation directed at his behavior, it is less intense than Jean-Jacques's. Furthermore, Emile learns about property through his own claim to the product of his labor. He learns first that labor is the source of just claims to property and second that this claim must be modified in the light of the claim of the first possessor. He learns to make advantageous contracts that avoid conflicts between his desires and those of other people. Thus, before reaching the age of twelve, Emile learns to accommodate a natural right to property with a more conventional right.

In Jean-Jacques's case there is a similar connection between property and the feeling of injustice, but there are two major differences: Jean-Jacques's anger has already been developed, and rather than attempting to assuage the boy's anger and teach him the natural foundation of property rights, M. Ducommun capriciously flaunts his possessions without showing his right to them. This conspicuous consumption stimulates a desire for equality in the apprentice. As a result Jean-Jacques learns to covet and to steal. This is the first example of a serious misdeed in the *Confessions*.

This incident not only distinguishes Jean-Jacques from Emile, it also marks a close parallel between Rousseau's *Confessions* and Augustine's *Confessions*. A story of a theft plays an important part in Augustine's account of his childhood. A comparison of the thefts can help to identify the difference between these two pictures of exemplary human experience.[35] The whole of Book II of Augustine's *Confessions* is a meditation on the significance of his childhood theft of some pears.[36] Augustine precedes the discussion of this particular theft with the admis-

---

35. For a treatment of this episode, see Hartle, *Modern Self*, pp. 24–25.
36. On the parallels between the events, see Starobinski, *Transparence*, p. 101.

sion that he occasionally stole from his parents' cellar and table out of greediness and from a desire to please his friends. He also mentions that he frequently lied.[37] Augustine interprets these actions as signs of a natural tendency toward sinfulness. Rousseau, on the contrary, attributes his earliest faults of the same sort only to innocent desires such as a love of sweets (I, 10). Rousseau and Augustine begin from the same phenomenon, but each gives a different explanation. Rousseau's claim for the truth of his system is based on his superior ability to give an explanation of such phenomena.[38]

The differences between Rousseau and Augustine emerge even more clearly in the continuations of their discussions. Augustine presents a complex explanation of his later theft. First he dismisses the possibility that he undertook the theft out of need or even a desire for sweets.[39] Instead he concludes that he stole because of a combination of friendship and shame.[40] Augustine does not shift the blame to his friends; he blames his own feelings of friendship and shame rather than any external agent. Furthermore, he finds this sense of shame and "thirst for others' loss" to be a normal condition for a sinful being. He has no need to treat the genesis of these passions, because he regards them as innate. Rousseau's account of stealing at the end of Book I focuses on the motive of friendship and omits shame. In other respects, however, his discussion is more complex than its counterpart in Augustine. Rousseau is not concerned with simply understanding the immediate motive for the theft. Such an account is sufficient for him in his earlier story of stealing sweets because in that instance the motive is supplied by a natural desire. But now he wishes to show the origin of an artificial motive. While he traces the origin of his willingness to steal to his resentment at the conspicuous consumption of his master, he indicates how unnatural theft is by insisting that he lived under M. Ducommun for more than a year without committing a theft. Even after a year, the immediate cause of his career of crime is not the frustration of the desires aroused by his master. His first theft is undertaken merely to oblige a fellow worker.

Like Augustine, Jean-Jacques derives no benefit from this theft.

37. Augustine, *Confessions*, I.xviii.
38. Lejeune argues that Rousseau here gives an alternative myth. This characterization conforms with Rousseau's intention of writing a moral fable, but not with his philosophy; see *Pacte*, p. 88.
39. Augustine, *Confessions*, II.iv.
40. Ibid., II.ix.

Unlike Augustine, Rousseau is willing to place blame on his friend and takes none for himself. While Augustine sees a natural tendency in himself toward sin, a tendency exacerbated by shame in the face of his friends, Rousseau excuses both himself and human nature by saying, "It is nearly always generous feelings misdirected that lead a child into taking his first steps in crime" (I, 32). Whereas Augustine allows no mitigating factor, such as desire for an object, to interfere with his description of sinfulness, Rousseau insists on both the mitigating factor of his master's ill treatment and the goodness of his own motive in committing the "crime."

It is only after his initial theft that less pure motives enter Jean-Jacques's mind, but even at this point Rousseau does not attribute sinfulness to himself. After his first success, Jean-Jacques concludes that stealing is not terrible. As a result he begins to steal objects that tempt him. These thefts resemble his infantile thefts; that is, they are undertaken out of a desire for food. However, this natural desire has been inflated by his master's bad treatment. Occasionally the thefts are detected and he is punished. The punishment merely increases the resentment that triggered the desire to steal. Thus, far from emphasizing a natural tendency to sinfulness, Rousseau focuses on the circumstances in which he found himself to explain the thefts. Rousseau's *Confessions* could hardly be more opposed to those of Augustine.

It might be expected that when these circumstances changed and Jean-Jacques no longer found himself under a tyrannical master, the desire to steal would disappear. If the environment causes crime, a change in the environment should prevent crime. To some extent this corresponds with Rousseau's presentation. Later, when he is in a situation in which all of his desires are fulfilled without theft, he does not steal (I, 268). But a mere change of circumstances is not sufficient to reverse what has become habitual. Even when the cause is removed, the effect remains, and Rousseau admits that he has been addicted to petty thievery for his whole life.

Even with this admission, Rousseau argues that his thefts are not a sign of complete denaturing or corruption. He insists that he is never tempted to steal money—the object of most civilized peoples' desire. He calls this "one of the singularities of my character" (I, 36). The combination of a willingness to steal and a lack of interest in money stems from his "very ardent passions." Although he is usually very shy, the arousal of passion changes his normal character. Of such occasions he says, "Outside of the sole object that occupies me the universe is no longer anything for me." The reason that money cannot be the "sole object" of his passion is that, rather than being an object of desire in itself, money is only a means to the satisfaction of desire. Money mediates between the desire and the object. To think about stealing money in order to acquire future or present objects of desire requires being occupied with more than a single object. Stealing money requires foresight, but Rousseau emphasizes the spontaneous character of his whims (I, 40).

One might argue that, rather than precluding the possibility of stealing money, this presentation in fact opens the possibility. Although Jean-Jacques might not steal money while under the influence of his ardent passions, when he is calm he could anticipate that his passion will be aroused again. This calm anticipation could lead to stealing to prepare for these onslaughts of passion. Rousseau begins to answer such objections with his statement, "Money that one possesses is the instrument of liberty: that which one pursues is that of servitude" (I, 38). In healthy political regimes money would be dispensed with as much as possible.[41] When Jean-Jacques is calm, he feels the servitude involved in pursuing money; when he is aroused, he forgets about money altogether. Rousseau also argues that the mere possession of money without any need to acquire it represents a sort of servitude. Money does not lead directly to the satisfaction of a desire. Money can be exchanged for a desired object only through a complex relation of services purchased from other people. One is then dependent on these people. The need to enter such a relation in order to satisfy a simple desire stands in the way of, and even renders impossible, the direct enjoyment of the desired object (I, 36–37). As with his sexual passions, Jean-Jacques's shame prevents him from making overtures to other people. In effect, one could say, his thefts substitute for the use of money. He acquires through a more direct action rather than a less direct one. Thus, whereas the objects of his passions distinguish him from a natural man and link him with corrupt civilized humans, the singular intensity of these passions makes him behave like a natural man rather than a corrupt civilized one.[42] Just as with sexuality, the very peculiarity and intensity of his desires leaves him in a position that resembles the natural one.[43]

41. On the political problems caused by money, see III, 1003–12, 920–36.
42. On the question of money and immediacy, see Starobinski, *Transparence*, pp. 129–37.
43. See Jean Starobinski, *L'Oeil vivant* (Paris: Gallimard, 1961), p. 104.

Jean-Jacques's quasi-naturalness with respect to property, like his quasi-naturalness with respect to sexuality, has a foundation unlike that of Emile's similar naturalness. Emile has quiet passions like a natural man, but learns to calculate about their future satisfaction; he learns to give up beans today to have melons later. Jean-Jacques's intense passion prevents him from calculating in this way. Both Emile and Jean-Jacques can be distinguished from the natural man, who has neither strong desires nor foresight; each can also be distinguished from most corrupt civilized humans, whose fairly strong desires stimulate their foresight. The civilized love of money requires a calculating foresight based on an imagination that can substitute a neutral token for the object of desire. Civilized people's constant desire for more prevents them from having either the self-sufficiency of Emile or the immediate satisfactions of Jean-Jacques.[44]

Once again Jean-Jacques's radical unnaturalness supports something resembling naturalness. Rousseau shows the genesis in himself of what Augustine would call sinful desires and what he himself would identify as unnatural. These unnatural desires lead Jean-Jacques to a career of petty theft which would not be undertaken by a natural human or Emile. Nevertheless, the very intensity of Jean-Jacques's desires preserves him from the sort of calculating exploitation of others that characterizes corrupt civilized life. His unnaturalness coexists with and supports a quasi-naturalness just as it does in the case of his sexual passions. This is what saves him from being completely corrupted by his first exposure to the social order.

In its lack of calculation, Jean-Jacques's distaste for money may appear natural, but its effects are not. His distaste extends beyond money to anything that would mediate between his desires and their enjoyment. Natural humans have similar desires for immediate pleasures, but their idleness and limited needs make it easy for them to do without any pleasure that cannot be gained effortlessly. After a brief moment of frustration, they simply forget about the unobtainable object unless it relates to a pressing natural need. Jean-Jacques's frustrations, however, lead him to the imaginary world where all desires are satisfied without effort. The lack of a real satisfaction keeps him in a state of endless longing very different from the placid calm of a natural

---

44. Rousseau admits that he did once steal a small sum of money, but he claims that this exception did not violate the rule. He attributes it to "a sort of delirium" rather than to calculating foresight. There was no point to the theft and no hope of avoiding detection (I, 38–39).

human. As is true of his sexual desire, Jean-Jacques forms an intense insatiable desire and then retreats into his imagination to dispose of things at his will. Once again, the same thing that keeps Jean-Jacques in a quasi-natural condition in one respect is an additional stimulus to his unnatural imagination.[45]

Imagination and the Disruption of Civilized Wholeness

To this point the *Confessions* shows how Jean-Jacques's unusually strong imagination disrupts his natural wholeness. The mistakes made by his educators and master increase this disruption. These mistakes also keep Jean-Jacques from being absorbed into a healthy political order. To conclude this chapter, we can look at Jean-Jacques's prospects for participating in a social whole that can compensate for his loss of natural unity. We can then reach some broad but tentative conclusions about his treatment of the imagination which can guide the rest of this inquiry.

To begin the analysis of Jean-Jacques at sixteen, we can take a final look at Emile. At the conclusion of Book III of *Emile* Rousseau summarizes what Emile is like at fifteen. His knowledge is restricted to physical relations; he knows nothing about moral relations with other people. Perhaps most important, his "imagination is in no way inflamed," and his amour-propre "is still hardly aroused" (*Emile*, 208). Because he understands physical relations so well, he is not physically dependent on the cooperation of other humans. Because his imagination and amour-propre are so limited, he is not psychologically dependent. It is this twofold independence that allows him to preserve his natural freedom even though he lacks the external appearance of a savage.

If Emile's life up to the age of fifteen is a study in the preservation of natural freedom in civil society, Jean-Jacques's life can only be a study in the development of unnatural dependence. His physical dependence is emphasized from the first moment of his life: "I was born almost dying, they had little hope of preserving me" (I, 7). Emile's tutor would never undertake to bring up such a child (*Emile*, 53). Although Jean-Jacques survives, his education gives him little knowledge of the physical relations that could allow him to establish natural independence. His psychological dependence is even more severe. Emile at fifteen has

---

45. Whether or not Jean-Jacques continues to steal depends entirely on the circumstances in which he finds himself (I, 268–69).

learned to look at the world in terms of "the relations which are connected with his interest." Jean-Jacques has learned to look at the world
through the distorting lenses of imagination, sexual desire, anger, and
vanity. Each of these artificial acquisitions puts him into relations with
other people which threaten his freedom. This physical and psychological dependence is the root of a potential political dependence.[46] Jean-
Jacques's artificial passions are easily transformed into a slavish passivity and resentment. They quickly lead to forms of imaginative flight
from the world and petty crimes—the marks of subjects of unjust political orders. Rousseau here gives the basis for a psychology of personal
and political repression.

After the extended discussion of stealing and money, which disrupts
the narrative, Rousseau returns to the account of his apprenticeship.
His survey reinforces his assertions that he was reduced to a condition
in which he partook of the characteristics of subservience, but that he
was preserved from some of the effects of these vices by his very different tastes. His lack of taste for the amusements of his fellow appren-
tices led him back to his own first amusement of reading.

This return to the initial theme of Book I reveals a further development of Jean-Jacques's imagination.[47] Earlier, Jean-Jacques became the
character about whom he read. After his first experience of sexuality he
is able to put himself into imaginary situations rather than losing his
own identity completely. Now he attributes to himself a new imaginative ability.[48] Of this new ability he says:

> It was to nourish itself on the situations which had interested me in my
> reading, to recall them, to vary them, to combine them, to appropriate
> them to me so much that I became one of the personages that I imag-
> ined, that I always saw myself in the most agreeable position according
> to my taste, so that the fictional state in which I came to put myself made
> me forget my real state with which I was so discontent. This love of
> imaginary objects and the facility in occupying myself with them suc-
> ceeded in disgusting me with all that surrounded me, and determined
> that taste for solitude, which has always remained with me since then.
> (I, 41)

This description both preserves and extends the account of the imagination given earlier. Jean-Jacques is still able to become another

---

46. A subpolitical version of such dependence is shown in the account of Jean-
Jacques's apprenticeship.

47. On this return to the introductory theme, see Lejeune, *Pacte*, p. 92.

48. This passage also represents a development in Jean-Jacques's sexual desire.

character, but he shows a much greater ability to manipulate the images he forms. In effect he is able to make an imaginary world to suit his desires.

This description of a poetic, or formative, imagination is of immense importance for the *Confessions*, for Rousseau's thought in general, and for his influence on later thinkers. In Rousseau's presentation, the imagination is the source of the richest and most human pleasures, but it is also the source of the greatest pain and delirium. No aspect of civilized life is untouched by it. Perhaps the most important reason that Rousseau is able to present his own life as paradigmatic, as more instructive than the lives of Jacques or Pierre, is that he understands his own life as a constant grappling with the deepest effects of an extremely developed imagination. The particular forms this struggle takes are unusual or even unique, but its significance is general. Imagination is what allows humans to make a world for themselves, but in using this power they remove themselves from what is most natural.

The ambivalence of Rousseau's view of the imagination is dramatized at the end of Book I. After being locked out of the city at night, Jean-Jacques decides to abandon Geneva to avoid further beatings from his master. He characteristically presents this fateful step as the result of a guard's laziness and his uncle's lack of concern, not as the consequence of his own decision. He concludes Book I by reflecting on what his fate would have been had he remained in Geneva and succeeded in his profession of engraving: "I would have been a good Christian, a good citizen, a good father of a family, a good friend, a good worker, a good man in every respect" (I, 43). This description could equally well apply to the citizens of Neuchâtel described in the *Letter to d'Alembert*, or to the life planned for Emile at the end of his education.[49] It is the life of a civilized human who has been preserved from most civilized corruption.

The prominent feature shared by each of these three pictures is self-containment. The people of Neuchâtel live with little contact with the outside world and in particular with no stimulation to their imagination from the theater. The argument against the introduction of a theater to Geneva in the *Letter to d'Alembert* is in part that such an institution would open a horizon for ambition, vanity, and fantasy which would destroy religion, citizenship, and family life. Emile similarly plans to live in the

---

49. As is shown by "Emile and Sophie," the sequel to *Emile*, these plans are not fulfilled.

country and center his life around his family. His imagination is directed toward his wife and unborn children. Rousseau describes his own lost opportunity in similar terms: "This station, lucrative enough to give an easy subsistence but not enough to lead to fortune, might have limited my ambition for the rest of my days and leaving me an honest leisure to cultivate moderate tastes, it might have contained me in my sphere without offering many means of leaving it" (I, 43). In this passage he stresses that ambition must be limited to a finite sphere so as not to destroy wholeness or self-sufficiency. By living in the self-contained sphere of family, friends, and city, Jean-Jacques might have avoided the tendency of corrupt civilized humans to live outside themselves, or while living outside himself, he might have been a part of a larger whole.

This position could be regarded as a civilized approximation of the wholeness of a natural man in the state of nature. This passage shows that the sphere is maintained by external supports and limits imposed on it. Rousseau describes a comfortable but modest subsistence that offers no opportunity for advancement. Yet in the same context he insists that there would be no internal barriers on his imagination. He says, "Having an imagination sufficiently rich to adorn all stations with its chimeras, sufficiently powerful to transport me, so to speak, at my whim from one to another, it mattered little to me in which I might be in fact" (I, 43). This discussion of the charm offered by the imagination, specifically its ability to transport one out of one's station, hints that the position of citizen, friend, and father might be insufficient for Jean-Jacques. This hint becomes stronger at the beginning of Book II immediately after this nostalgic account of the lost opportunity for an ordinary life in Geneva. Rousseau describes his feeling of independence and great hopes for the future outside his native city rather than his sense of loss. While under his tyrannical master, his imagination forms a fantasy world in which he can live, but ultimately it causes him to embrace the opportunity to fulfill these fantasies in another part of the real world. Given Rousseau's repeated assertions in his other works of the need to avoid stimulating the imagination of ordinary decent citizens, it is difficult to maintain that the harshness of his master is the sole reason for his departure.[50]

This hint is given confirmation in Book IV when Rousseau recounts his rejection of another opportunity for a peaceful family life (I, 145–

50. Cf. Starobinski, *L'Oeil*, p. 135.

46; see also 153). In this context he admits his tendency to abandon himself to hopes for future adventures as long as these hopes demand little application for their fulfillment. He also says that frequently the smallest immediate pleasure causes him to sacrifice long-term plans and commitments (I, 99–100). In these passages he also discusses the pain that ultimately resulted from the lost opportunities for a settled life. These discussions differ from the passage at the end of Book I in one way, however. In the earlier passage Rousseau claims that a powerful imagination that takes one outside oneself causes contentment with one's actual lot; in the later passages he argues that such an imagination causes one to abandon one's stable condition. In Book I Rousseau attributes his unhappiness to bad fortune; in Book IV he attributes it to his own imagination.

That the passage in Book I is less straightforward about the completeness of Jean-Jacques's departure from wholeness than later passages is typical of the narration of events in the opening book. Rousseau consistently presents each departure from nature or wholeness as the result of accidents beyond his control. Each arbitrary event is initially presented as an absolute departure from naturalness imposed from outside. At the same time, the elaboration of the consequences of each event reveals the ultimate effect on Jean-Jacques's character to be conditioned by the preceding "absolute" departure from nature. By combining the two aspects of repeated absolute departures and a series of events in which the later build on the earlier, Rousseau succeeds in keeping open a number of important issues. First, he is able to stress the importance and riskiness of every childhood experience, while at the same time leaving some question about how successfully the effects of this experience might be removed or mitigated. Second, he is able to argue that early events condition what comes after, while at the same time suggesting that future events can channel earlier tendencies in a variety of directions. In short, Rousseau presents departures from nature as closed and variable at the same time. A departure from nature opens a potentially infinite horizon that is constantly reshaped at each subsequent departure. Civilized humans have an apparently enormous realm of freedom in that they can be shaped in many ways, but each step in this realm forecloses some possibilities even as it opens new ones. Just as the imagination is the source of both extreme pleasure and extreme pain, the departure from nature presents an aspect of liberation and one of servitude.

The issue implied in Book I of the *Confessions* reflects the issue implied in the *Second Discourse*: once natural independence and whole-ness have been lost, can they be restored? If they cannot be restored, can they be approximated? In the *Second Discourse* the answer to the first question is unambiguous: once natural independence is gone, it is gone forever (*Discourses*, 160). This answer, however, applies only to the species as a whole. The variants of these questions in the *Confessions* apply only to a single member of the species. By the end of Book I their answer is ambiguous. Rousseau presents each individual departure from nature as an absolute and irreversible rupture. The very existence of a sequence of such ruptures, however, calls into question the abso-lute character of each of the members of the sequence. Furthermore, while each later break is conditioned by each former one, the later breaks also modify the effects of the former. To put this another way, Rousseau's account of his faulty education is much clearer about the natural point of departure than it is about the direction of the destina-tion. This destination, or one possible destination, is revealed in the remainder of the *Confessions*. The role played by the imagination in Rousseau's account of the destruction of natural wholeness is im-mensely significant and is an important indication of the importance of this faculty for his thought as a whole.

The imagination plays a much more complex role in Rousseau's thought than it does in the thought of his contemporaries who sup-ported the goals of the Enlightenment. One of the hallmarks of the Enlightenment is the presentation of the imagination as the fundamen-tal source of dangerous errors. One of the best examples is found in Condillac's *Essay on the Origin of Human Knowledge*, the publication of which Rousseau greatly assisted. Condillac identifies three important features of the imagination.[51] First, in its developed form, the imagina-tion is the predominant source of human errors. Second, also in its developed form, it is one of the major sources of knowledge. Finally, to avoid the errors while receiving the advantages, one must learn how to regulate the imagination. The mastery of the imagination is what Con-dillac offers to teach. He is particularly concerned with mastering what he calls "the vices" of the imagination, which include shame at suffering an affront, courage at avenging affronts, prejudice in judging other people, and the different forms of madness.[52] The first three vices are

51. Abbé Etienne Bonnot de Condillac, *Essai sur l'origine des connaissances humaines* (Paris: Editions Galilée, 1973), pp. 121, 142–43.
52. Condillac, *Essai*, pp. 145–46.

the major sources of disagreements and quarrels that issue in the destruction of life rather than its preservation.[53] The final dangerous
idea, madness, is of particular interest. The first form of madness Condillac mentions is seeing oneself as the hero of a novel, the experience
Rousseau identifies as the origin of his own self-consciousness.[54] To
novels Condillac adds books of devotion that open readers to religious
illusions. With these two examples, Condillac indicates that by madness
he means being under the influence of the authority of books and their
authors. Regulating the imagination properly means overthrowing the
imaginary understanding of the world presented in traditional au-
thoritative books that present exemplary figures for emulation. The
Abbé Condillac is no friend of exemplary lives, particularly those of a
religious nature.[55]

This account of the dangers of imagination closely resembles the
negative aspects of Rousseau's treatment, although it is somewhat less
complete in its list of complaints. Yet, as is shown by his attack on books,
Condillac grants the imagination no positive role beyond that as a
pleasing and harmless embellishment to life.[56] Rather than attributing
a potentially important political function to the arts as Rousseau does,
Condillac reduces them to ornamentation.[57] Thus in Condillac's treatment the imagination begins as an absolute ruler who tyrannizes over
humans by deceiving them with notions like shame and honor and by
making them submit to the illusory authority of books and their authors. After deposing the tyrant by regulations that confine it to the
humble service of useful ideas, Condillac grants the former tyrant the
right of embellishing. He grants this right conditionally, however: the
imagination must "seek only to please," not to enslave. Condillac's proposal is in complete accord with the spirit of the manifesto of the
Enlightenment, Diderot's *Encyclopedia*; in the frontispiece of the *Encyclopedia*, Imagination is depicted as adorning a triumphant Truth with a
garland of flowers.

Rousseau agrees that imagination is the source of dangerous errors.

53. Consider Hobbes, *Leviathan*, chap. 11, on the causes of contention among men,
and chap. 12 on the passions that incline them to peace.
54. Condillac, *Essai*, p. 145. Descartes gives a similar argument in the *Discourse on
Method*, Part I.
55. Condillac's outright hostility to exemplary lives sheds light on his reception of
Rousseau's autobiographical works (I, 981–82).
56. Condillac, *Essai*, p. 148.
57. For a useful account of the relation between Rousseau and his contemporaries on
this issue, see Eigeldinger, *Réalité*.

He also argues that it is necessary to regulate it to avoid important vices. The first part of Emile's education is a good example of Condillac's project of avoiding illusions and acquiring knowledge by means of the proper direction of this faculty. As we have seen, however, Rousseau is much more willing to attribute advantages to the role of the imagination in emulation. The reason for this difference is that Rousseau, unlike Condillac and other members of the Enlightenment, thinks that it is neither possible nor necessary for social humans to master the imagination completely. It can neither be prevented from emerging nor uprooted once it has emerged in the majority of people. It must therefore be directed into the formation of a true political life. Such a life does not require a simple acceptance of the madness Condillac attributes to emulation; rather, it is an improvement on the mere selfish calculation of interest on which earlier modern thinkers tend to rely. Because Rousseau does not share the view of Condillac and the rest of the Enlightenment about the ease with which the imagination can be mastered, he seeks for ways to accommodate this faculty and the illusions that arise from it when they are unavoidable. As a result he does not and cannot relegate the imagination to the primarily decorative function of embellishing the truth. For Rousseau, the imagination is the single most important constitutive factor of human social life.

The *Confessions* has an important place in conveying Rousseau's teaching about the imagination. The Jean-Jacques of the *Confessions* is neither a natural man who has no imagination nor a good citizen who has a well-directed imagination. What the *Confessions* explores are the dangers and possibilities open to those for whom the Enlightenment project of mastery of the imagination is impossible and for whom citizenship has ceased to be an option. The task that Rousseau sets himself in the *Confessions* is to present the working out in his own life of the conflicting tendencies arising out of the imagination. The remainder of the *Confessions* shows whether Jean-Jacques is able to find a way to overcome the corrupting education he receives in Book I or to combine his new civilized attributes with something analogous to a return to natural wholeness.[58]

58. Williams gives a good statement of this problem in *Romantic Autobiography*, pp. 91–92.

[4]

The Alternatives for Civilized Life (Books II–VI)

The Consequences of a Positive Education

Book I of the *Confessions* is perhaps the best defense Rousseau could give for the first part of Emile's education. The latter's so-called negative education contrasts sharply in two ways to the positive education given to Jean-Jacques. First, Jean-Jacques's education develops prematurely those attributes such as imagination and sexual desire which emerge very late in Emile's education. Second, Jean-Jacques develops other characteristics, such as anger and vanity, which Emile never acquires or does so only to a small degree. Thus Rousseau shows through his own example that an attempt at more than a negative education in a child is likely to lead to alienation from oneself, contradiction within oneself, dependence on others, and vice.

As the *Confessions* proceeds, it is almost inevitable that the parallels with *Emile* become less and less precise. Accidental occurrences necessarily play a part in the life of a real person, and they must be taken into account even in a report that focuses on the "chain of sentiments" rather than on mere external events. Book I alone has already supplied abundant evidence about the power of accidents to cause feelings. The remainder of the *Confessions* continues to display such complications, which are avoided by Emile's omniscient tutor. This difference between the two books can be explained in terms of Rousseau's claim at the beginning of *Emile* that any education is made up of three parts: nature, men, and things (Emile, 38). A natural education harmonizes the student's experience of men and things with the unavoidable natural development. An unnatural education such as Jean-Jacques's mixes and confuses the three elements. Experiences with other people conflict with natural development, and "things" or events intrude because they are not subject to control.

A second reason for the progressive divergence of the two books is the very different points of departure established in the two students by the age of fifteen. Even if the events occurring to each were identical, for example, if Jean-Jacques met Emile's Sophie instead of Mme de Warens, the two boys' responses to the identical events would differ. Rousseau presents himself as being denatured in the way that a corrupt civilized human is. He has inflamed, contradictory passions that cause him to behave very differently from Emile.

Finally, from the beginning there has been another difference between the two youths. Emile is by nature ordinary. He has no special talents or faculties except those that have come to him from his education. Rousseau, on the other hand, presents himself as extraordinary, not because of his early education, but prior to it. In the terms used in Emile, he is one of those who "raise themselves in spite of what one does" (*Emile*, 52). This formulation reveals the great advantage of Emile's commonness. His education requires much manipulation by the tutor, and it is imperative that he remain unaware of the manipulation. If he had extraordinary capacities he could not be so easily led. A young Socrates would not be deceived by the tricks of the magician "Socrates" (*Emile*, 175). Even in the *Second Discourse* the more talented humans lead the departure from the state of nature (*Discourses*, 159). In effect this means that, whereas Emile can be given a natural education, Jean-Jacques cannot. His very superiority to Emile is the cause of his premature departure from nature. It remains to be seen how capable Jean-Jacques is of educating himself and where this education can lead.

The differences between Jean-Jacques and Emile notwithstanding, it is possible to identify some broad parallels in the development of the two books. Some of these are shown by simple chronology. Book IV of *Emile* covers the period from age fifteen to age twenty, which corresponds to the period covered by Books II–IV of the *Confessions*. In the draft of *Emile* this period is called the "age of force" (IV, 60). During this time Emile's abilities exceed his desires. The *Confessions* differs in showing Jean-Jacques at the same age tormented by desires he cannot satisfy. Book V of *Emile* covers the years from twenty to twenty-five, which corresponds to the period covered by Book V of the *Confessions*.

In the draft of *Emile*, this is called the "age of wisdom." In the *Confessions*, Rousseau begins the corresponding book by addressing himself to the question of his own wisdom at this age. He says, "I was sufficiently formed for my age on the side of mind, but judgment was hardly there" (I, 176). Book V of both *Emile* and the *Confessions* gives an account of an experience with a woman who fixes the student's character. Finally, the draft of *Emile* distinguishes the remainder of Emile's life as the "age of happiness" (*âge de bonheur*). Book VI of the *Confessions*, the concluding book of Part One, virtually begins with Rousseau's assertion that "here begins the short happiness (*bonheur*) of my life" (I, 225). This general similarity in structure can guide the analysis of the development of Part One of the *Confessions* as Jean-Jacques departs further and further from the natural standard. This similarity also signals a more radical departure in Part Two, which presents itself as the "age of misfortunes" (*malheurs*, cf. I, 278).[1] Thus Part One completes what could be called the reversal of Emile's education and Part Two shows the consequences of that reversal as well as an attempt to reverse the reversal, or to return to naturalness.

Although Jean-Jacques's early education is "positive" when compared to Emile's, it can accurately be called negative when compared to the education of a citizen. A citizen's education is positive both in that it allows the formation of artificial characteristics and in that it encourages the establishment of a fixed communal identity. Humans are made into citizens by their identification with their community and its exemplary figures. Jean-Jacques, on the contrary, has such a variety of conflicting and unsettled characteristics that he is nothing in particular; that is, this early education reveals far more about what Jean-Jacques is not than about what he is. Even though he has lost natural wholeness and independence completely, he has not developed the social wholeness of a citizen. His active imagination drives him beyond the social sphere. What he will become remains open.

Although or because Jean-Jacques has not yet become anything definite, he is capable of becoming any of several things. The remainder of Part One of the *Confessions* is an exploration of the options available to those who have neither preserved their naturalness nor become citizens. In Books II–IV Rousseau shows the continued development of the artifical characteristics that began in Book I. This section continues the undirected progress of these corrupt characteris-

---

1. This age should be compared with Emile's life in "Emile and Sophie."

tics; hence it portrays in an extreme form some of the typical attributes of a corrupt civilized human. In Book V Rousseau shows an attempt to establish or fix Jean-Jacques's character in a particular way. This book shows him as a part of a social whole that does not make the same rigorous demands that citizenship would; hence it reveals a social option for mitigating the corruption and dividedness of civilized humans who are too corrupt to become citizens. Finally, in Book VI Rousseau shows a sort of return to nature. This book shows the reversal of his most damaging artificial characteristics; hence it portrays the possibility of reestablishment of natural wholeness and independence within a civilized context.

Imagination continues to play the dominant role in the course of these books, as it did in Book I. Part One of the *Confessions* progressively shows the development of greater and greater power in the imagination, culminating in Rousseau's suggestion that it is almost capable of creation out of nothing (I, 172). Rousseau's use of the term "creation" suggests a quasi-divine power.[2] Human imagination can, of course, create only images, but it can create. Thus Rousseau prepares the way for conceiving of creativity as the highest human activity. This replacement of divine creativity by human creativity is one of the revolutionary characteristics of the *Confessions*. To teach people that they possess an almost divine ability is to transform their understanding of what it means to be human and what the highest human possibilities are. For example, it presents a new understanding of what an artist is. On the basis of this understanding, art can be considered creative rather than representational. Thus, in the old question of the rivalry between philosophy and poetry, Rousseau gives new arms to the poets. If the dispute between the two activities is decided on the basis of which activity represents the world most accurately, philosophy is always able to muster a powerful argument.[3] If the dispute is decided by creativity, by who is most capable of introducing new, undreamed of possibilities, poetry is on much more advantageous ground.[4] Thus, even though Rousseau himself tends to resort to the traditional grounds of philosophic judgment, he ultimately adds new fuel to the artistic fire.

2. This assertion of creativity is all the more startling because creation out of nothing is an ability Rousseau is reluctant to attribute even to God (IV, 956–57).

3. See Plato, *Republic*, 607b.

4. For an account of Rousseau's profound influence on English romantic poets, see Paul A. Cantor, *Creature and Creator: Myth-Making and English Romanticism* (Cambridge: Cambridge University Press, 1984).

The *Confessions* also shows that creativity is not the exclusive preserve of artists. Imagination makes all social humans creative. Each social human creates a personal view of the world, a personal inner life. Karl Barth has captured this aspect of Rousseau's revolutionary impact well: according to Rousseau's teaching, "existence was a beautiful, rich and lively inner life of its own, so beautiful, rich, and lively that anyone who has once discovered it no longer attributes any worth to any life which differs from it, and can only honor and love anything different from it as it is connected with this life; but he really could honor and love it now in this connexion."[5] The creative imagination can produce a fascination with one's inner experience of its products far more alluring than any contemplation of external objects. Rousseau teaches that external beauty, in fact, has its source in us.[6] What is remarkable in Rousseau's presentation is his insistence on the many dangers as well as charms of this new understanding. In his works, the imagination receives the greatest condemnation and the highest possible praise. He presents it as an enslaving as well as a liberating power. Part One of the *Confessions* reveals both of these aspects but with an emphasis on enslavement.

Books II–IV: Living outside Oneself

Books II–IV of the *Confessions* dwell on the same themes as Book I: the imagination and its effects on sexuality, anger, and vanity. In Book I the emergence of these artifical characteristics in Jean-Jacques comes against the background of the confined worlds of Bossey and Geneva. In Books II–IV, as Jean-Jacques moves physically beyond the Alps, he also moves mentally far beyond the bounds of family and city. His physical existence is extremely unsettled. He finds himself moving rootlessly from place to place and even from social class to social class. He first takes refuge with a Catholic priest, who sends him to the convert Mme de Warens, who in turn sends him to Turin for his instruction and conversion. After a brief period he finds employment as a sort of secretary to the Countess de Vercellis, after whose death he enters the service of the Count de Gouvon. Finally, he returns to Mme de Warens to a life alternately settled and unsettled. During the period covered by Books II–IV, Jean-Jacques is literally a boy without a country because

5. Barth, *Protestant Thought*, p. 110.
6. See Williams, *Romantic Autobiography*, p. 39.

his conversion to Catholicism causes him to lose his Genevan citizenship. Furthermore, his imagination continues to develop its power in ways incompatible with citizenship. His mental existence is almost as turbulent as his physical existence.

During this period Jean-Jacques's imagination progresses through a series of fairly clearly definable stages. This progression intensifies his experience of the artificial passions. By the end of Book I his imaginative ability has already extended beyond passive identification with others to an active appropriation and combination of situations about which he has read. Rousseau's references to appropriating and combining suggest a desire and ability to control or own things. This stage of development could be called a "constructing" stage. Books II–IV further develop the implications of this constructive ability. Then these books move on to a "generating" stage in which Jean-Jacques does more than combine materials given to him from outside. Finally, he goes on to a "creating" stage in which he makes images, as it were, out of nothing. The attainment of a new stage does not entail the abandonment of the abilities characteristic of the earlier ones.

Once again, the parallel with Emile can guide the analysis of Jean-Jacques's progressive departure from nature. Emile's life as he approaches adolescence is an "age of force," because during this period his abilities far exceed his desires. Rousseau introduces this age with an explanation: "From where does man's weakness come? From the inequality between his strength and desires. It is our passions that make us weak, because to satisfy them we would need more strength than nature gives us. Therefore, decrease desires and you will increase strength" (*Emile*, 165). Emile is strong because his desires are weak, and his desires are weak because his imagination has not yet awakened. His sexual desires remain quiet, his anger has been calmed, and he is now only vulnerable to vanity, for which he is soon to be inoculated.[7] On every count Jean-Jacques is Emile's opposite. During what should have been his own "age of force," Jean-Jacques becomes progressively weaker as his desires continue to grow along with his imagination.

Jean-Jacques's imagination both causes his weakness and attempts to compensate for it. At the end of Book I (during the constructing stage of his imagination) Rousseau emphasizes a complete split between the "fictive state" made by his imagination and his "real state" of apprenticeship. In response to his weakness in the real world Jean-

---

7. On the question of inoculation, see *Emile*, 131.

Jacques constructs an imaginary world in which his desires are fulfilled. This imaginary world, in which he is strong, ultimately causes him to become still weaker in the real world by stimulating his desires even more. Rousseau says that he is "devoured by desires whose object [he] did not know" (I, 41). He is ignorant of the objects in the real world which could satisfy his imagination-inspired desires. In fact, novels have given him desires that simply cannot have any real objects. As a result of this disproportion between his desires and his ability to satisfy them, he is weak. Thus the imagination makes possible an unsatisfying flight from the real state. It can recall, vary, combine, and appropriate objects in such a way that it constructs a completely fictive state, but in doing so it forms a desire to make the fictive state real. The imaginary world is not only a place where all frustrated desires can be satisfied, it is also a place where new desires are formed.[8] These new desires then set off another cycle of frustration, flight to an imaginary world, and formation of new desires. The ability to combine imaginary objects is both a consolation in the fictive state and a curse in the real one.

At the beginning of Book II Rousseau shows that the constructive imagination can respond to weakness by doing more than making an imaginary world. It can also prevent one from seeing the real world as it is. In effect, the split between the real world and the imaginary world is resolved by making the real world into an imaginary world. Rousseau shows this effect by describing first his real condition and then its appearance to him at the time. For example, at the end of Book I he warns the reader of the miserable consequences of his flight from Geneva. This warning is obviously the fruit of hindsight, but misery is a reasonable outcome of leaving one's home at a penniless young age. Later in Book II, after Rousseau's account of his conversion to Catholicism, he says, "It is easy to judge what a sudden revolution must have happened in my ideas, when from my brilliant projects for the future, I saw myself falling into the most complete misery, and that after having deliberated in the morning upon the choice of palace in which I would live, I saw myself in the evening reduced to sleeping in the road" (I, 70). This is Rousseau's presentation of what the reader should judge his condition to have been. In both of these cases Rousseau gives a sober unimaginative appraisal of his real condition. In the first case he does this by the use of hindsight and in the second by adopting the perspective of the

8. For a useful account of Rousseau's analysis of the imagination, see Eigeldinger, *Réalité*.

reader.[9] In both cases he immediately contrasts the realistic picture of his weakness to the way his condition appeared to him at the time. After describing how he should reasonably have looked at his departure from Geneva, Rousseau says, "The independence that I believed I had acquired was the sole feeling that affected me. Free and master of myself, I believed that I could do everything, attain everything: I had only to throw myself to ascend and fly through the air" (I, 45). His imaginary hopes are more real than his actual predicament. Similarly, after leaving the hospice for catechists he says, "The first feeling that I tasted was that of the liberty which I had recovered" (I, 70). In both cases the exhilaration of independence is accompanied by great hopes for immediate success. First he says, "I entered the vast space of the world; my merit was going to fill it" (I, 45). Later he declares, "Far from giving myself up to discouragement and tears, I had only to change hopes, and amour-propre lost nothing by it" (I, 70). In both cases Rousseau shows that his imagination transforms the appearance of the world and in particular forms hopes based on this transformed appearance.[10] He is strong in his imagination but weak in fact.

Another passage in Book II describes even more clearly how the imagination transforms the appearance of the world. This passage, occurring between the two cited above, sums up the stage of imaginative development in which Jean-Jacques finds himself at this point. Rousseau describes his trip across the Alps to Turin, where he is to enter the hospice: "I was in the happiest situation of body and mind in which I had been in my life. Young, vigorous, full of health, of security, of confidence in myself and others, I was in that short but precious moment of life in which its expansive fullness extends so to speak our being by all our sensations and embellishes for our eyes all of nature with the charm of our existence" (I, 57–58). This instance can be distinguished from the account of the constructive power of the imagination in Book I. When he is apprenticed to M. Ducommun, Jean-Jacques's imaginative life is a flight from, a rejection of, the real world. This case differs first in that the real world itself is embellished. The split between the fictive state and the real state does not exist, because the real state is secure and pleasurable. Such a condition would seem to

9. On Jean-Jacques's position in Book II, see François Chedreville and Claude Roussel, "Le Vocabulaire de l'ascension sociale dans le livre II des *Confessions*," *Annales de la Société Jean-Jacques Rousseau* 36 (1963–65): 57–86.
10. Emile would not become discouraged in these circumstances, but he also would not need to manufacture imaginary hopes.

require no imaginative response. Jean-Jacques has no needs that cannot be easily fulfilled. All he must do is enjoy the present moment. Instead, his awakened imagination embellishes the real world. It transforms the world to correspond with his internal feelings. Where there are houses, Jean-Jacques imagines rustic festivals. Where there are shade trees, he imagines voluptuous tête-à-têtes.[11] He is simply incapable of seeing things as they are.

Rousseau has now revealed two important powers of the imagination. It can draw one out of the real world into the land of chimeras where real desires are satisfied without effort and where new, impossible desires come to be. Alternatively, when the real world does not drive one away, the imagination can transform it by embellishing it in accordance with imaginary desires. Thus, when one sees the world as it is, the imagination helps one to flee it, and when one returns to the world, the imagination prevents one from seeing it as it is.

Rousseau goes on to show that at this stage it is still possible to limit the imagination by fixing its attention on a real object. He says, "My sweet inquietude had an object which rendered it less wandering and fixed my imagination." This object is Mme de Warens, whom Jean-Jacques had just met. He now regards himself as her "product, student, friend, almost lover." Here we see that it is possible to "fix" even a very lively imagination. Jean-Jacques's imagination does transform the world, he does "dream deliciously," but this transformation and dream is limited by a real object. It is this real object that keeps him from the land of chimeras. This adds yet another element to the characterization of the imagination. Although the awakened imagination cannot be prevented from being active, its activity can be directed.

Subsequently, however, Jean-Jacques's imagination reaches a condition of almost boundless power that is much more difficult to fix on a particular object.[12] First, he reaches what is referred to above as the generating stage. The increased power of his imagination allows him to generate images that cannot be imposed on the real world. As a result he renews the split between his imaginary world and the real world. In giving an account of his first trip to Paris after a separation from Mme de Warens, Rousseau says that his bitter experience had caused him to moderate "little by little my romantic projects." This moderation, which

11. In the same setting, Emile or a natural human would see only a convenient spot for lunch.

12. In this connection, see Williams, *Romantic Autobiography*, pp. 91–92.

might be expected to lessen the power of his imagination, has exactly the opposite effect. His lack of romantic projects causes him to form the more Roman project of military glory. He imagines himself as Marshal Rousseau. "My sweet chimeras kept me company," he says, "and never has the heat of my imagination given birth to more magnificent ones" (I, 158). He gives birth to chimeras rather than simply embellishing the world or recombining existing images. Because of the magnificence of his chimeras, he finds the reality of Paris to be extremely disappointing: "Such is the fruit of a too active imagination which exaggerates beyond the exaggerations of men and always sees more than is said to it." He has generated his own image of Paris, and it does not correspond to the real one. He has done more than combine images based on what he has read or been told; he has added something new. There is no object that has first fixed his imagination and then allowed it to transform the appearance of the real world, as there was when he crossed the Alps. His imagination is too powerful to be connected to a specific object after the fact.

Once again, however, his imagination is calmed by its focus on Mme de Warens. As he returns to the provinces to seek her, Jean-Jacques again projects his feelings onto his surroundings (I, 162–63). On this journey, he both "busies [himself] in the land of chimeras" and "identifies" himself with his surroundings. When he approaches her, his imagination is calm aside from the anticipation of their reunion. He focuses so much on the object he seeks that he imagines nothing else. He sees houses and trees rather than festivals and tête-à-têtes and enjoys his surroundings for what they are rather than for what he makes of them. Because he is no longer in a position in which his imagination demands embellishment or creation, his surroundings "paint themselves at most as they are" (I, 171–72).

In this same context Rousseau refers to a still greater power of his imagination to make objects out of nothing. This is the creative stage referred to above. He says that in some circumstances his head "would not know how to embellish, it wishes to create." Rousseau's contrast between embellishing and creating here is an important one even if it is an exaggeration. Now he suggests for the first time that it is possible for him, not only to construct and give birth to images, but also to create them. He can form entirely new images using virtually no material from outside. A fully developed imagination is a creative faculty.

How the increasing power of his imagination affects his artificial passions remains to be seen. In Book I his sexual desire and his anger

develop quickly. Each of these begins to develop with the earliest stir-
rings of the imagination. They could be considered the most primitive
of the unnatural social passions. Vanity, which depends on an ability to
make rather complex comparisons, depends on a more sophisticated
imaginative ability. All three can be expected to undergo modifications
under the influence of Jean-Jacques's developed imagination.

In general, Rousseau's account of his developing sexuality in Books
II–IV follows that of his developing imagination. It begins with passive
observation, moves to an attempt to find a real satisfaction for an imaginary desire, and concludes with an attempt to construct images to give
an imaginary satisfaction. Jean-Jacques's sexual imagination stops short
only of generating or creating completely new images. The passive bent
given to his experience of pleasure keeps him in a relatively chaste
condition, but it is also the cause of the stimulus to his imagination.
Because his specific desires require him to be inactive, to make no
overtures, Jean-Jacques's sex life takes place almost entirely in his imagination.

The first important sexual escapade in this section of the *Confessions*
takes place in Book II. After being released from the hospice at Turin,
Jean-Jacques finds employment with Mme Basile, a charming shop-
keeper with whom he soon becomes infatuated. Rousseau calls his relations with Mme Basile a romance "in which if I had brought it to its end
I would have found pleasure a thousand times more delicious" than he
could have found with a young princess (I, 72). His "natural timidity,"
(I, 77) however, presents him from bringing this romance to its conclusion.

The effect of his passive taste is clearly manifested in this failure.
The decisive moment in this romance occurs when Jean-Jacques, believing himself unobserved, watches Mme Basile comb her hair: "Her
attitude was gracious, her slightly lowered head allowed the whiteness
of her neck to be observed, done up with elegance her hair was adorned
with flowers. In all her visage there reigned a charm that I had the time
to consider and which put me outside of myself" (I, 75). Jean Starobinski remarks that "Jean-Jacques disposes of each feature, of each
gesture, of each sigh of the young woman. No more was necessary for
him. He does not dream of carnal possession: visual possession suffices
for him."[13] Starobinski's description is in general accurate, but it exaggerates in two opposite ways. First, he refers to Jean-Jacques as "dis-

13. See Starobinski, *L'Oeil*, p. 109.

posing" of what he sees. This is a more active description than Rousseau's language suggests. Rousseau emphasizes losing himself, being outside himself, because of what he sees. He is lost in passive observation. Second, Starobinski says that "visual possession suffices" for him. This is true to a point, but this sufficiency would depend on his ability to dispose of or possess what he sees. Rousseau says, however, that after he realized that Mme Basile was observing him in her mirror, "I did not dare to undertake anything." Even before this he throws himself on his knees behind her. Thus he observes a real, desirable object, but his passive sexual taste does not allow him to act as he would like. He remains in a "ridiculous and delicious state" (I, 76). Starobinski underestimates Jean-Jacques's real desire and lack of satisfaction because he overestimates his ability to find imaginative satisfaction at this stage.[14]

The next example, which occurs at the beginning of Book III, reveals a slight advance over the romance with Mme Basile. At this stage Starobinski's picture of Jean-Jacques is more appropriate. Rousseau now says, "My inflamed blood incessantly filled my brain with girls and women, but not feeling their true use, I occupied them in idea bizarrely at my whims without knowing how to do any more" (I, 88). Now, he does not have an object of attraction present. He merely imagines objects of his desire. Furthermore, this time he acts on or disposes of the objects of his desires. He attempts to do so in action as well as in his ideas. He exposes himself to women as they are drawing water from a well. This might appear to be a radical departure from his passivity, a sort of aggression, but Rousseau insists that this is not true. He says that he exposed himself "in the state in which I would have wished to be near them," that is, he exposed "the ridiculous object" rather than the "obscene object." As Starobinski says, "exhibitionism, masochism are, by equal title, attempts destined to invert the direction of movement which goes from the consciousness to the desired beings."[15] Far from being aggressive, Jean-Jacques acts in the hope that he can inspire approaches to him. His action from afar is the most his passivity allows.[16] This attempt to elicit a first step from a woman fails. Jean-Jacques is apprehended and escapes only by pretending to be the de-

14. Another incident that should be compared with both this one and Jean-Jacques's earlier attachment to Mlles Goton and de Vulson (I, 26) is his brief idyll with Mlles de Graffenried and Galley (I, 136–39).
15. See Starobinski, *L'Oeil*, p. 107.
16. See Lejeune, *Pacte*, p. 75.

ranged child of a nobleman. This checks his attempt to join the image in his mind to action in the real world.

This event also leads to another important step in Jean-Jacques's sexual development. After this point, he never refers to any efforts to satisfy his masochistic tastes. It is only after this point that Starobinski's description of him as "disposing in his mind of the object of his desire" should be applied. After recounting his return from Italy to Mme de Warens, Rousseau says, "I carried back not my virginity but my maidenhood" (I, 108). His loss of virginity is caused by masturbation, "this dangerous supplement which fools nature" (I, 109). This vice, Rousseau says, is appealing to the timid and shameful and particularly to those with lively imaginations. He describes its aim as "to dispose so to speak of all of the sex at one's pleasure." This formulation matches his description of his constructive imagination, which allows him to "appropriate at my pleasure" and to "dispose of all of nature as its master" (I, 162). Masturbation is a doomed attempt to overcome the separation between an imaginary world and the real world.

It might seem that masturbation is a way of maintaining a quasi-natural independence, a way of satisfying natural sexual desire without being dependent on other humans. Rousseau's account suggests exactly the reverse (Emile's sexual development is carefully supervised to prevent him from acquiring this habit; *Emile*, 333–34). Rousseau argues that natural sexual desire is stimulated only by real objects. Masturbation, on the contrary, depends on the development of civilized imagination. Furthermore, because it is linked with the imaginative ability to combine, choose, and appropriate objects, it creates virtually limitless desires. A natural man may desire any woman he happens to see, but he seldom encounters women. Masturbation involves the constant accessibility of an endless number of objects for desire. Thus, while it may grant the appearance of independence from others, it entails an extreme degree of dependence on or enslavement to the imagination. Because it attempts to fool nature and leads to dependence, masturbation is far less satisfactory from a natural standpoint than Emile's attachment to a single woman who is able to satisfy his limited desires.

Rousseau later says that he was temporarily cured of his habit after being approached by a man who suggested that they "amuse [themselves] together" (I, 165). Jean-Jacques's revulsion at this proposal stems from the fact that the presence of the other man would focus attention on the physical act rather than on the imaginary object of desire.[17] By removing the imaginative dimension of the act, this amusement would fail to amuse. This proposal destroys the illusion of the harmony between the imaginary desires and the physical activity intended to satisfy them.

In sum, Rousseau's account of the development of his own sexual desire continues to stress the way the imagination transforms natural desire. This process, which takes place in all civilized humans, is carried to an extreme by the initial bent of Jean-Jacques's desires. First, his lively imagination makes him susceptible to a premature stimulation of the senses. Second, his initial passive taste makes him incapable of satisfying his desires directly. Consequently, he seeks satisfaction entirely in his imagination. Yet the physical nature of his desire demands a real satisfaction. After several attempts to elicit the desired overtures from women, he resorts to masturbation, which appears to allow a combination of imaginary and physical pleasures without violating his passivity. Jean-Jacques can receive physical pleasure while being imaginatively active and physically passive. This attempt to combine the imagination and physical pleasure is shown to be an unsatisfying illusion. In the end, Jean-Jacques is left with his unsatisfied imaginary and physical desires.

The development of Jean-Jacques's imagination affects his experience of anger as well as his sexual desire. It does so, however, not exactly by throwing him into an imaginary world, but by increasing his ability to sympathize with someone else. The "feeling of violence and injustice," first shown in Book I in the account of Jean-Jacques's ability to attribute intentions to the Lamberciers, shows anger derived from the ability to imagine, however erroneously, what someone else feels. The feeling of injustice does not arise from a simple identification with another person; rather, it involves concern with how this person is looking at oneself. In its origin it is a sign of an attempt to make the world revolve around oneself. Thus, at first, Jean-Jacques's hatred of injustice is restricted to injustice inflicted against himself. This anger at injustice can be turned into a healthy passion only by being extended to injustice inflicted on others.

Although in Book I Rousseau assures the reader that he quickly accomplished this extension, his first real step in this direction does not occur until the conclusion of Book III. This happens while he is helping M. Le Maître leave Chambéry. Le Maître wishes to leave because he

17. A similar event occurs in Book II (I, 66–68).

has received an affront from his ecclesiastical employer. Jean-Jacques helps him gain revenge by aiding his departure at a moment that will cause embarrassment to Le Maître's employer. Jean-Jacques's sympathy for Le Maître inspires him with the uncustomary boldness to perform a daring imposture and aid the escape. Such behavior runs counter to his normal timidity and requires explanation. Rousseau says, "I believe I have already remarked that there are times when I am so little like myself that one would take me for another man of a completely opposite character" (I, 128). He gives no explanation of where the boldness comes from, but it is noteworthy that it is in defense of an innocent victim, the persecuted Le Maître. This boldness is the result of Jean-Jacques's identification with Le Maître and his recollection of his own rage at mistreatment. Jean-Jacques is not only unlike himself, he has temporarily become Le Maître. The spiritedness of Jean-Jacques's reaction is reminiscent of the spiritedness he attributes to citizens. The anger of a citizen is directed at the enemies of the community and is based on an identification shared with the community as a whole. Jean-Jacques no longer feels a merely selfish anger, but he still hates only injustice directed against a single acquaintance. He has not yet generalized his feelings.

The episode with Le Maître ends with the confession of a misdeed, which indicates the weakness of Jean-Jacques's feeling of justice: "Thanks to Heaven I have finished this third painful confession (*aveu*); if many similar ones remained to be made, I would abandon the work that I have begun" (I, 129).[18] In Lyon, Le Maître suffers an illness and collapses in the street. Jean-Jacques becomes fearful, calls for help, and then simply abandons his companion. After narrating this story, Rousseau says that he felt no pangs of conscience or shame until much later. At the time, he rationalized his flight by arguing that he could be of no further assistance and would be a drain on Le Maître's finances. He concludes, "That is how I saw the thing then; I see it otherwise today" (I, 132). His desertion of Le Maître carries with it the punishment of remorse. His sentiment of justice, the compassionate identification with Le Maître, evaporates with the first real crisis. This sentiment requires further stimulus for development.

A further step in the generalization of this anger occurs in Book IV. Jean-Jacques encounters a farmer who is obliged to live with the ap-

18. This confession is by no means as complete as either of the other two. A second, earlier confession is discussed in the following section. See also "Imagination, the Political Order, and Nature" in Chapter 5.

pearance of abject poverty because of confiscatory taxes. Here Rousseau says, "All that he said to me on this subject, and of which I had not had the least idea, gave me an impression which will never be effaced. Here was the germ of that inextinguishable hatred which has since developed in my heart against the vexations which test the unfortunate people and against their oppressors" (I, 164). This additional step must not be overestimated. Jean-Jacques now has a more general object for his compassion and his anger, but he has only the "germ" of a generalized hatred of injustice. This germ requires other occasions for its development. For now he is left with his hatred of particular injustice inflicted against both himself and other individuals.

This anger develops more haphazardly than sexual desire does. Sexual desire forces its own development (although not necessarily the form this development will take) because it is derived from a purely physical need. Once the senses are aroused by the imagination, sexual desire moves ceaselessly from stage to stage unless it hits upon a final satisfying form. Anger is more likely to remain fixed in a particular direction or to disappear. At times Jean-Jacques becomes another man, transported by indignation. Because there is no constant spur to this sort of transport, however, he lapses into his ordinary character. His citizenlike spirit is aroused only intermittently.[19]

Whereas civilized sexual desire is derived directly from a natural need and anger emerges from the first experiences of the imagination, vanity is a very late development that depends completely on concern for images. In Book I vanity is in many respects the least significant of the artificial passions in Jean-Jacques's development. Rousseau describes his first experiences of sexual desire and indignation with great intensity and seriousness; he describes vanity in a playful tone. There his vanity takes the form of the desire to gain glory by surpassing his tutor. Beginning in Book II Rousseau very much changes his emphasis. The new importance of vanity can be seen in the examples of his imaginative activity, which are filled with dreams of glory. Vanity is perhaps the passion that most demands the creation of imaginary worlds and the transformation of the real world. After leaving Geneva, Jean-Jacques

19. The consequences of the development of anger are important in Jean-Jacques's diversion from the path followed by *Emile*. Because Emile's anger is so quickly calmed, his attachment to justice is based on his compassion (*Emile*, 253). Emile has more pity than hatred for the wicked (*Emile*, 244). His speech on behalf of justice is "simple and hardly at all figurative" (*Emile*, 252). Jean-Jacques's attachment to justice is based on both compassion and indignation. He hates "our foolish institutions" (I, 327). His attacks on injustice are "divine bursts."

thinks that his merit will fill "the vast space of the world" (I, 45). He says that "to follow Hannibal across the mountains appeared to me a glory beyond my age" (I, 58). On the way to Paris he sees himself attaining military glory as Marshall Rousseau (I, 158–59). He sums up his condition when describing his arrival at Turin by saying, "Already the fumes of ambition excited me" (I, 59). Now a wish for celebrity is at least as strong as his other artificial passions. Jean-Jacques's increased ability to form images has increased his susceptibility to images of his own glory. He moves from seeing himself as Hannibal to constructing images of a completely new military hero.

That Jean-Jacques's vanity can lead to him to attempt to exploit others is shown by his actions following his departure from the Gouvon household. Jean-Jacques founds his hopes on a mechanical toy that he and his friend Bâcle wish to use to dupe peasants and thereby finance their travels. The use of a knowledge of science to gain esteem from the ignorant is the source of "the first movement of vanity" in Emile (*Emile*, 175). Thus vanity, to a much greater degree than sexuality or anger, calls forth conscious reflection on one's relations with others.

A further illustration of the self-conscious exploitation of others characteristic of vanity occurs in Book IV. This example shows the difference between a proud identification with another person and a vain imitation. After he abandons Le Maître and returns to Annecy to find Mme de Warens gone, Jean-Jacques undertakes his first attempt at teaching music. In the beginning of this career, he labors under several disadvantages. For example, he finds himself a Catholic convert in Lausanne, a Protestant city. Furthermore, he is almost completely lacking in knowledge of music. In an attempt to remedy both problems he claims to be a Parisian musician named Vaussore de Villeneuve. As a Frenchman and hence Catholic from birth he hopes to avoid hostility directed toward an apostate. As a Parisian he hopes to acquire a reputation for sophistication that will substitute for real knowledge. This substitution of appearance for substance is characteristic of vanity, which seeks to manipulate opinions.

The essence of this vanity is shown by the sort of imitation it entails. Jean-Jacques's choice of name for his masquerade is a combination of an anagram of Rousseau and the name of a friend, Venture de Villeneuve, who had successfully posed as a musician at Annecy.[20] Jean-Jacques is himself and someone else at the same time.[21] He conceals his

20. Jean-Jacques is insufficiently aware of the fact that Venture's success comes from his ability to display real talents when his frauds are suspected.

21. For a discussion of this event, see Raymond, *Quête*, p. 22.

own identity while imitating but not becoming another person.[22] Unlike his identification with citizens, in this instance he is aware of his own true identity. He merely wishes to impose on others. After a brief initial success, the imposture is discovered in a most humiliating way: Jean Jacques is obliged to compose a piece of music for public performance. This public humiliation has the same effect on Jean-Jacques as Emile's humiliation by a magician after his first movement of vanity. Both young men attempt to impress people with false displays of ability and both are publicly humiliated. Jean-Jacques is distinguished from Emile by his greater degree of pretense and the short duration of his cure. It is only a few months after his public humiliation that he imagines himself as Marshal Rousseau on his way to Paris. The final resolution of the problem of vanity and the conclusion of the alternation between pride and vanity awaits Part Two of the *Confessions*.

In sum, Books II–IV demonstrate a further development of the artificial characteristics of imagination, sexuality, indignation, and vanity after their emergence in Book I. In the treatment of each, Rousseau gives a picture of what it means to live outside oneself. The continuous extension of his imaginative ability is the development of an internal life, or self-consciousness. The rich internal life displayed here, however, is a life of longing for and creation of imaginary worlds. Furthermore, the created images cause the formation of very real desires that demand fulfillment in the real world. The development of sexuality, for example, leads Jean-Jacques to retreat into himself, but it also forms longings for contact with others. His anger, which initially grew out of a misreading of others' intentions, leads him to compassionate concern for the weak and hatred for the unjust strong. Finally, his vanity leads to a desire for recognition from others and a willingness to manipulate them to achieve or maintain the proper image in their eyes. In short, the young Jean-Jacques fits Rousseau's own description of a corrupt civilized man whose natural unity is destroyed but who is not incorporated into any social whole.

Natural, Conventional, and Imaginary Places in the Political Order

To this point in this chapter the focus has been on Jean-Jacques's internal development. This perspective is necessary to identify the fur-

---

22. For another example of such an imitation, see the discussion below of Jean-Jacques's pose as M. Dudding.

ther development of his unnatural social characteristics. Still, it should be kept in mind that these are social characteristics; that is, they bring him into relations, however contradictory, with other people in a political order. Jean-Jacques's relations to others can be analyzed on two issues. First, there is Rousseau's account of the relations among Jean-Jacques's now developed abilities, his position in the world, and his view of his position; in other words, the relations among talent, convention, and imagination. Second, there is the continued development of the themes from Book I, indicated by the confession of another theft.

Rousseau begins to explore the relation between the superiority of his talents and his conventional inferiority in Book II. His first employment after his brief encounter with Mme Basile is as a servant to the Countess de Vercellis. He describes the jealousy of the other servants, who "saw very well that I was not in my *place*" (I, 83, emphasis added) as a lackey. Here the opposition between his natural talents and his actual position adds another dimension to the opposition between his imaginary desires and his actual position. Jean-Jacques is in one position, his natural ability warrants another, and his desires make him wish for a third.

In Book I the opposition between Jean-Jacques's desires and his demeaning position led to his brief career as a thief. At the end of Book II he mentions his desire to expiate a crime that "in some fashion has contributed very much to the resolution that I have taken to write my confessions" (I, 86).[23] The crime that must be confessed occurs when Jean-Jacques is employed by Mme de Vercellis. In some respects this employment returns him to the conditions of apprenticeship. In both instances Rousseau says that he was regarded as a lackey (I, 32, 82). In this case he claims that the jealousy of the other servants prevented him from receiving the recognition he deserved from his employer. After her death, Jean-Jacques, who received no mention in her will, steals a ribbon from the estate with the intention of giving it to another servant, Marion. When this theft is detected and the ribbon found in his possession, he blames the theft on the intended recipient of the ribbon. Years later he still feels guilty for the possible consequences to the innocent Marion.

As is mentioned in Chapter 1, Sebastien Mercier argues that the *Confessions* should be understood as a novel presenting a series of parables rather than as a factually truthful narration. According to Mercier,

23. For the significance of "confession," see Chapter 1.

the confession of this theft is "a parable to put in a moral light all the force and all the tenacity of remorse which could be entitled 'the combats of bad shame.'"[24] Mercier regards this narration simply in terms of its moral effect on the reader. The fable teaches the horrible consequences of lying merely out of a sense of shame. It conveys the lesson that the conscience punishes injustice and at the same time that remorse for a youthful transgression can lead to a blameless life thereafter.

Rousseau's narrative of the incident does aim at this moral effect, but it has a very different function as well. It reveals one of the changes he has undergone since the incident of the broken comb in Book I. In the earlier event Jean-Jacques is the object of an unjust accusation; in the later he is the unjust accuser. The key to his reaction in the first story is his inability to see that appearances are against him. He regards the Lamberciers as willful torturers. In this second story appearances also play the decisive part. Jean-Jacques's insistence and Marion's moderation in her defense put the appearances on his side: "It did not seem natural to suppose such a diabolical audacity on one side, and such an angelic sweetness on the other" (I, 85). Jean-Jacques has learned to manipulate appearances to take advantage of them.

The events reported in this confession reverse the case of the broken comb.[25] Jean-Jacques was the accused, now he is the accuser. He was the dupe of appearances, now he is their manipulator. There is a respect in which the stories are not opposites. In both cases the appearances implicate an innocent victim. Furthermore, in both cases the same appearances implicate the accuser when viewed from another perspective. Rousseau says that he regarded the Lamberciers as torturers when in fact they were simply deceived. Similarly, Marion and perhaps the reader interpret Jean-Jacques's false accusation as diabolical audacity. The Lamberciers are exculpated by a proper understanding of what they saw. Jean-Jacques, however, cannot be cleared in the same way; he knew that Marion was innocent.

Rousseau claims that he does not wish to deny the wrong he did in slandering an innocent girl. He goes on to say, however, "I would not fulfil the goal of this book if at the same time I did not expose my interior dispositions and if I feared to excuse myself in what is in conformity to the truth." His appearance is at first glance that of a just

24. Mercier, *Auteurs*, p. 268.
25. On this point, see Lejeune, *Pacte*, p. 55.

accuser and at second glance that of an audacious devil. Rousseau argues that both appearances are wide of the truth. He merely excused himself "on the first object that offered itself" and persisted in his accusation out of shame. His introduction of shame into the discussion raises the question of the appearances in a third way. Rousseau says, "I saw only the horror of being recognized, declared publicly with myself present to be a robber, liar, calumniator" (I, 86). He concludes that if he had been allowed to return to himself he would have declared all. His sense of shame makes him live outside himself. He cannot help being concerned with how he appears to others. It is his ability to project himself into others which makes him concerned for their opinions about him.

Jean-Jacques has committed a small crime (the theft) out of generous motives. He manipulates appearances to avoid detection and turns the small crime into a large one. To be successful, he must adopt the false appearance of complete innocence. Forty years later, he confesses his misdeed to restore the truth. By itself this confession creates an equally false diabolical image, which he must replace with a true account that relies on what is internal rather than external. The final purpose of the confession is to reveal what has been concealed and to correct false appearances. Even the exculpation that comes from the explanation of Jean-Jacques's sense of shame reveals him to be a corrupt social being who is willing to sacrifice others for his own benefit.

In Book III the strains among talents, social convention, and imagination are intensified. The focus is first on the opposition between Jean-Jacques's talents and his position. After his departure from the de Vercellis household, Jean-Jacques abandons his fanciful ambitions because of the influence of the Savoyard abbé Gaime.[26] He summarizes the effects of M. Gaime's influence: "In the successive order of my tastes and of my ideas, I had always been too high or too low; Achilles or Thersites, first a hero then good-for-nothing.[27] M. Gaime took the trouble of putting me in my place" (I, 91). By putting Jean-Jacques in his place, M. Gaime causes him to abandon his imaginary hopes for advancement. He restricts the boy to realistic hopes. He "very much killed my admiration for greatness by proving to me that those who dominated others were neither wiser nor happier than they." Rousseau

26. M. Gaime and a M. Gâtier are the sources for Rousseau's Savoyard vicar (I, 91, 119).
27. In the Neuchâtel manuscript Rousseau adds "never man" (I, 1276; see also I, 39).

thus admits that he has been afflicted with a desire to dominate. Although M. Gaime is to some degree able to put Jean-Jacques in his place by curing him of his exaggerated flights of virtue as well as his vanity, he unfortunately "did not have enough credit to place" (I, 90) Jean-Jacques in a position that would correspond to his natural talents. Thus he mitigates the opposition between Jean-Jacques's imagination and his condition but aggravates the opposition between his talent and his condition.[28]

Soon, however, the Gouvon family offers the boy a position that promises to remedy the latter disproportion. He is to begin only slightly higher than a lackey, but he will later be advanced in a political career. Of his low starting point Rousseau says, "I felt myself too little made for that place to fear that they would leave me there" (I, 93). In order to advance, Jean-Jacques shows himself to be a good servant, keeping himself in his "place" (I, 94) with regard to the attractive Mlle de Breil. He controls his desire to imagine himself as her lover. This time his dutifulness is rewarded and he is given the opportunity to show his abilities. He does so in what he calls a "novel" (I, 96) in which his conventional place as a servant is transformed into his natural place.[29] At a dinner party he is encouraged to display his learning and wit by explaining the Gouvon family motto. He describes his triumph as "one of those too rare moments which *replace* things in their natural order and avenge merit debased by the outrages of fortune" (I, 96, emphasis added). Thus, in the short space of a half-dozen pages, Rousseau portrays the imaginary place that he wishes for, his conventional place as a servant, and his superior place in the natural order.[30]

After this triumph Jean-Jacques is "generally regarded in the house as a young man of the greatest hopes, who was not in his place and whom one expected to see arrive there" (I, 98). It seems that the disproportion between his conventional position of inferiority and his natural superiority is about to be overcome. However, Rousseau quickly introduces yet another notion of "place": "But my place was not that which had been assigned to me by men, and I was obliged to arrive at it by very different roads" (I, 98–99). This statement is all the more striking be-

28. Compare the alternative account of Rousseau at this period given in *Emile* (*Emile*, 260–65).

29. Starobinski discusses some of Rousseau's uses of "place" in *Relation*, pp. 106–9.

30. The motto Jean-Jacques explains is "*Tel fiert que ne tue pas.*" His explanation that "fiert" derives from *ferit* (strike) allows Jean-Jacques to strike a blow at social conventions that do not allow him his true place.

cause of its context. In the preceding sentence Rousseau asserts that the Gouvon family is aware that his conventional place of inferiority is not his natural place. Now Rousseau refers to a different "place," one that does not correspond to either his conventional inferiority or his natural superiority. It is by no means clear whether this new place is one of even greater superiority, a return to natural equality, or one of great misery.[31] It is tempting to suggest that this is the place assigned to Jean-Jacques by fate or providence, rather than by nature or society. However this may be, he goes on to give a very precise account of the reason for his abandonment of his place in the Gouvon household.

This account emphasizes Jean-Jacques's unwillingness to reconcile himself even to a very promising condition in the real world. Rousseau refers to his unwillingness to undergo the constraint necessary for a sure but slow advancement. The cure begun by M. Gaime is not complete. Jean-Jacques's imaginary hopes begin again: "My mad ambition did not seek fortune except through adventures" (I, 98). Jean-Jacques's "fate" is dealt by the strong imagination that is the source of his romantic hopes. A [...] imaginary worlds and [...] er people. The immed [...] es into an imaginary w [...] an empty bottle" (I, 1 [...] his natural place.

Roussea [...] his section: the place h [...] n by social convention [...] the place fated for h [...] world. This section of [...] opposition between co [...] it is a brief but powerf [...] tion and an important [...] ately, Jean-Jacques's in [...] n. Bringing his conven [...] ot enough. Jean-Jacqu [...] place warranted by his talents in favor of an indulgence in his unnatural, imaginary hopes. By showing the differences among nature, convention, and imagination in his retrospective comments, Rousseau reveals that the young Jean-Jacques confuses them. He fails to distinguish between his

31. This final "place" is discussed in Chapter 6.

natural capacities and his romantic hopes. Learning to make this distinction is slow, and success is by no means inevitable. Perhaps the major task of Jean-Jacques's self-education is to sort out the precise relations among nature, social position, and imagination.

At first glance Rousseau's account of the exalted place in the political order that he would be justly accorded on the basis of his talents seems to be in conflict with his egalitarian politics. Even if it is conceded that his talents are based on a natural superiority, it remains the case that the just political order described in the *Social Contract* "substitutes a moral and legitimate equality for whatever physical inequality nature may have placed between men, and that although they may be unequal in force or in genius, they all become equal through convention and right" (*S.C.*, 58). This legitimate equality does not, however, imply that genius has no status. In the *Second Discourse* Rousseau refers to four different bases for political inequality: wealth, rank, power, and personal merit (*Discourses*, 174). Further, he claims that observation of the relative importance of these different bases "can permit a rather exact judgment of the extent to which each people is removed from its primitive institution, and of the distance it has traveled toward the extreme limit of corruption." A political order that would make use of the talent of a Jean-Jacques would be at the farthest remove from corruption as long as this use of his talent did not release him from the dependence on the laws shared by all citizens. The actual order in which he finds himself degrades talents beneath wealth and rank. Rousseau's attack on social convention in the name of offended talent is one of the sources of his powerful revolutionary appeal.

The importance of this aspect of Rousseau's thought should not obscure the fact that Jean-Jacques's imagination does not allow him to accept a chance to rise to the position his talent deserves. Unlimited imagination would drive him out of a just political order as well as an unjust one. To be sure, his imagination does not make him contemn political and social status. In fact, this status is precisely what his vanity demands. Imagination does, however, keep him from making the effort to acquire social status. In short, imagination forms the desires that can support either just or unjust political orders, but it can also drive an individual who shares these desires out of those orders. The imagination may make one think that one longs for independence; it may even make one think that one is independent. But as long as it stimulates social passions like sexual desires, anger, and vanity, it in fact makes one dependent.

The history of Jean-Jacques's soul is the history of the development of his artificial passions and of the imagination that sets them in motion. His actions and feelings are all the products of these passions. Book I describes their origin; Books II–IV record their progress. There are three ways this description of the young Jean-Jacques differs from that of more ordinary corrupt humans. The first is simply his natural ability, which is shown most clearly by the intensity and facility of his imagination. As is show in Chapter 1, Rousseau presents himself as one of those exceptional people who educate themselves in spite of their teachers. By the end of Book IV, of course, he is only an exceptional boy on the verge of adulthood. Far from being complete, his self-education has barely begun. Already, however, he has shown capacities such as a reasoning ability that derives from his imagination. Such capacities intensify his corruption beyond ordinary levels and in some instances preserve him from delusion. In his actions he fluctuates between natural goodness and vice, between passivity and boldness. Jean-Jacques is also atypical in that, because of his unusual abilities and very unsettled life, he is much less formed than an ordinary eighteen-year-old. Time and again he presents a moment as decisive in forming his character only later to minimize its importance. This series of intense, extreme experiences makes him an example of certain forms of civilized corruption, but it also shows him to be less defined, more open to change in various directions for good and bad, than is the case for most civilized humans. Finally, the peculiar forms taken by some of his most artificial characteristics preserve Jean-Jacques from some types of civilized corruption: his sexual passivity and imagination preserve him from promiscuous libertinism, his intense desires for immediate pleasure preserve him from love of money, his initial experience of injustice prevents him from being unjust. In certain respects, Jean-Jacques has developed unnatural characteristics resembling the natural characteristics that disappear altogether in most civilized humans.

Because of these three unusual attributes—his unique abilities, his unfixed character, and his possession of some characteristics that appear natural—several possibilities are open to Jean-Jacques at eighteen. It is possible to conceive of him simply intensifying the civilized characteristics he has acquired. It is possible to imagine him becoming integrated into a domestic or political community under the right circumstances. Finally, it is possible to see him undertaking a more complete return to nature. The first of these possibilities represents a triumph of his imagination and vanity; the second, a triumph of either his capacity for love or his pride; the third, a triumph of nature over all of these attributes of civilization. The remainder of Part One of the *Confessions* (and indeed Part Two as well) presents Jean-Jacques grappling with these alternatives: Book V shows him as part of a domestic community; Book VI shows him achieving a sort of natural independence.

Book V: Subpolitical Social Wholeness

Book V of the *Confessions* relates Jean-Jacques's successful but short-lived experience as a member of an unusual subpolitical community. By exploring how someone with a stimulated imagination can become integrated into a social whole, Rousseau gives an indication of a possible basis for subpolitical institutions that support, or at least do not destroy, healthy political life. Thus he shows a social position midway between the denaturing of citizens and the complete corruption of other civilized humans. By showing how fragile such a community is, he begins to point to a way of life that is psychologically independent of any political order. Once again the possibilities open to Jean-Jacques emerge most clearly in a comparison with Emile.

At the start of Book V of the *Confessions* Jean-Jacques's situation is somewhat more analogous to that of Emile at the same age than it has been earlier.[32] Both boys are beginning to lose their earlier moderation. Emile begins to feel natural sexual desire. Jean-Jacques's passivity is insufficient to protect him from the impressive array of attractive girls and their mothers whom he meets as a music instructor. Internal restraints are no longer sufficient for either boy; each needs an outside agent to preserve his morals.

In Emile's case, the tutor supplies the outside assistance by making his pupil fall in love. Emile is encouraged to construct a single imaginary object for his desires. It is through this object and his imagination that his senses are repressed. In addition, he is removed from contact with women as much as possible. When he is at last introduced to Sophie, he becomes interested at the first sound of her name. Thus the success of the plan to keep Emile from promiscuous enslavement to his imagination and senses depends on the restriction of his imagination to a single object and the prompt introduction of a real woman.

Emile's sexual initiation prepares his initiation into the social order.

---

32. In Book V Rousseau mentions his study of arithmetic, design, gardening, literature, and music. Jean-Jacques lags behind Emile in these accomplishments.

He falls in love with Sophie, learns to be a citizen for the sake of his future family, and cements the social bond by marrying. The first of these steps is the key to the others. It is because Emile's imagination is fixed on one object, Sophie, that he is willing to tie himself to a community. This step is both desirable and necessary at this stage of the education. It is desirable as a natural basis for a qualified attachment to a community. It is necessary because Emile's imagination makes it impossible for his sexual desire to remain purely natural as he moves into a world with other people. The tutor endeavors to "make him moderate by making him fall in love" because Emile's emerging sexual desires are much stronger than the naturally moderate desires of someone in the pure state of nature (*Emile*, 327). Because his imagination has stimulated his senses, it is necessary to repress his senses by his imagination. Thus Emile is both tied to a community and saved from a more enslaving sexual immoderation by his love for Sophie.

Jean-Jacques presents a comparable problem for his tutor, Mme de Warens. Rousseau says that her object was "to secure me from the snares to which my age and station exposed me" (I, 191). Although the purpose of Jean-Jacques's sexual initiation is the same as Emile's, the difference between the boys requires a different method.[33] Emile's senses are at the root of his problem; Jean-Jacques's imagination is at the root of his. An imaginary object alone is not enough to protect Jean-Jacques from constant temptation because he is surrounded by so many women with whom he might identify his imaginary creation. Rather than repressing Jean-Jacques's senses by means of his imagination, Mme de Warens attempts to repress his imagination by means of his senses.[34] She decides to satisfy his physical desires to keep them from stimulating his imagination.

Mme de Warens can satisfy Jean-Jacques's senses without stimulating his imagination because his imagination does not see her as an object of sexual desire: "Without desiring to possess her, I was very glad that she removed my desire to possess others" (I, 196).[35] Rousseau

33. Rousseau calls explicit attention to the educational method of *Emile* in this context (I, 194).

34. On the repression of Emile's sense by means of his imagination, see *Emile*, 329.

35. Rousseau says that he was unhappy in his first physical relations with Maman because he felt as if he had committed incest. This statement should be understood in relation to Rousseau's more general discussions of incest. In none of his accounts of the state of nature does he present the incest prohibition as natural. In the *Second Discourse* (*Discourses*, 148) and the *Essay on the Origin of Languages* (*Oeuvres*, Geneva, 1782–89, XVI, 230–32) it is quite clear that the earliest family relations are incestuous. Thus the signifi-

claims that because his attachment to her is not sexual in nature, their relations do not engage his imagination. Their physical relations preserve him from promiscuous relations with other women that could arise from his imaginative attractions to them.[36]

Because she curbs Jean-Jacques's sexual imagination, Mme de Warens is able to speak to his heart, or imagination, on other matters (I, 193). Although their sexual relations are purely physical, their other relations are not. Rousseau is attracted to Maman, as he now calls her, as "more than a sister, more than a friend, even more than a mistress" (I, 196). The weakening of Jean-Jacques's sexual imagination, which would have led him to other women, strengthens his less sexual imagination, which leads him into a community formed by Mme de Warens. It is her ability to separate physical and imaginary needs in order to satisfy each separately that allows Mme de Warens to construct her own unusual domestic community (I, 198).

Just as Emile's relations with Sophie lead him to form broader social ties, Jean-Jacques's relations with Maman bring him into a sort of domestic community. Even before his account of his own sexual initiation, Rousseau mentions his surprise at learning that Maman has a lover, her faithful servant Claude Anet. Her new intimacy with Jean-Jacques does nothing to change this other relationship. Thus, unlike Emile, Jean-Jacques finds himself a part of a peculiar ménage à trois. Rousseau does not exactly present this relationship as a model for imitation. He says, "There was established among the three of us a society possibly without another example on the earth" (I, 201). Nevertheless, the temporary success of this arrangement shows what Rousseau considers necessary for successful domestic relations. As a result, it sheds light on the problem faced by more ordinary domestic arrangements. This "unique" example also sets a pattern for domestic relations to be elaborated in Part Two of the *Confessions*. The recurrence of this theme is a part of the moral fable of the *Confessions* by which Rousseau encourages the building of even very unorthodox social ties as an improvement over mere corrupt, civilized selfishness.

---

cance of Rousseau's declaration in the *Confessions* is not that he has violated a sacred prohibition but that he feels the prohibition. After his sexual initiation Jean-Jacques suffers no additional pangs. For a useful account of Rousseau's presentation of incest, see Derrida, *Of Grammatology*, pp. 265–68.

36. Because these relations curb the imagination by satisfying the senses, they more clearly approximate natural wholeness than does masturbation, which attempts to satisfy the senses by stimulating the imagination.

This unique society of three can be judged by its ability to meet the standards for community life which Rousseau set out at the end of Book I. In that context he argues that he could have been both a good citizen and a good family man if he had stayed within the sphere of Geneva. He presents two different sorts of condition for maintaining the wholeness of the sphere: its physical independence and its effect on the imagination.

There are two aspects of the physical or material independence of the Genevan sphere. On one hand, Jean-Jacques's profession as an engraver would have made him self-sufficient by maintaining him in modest comfort. On the other hand, the profession would have imposed severe limits on possibilities for advancement or wealth. Thus the sphere is maintained because it is both self-sufficient and leads to nothing beyond itself.[37] These material features would have an effect on Jean-Jacques's imagination by limiting his ambition and greed. Rousseau insists, however, that the pleasantness of the sphere would be guaranteed by the relative lack of constraint on his imagination. His powerful imagination would have adorned his estate by transporting him out of it. Whereas the material support for the sphere both makes it comfortable and restricts it, the imaginative support adorns without restricting.

It is this relative lack of restraint on the imagination which threatens the wholeness of the sphere. Again and again in Part One Jean-Jacques is offered the chance to live in a limited sphere only to be driven out by his "unsettled heart," which "demands more" (I, 101, 145–46, 153). Rousseau always presents these rejections of limited spheres as accidents or mistakes. By doing so he encourages his readers to make wiser choices in their own lives, but his own behavior shows that these limited spheres cannot satisfy someone with a powerful imagination. Generally, the problem of maintaining wholeness in social relations is to provide material and psychological supports and restraints that simultaneously satisfy and limit.

The "little circle" of Jean-Jacques, Anet, and Mme de Warens described in Book V represents a somewhat different approach to the problem of maintaining social wholes. It resembles the Genevan sphere on the first point of fulfilling the external conditions necessary for maintaining the self-sufficiency of a sphere. For the first time Jean-Jacques engages in a moderately remunerative occupation in accord

---

37. These are also the conditions of the pure state of nature (*Discourses*, 104–41).

with his taste (I, 186). In addition to the subsistence it provides, Jean-Jacques's occupation as music master offers little hope for advancement. Thus there are no external obstacles to or temptations against maintaining the self-contained and self-sufficient character of the community.

This little circle differs from the Genevan sphere in the management of the psychological conditions for domestic unity. While in Geneva Jean-Jacques's imagination would have taken him out of the sphere, Rousseau now says, "All our vows, our cares, our hearts were in common. Nothing of them passed outside of the little circle" (I, 201). Their imaginations are entirely contained in the circle, both adorning the circle and restricting the members to it. Most important, this is accomplished by allowing much more scope to the imagination than is given in an ordinary political community.[38] Rousseau stresses the constant activity that absorbs the imagination: "I maintain that to render a circle truly agreeable, it is necessary not only that each does something there, but something which demands a little attention" (I, 202). The absorption in a constant variety of diverting tasks simultaneously frees and checks the imagination by offering an array of different objects for attention.[39] The little circle is a social unity which is compatible with an active imagination.

The shift of image from "sphere" to "circle" is very appropriate for the depiction of this social arrangement. It is a purely domestic, apolitical arrangement.[40] It lacks the dimension of citizenship: each of the three members of the circle is a religious convert in exile; each has forfeited citizenship. Its contact with the larger sphere is limited by the absence of children. Rousseau's series of geometric metaphors can be completed by adding a perfectly natural individual. A city may be regarded as a sphere, a purely domestic arrangement as a circle, and a natural human as a point.[41] Social relationships can be developed by turning from Rousseau's geometric to his mathematical image. One can say that, whereas a natural man is an integer and a citizen is a numerator of a fraction of which the city is the denominator, most civilized

38. For a Rousseauian discussion of the need to limit the imagination, see Alexis de Tocqueville, *Democracy in America*, vol. I, pt. 2, chap. 9.

39. Compare the boring circles of high society (I, 115–16).

40. For examples of Rousseau's use of "sphere," see Chedreville and Roussel, "Vocabulaire," p. 77.

41. For a discussion of the relation between this period of happiness and the "golden mean" of the *Second Discourse*, see Williams, *Romantic Autobiography*, p. 140.

humans are numerators with no known denominator. Such people are fractional beings who do not form part of a whole. For such people, unity is possible if they can unite with complementary fractions. As *Emile* shows, conventional families sometimes succeed in providing such a unity. Even extrafamilial arrangements that support political life are possible in some circumstances. In the *Letter to d'Alembert* Rousseau discusses Genevan "circles" or social clubs, which he presents as much more salutary sources of entertainment than the theater (*d'Alembert*, 104–13). By allowing gossip, pursuit of common interests, and drinking, these circles provide outlets for imagination without seriously threatening political life. When such subpolitical organizations are "public and permitted" (*d'Alembert*, 108), they help to tie their members to a broader community by extending their attachments. Nevertheless, Rousseau's praise is tempered with criticism of the degree of drunkenness and gambling (not good examples of republican virtue) that takes place in the circles. Furthermore, these circles are salutary only in so far as they limit the imagination. Rousseau insists that the Genevan circles are less dangerous than others because of their "order and rule," and he also stresses their segregation of sexes. Only such carefully circumscribed circles can be integrated into a sound political life. The example of Jean-Jacques in the *Confessions* shows that some fractional beings may require unusual arrangements to become whole.[42]

The success of the little circle depends largely on chance. It requires Maman's ability to unite people to her, Claude Anet's skill as a supervisor and manager, and Jean-Jacques's susceptibility to such wholesome influences. One is unlikely to conjure up such companions at will. Nevertheless, such domestic circles occur frequently in Rousseau's works in numerous variations.[43] Rousseau presents them as the best possible arrangements for civilized humans who do not live in healthy political communities. He gives an image of an admittedly unconventional life which offers hope for some semblance of wholeness for those who have developed imaginations.[44] The unique society of Book V itself has an entirely accidental end, just as it had an accidental beginning.[45] Claude Anet becomes ill on a botanical expedition and dies. As a result the little

42. For a discussion of Rousseau's thought as a whole which pays special attention to such strategies for civilized humans, see Shklar, *Men and Citizens*.

43. Such domestic circles occur in both in *Emile* and *Julie*.

44. For a more thorough account of one of the unconventional arrangements recommended by Rousseau, see Schwartz, *Sexual Politics*, pp. 114–41.

45. This is one of the sections in which Rousseau most altered the facts of his narrative (I, 1338–41).

circle loses its stability. Most important, Jean-Jacques begins to manifest a resurgence of the desire for distinction beyond the bounds of a
small community. Rousseau refers to his "foolish vanity" and his "nas-
cent emulation" (I, 218). The conditions for establishing an apolitical
social unity are gone.

Later in the *Confessions* Rousseau returns to the theme of the little
circle. With this first description he has outlined the elements that make
up such a social unity. The circle comprises denatured, fractional humans with no political allegiance. Their ties to each other are based on
natural sexual desire and an affinity among their imaginations. Their
imaginations are limited by the circle, but they are allowed much
greater freedom than is possible within a political community. In sum,
the little circle is a way of reconstituting wholeness for corrupt, civilized
humans. It requires both less radical denaturing than good political
communities and a greater leeway for the development of a variety of
unnatural capacities.

Book VI: Happiness and Natural Wholeness

Once the imagination of a civilized human begins to develop, the
process of denaturing is irreversible. While a natural human whose
imagination is quiet can maintain that wholeness and independence
indefinitely, a civilized human must find wholeness by participating in a
community. Such, at least, is the normal course of Rousseau's argument. In the *Second Discourse* he says that the origin of society "destroyed natural freedom for all time" (*Discourses*, 160). In *Emile* he takes
great care to retard the development of the artificial passions because
these passions will stifle nature (*Emile*, 48). Thus it seems that Jean-
Jacques's failure to absorb himself in either a domestic or a political
community irreversibly consigns him to the life of dependence, contradiction, and division that characterizes corrupt, civilized humans.

The immediate effect of the dissolution of the little circle confirms
this bleak prognosis. Aside from the stimulation given to his vanity and
imagination, this dissolution puts Maman's finances in an extremely
precarious condition. To complete the foundation of his misery, Jean-
Jacques is temporarily blinded by an explosion that occurs during a
chemistry experiment.[46] The resulting decline in his health is exacer-

---

46. In *Emile* Rousseau argues that the study of chemistry is dangerous because the
typical apparatus appeals so much to vanity (*Emile*, 182–83). Thus Jean-Jacques's study
may be a sign of his vanity at this period. The explosion helps to cure him temporarily.

bated by his renascent imagination: "My passions made me live, and my passions killed me" (I, 219). Because his imagination is no longer distracted by the circle's activities, he becomes obsessed with the "most puerile things in the world."[47] His trivial obsessions tax his strength. With this account, Rousseau indicates the complexity of the relation between the imagination and the body. In short, all factors, internal as well as external, emotional as well as physical, show the extent of Jean-Jacques's departure from natural health and wholeness. It is this condition that marks the beginning of what Rousseau calls "the short happiness of my life." Book VI, which describes this age of happiness, is a remarkable reversal of what one might expect from the conclusion of the book that precedes it. In this book Jean-Jacques, who has suffered from the most extreme development of artificial sentiments, accomplishes a sort of return to natural independence and wholeness. In describing his happiness Rousseau ceases to discuss particular events that further the development of his character. In large part his character has been fixed by his education with Mme de Warens (I, 179). He argues that his new condition is virtually indescribable: "If it had consisted in facts, in actions, in words, I would be able to describe it and render it, in some way: but how to say what was neither said, nor done, nor even thought, but tasted and felt without my being able to enunciate any other object of my happiness than the feeling itself" (I, 225). Jean-Jacques's happiness is indescribable because it consists solely in a feeling caused by no event or object in particular. Because this feeling depends on no particular event, his memory can recapture it entirely. This feeling is directly accessible to him in a way that the important events of his life are not.

After this beginning, the substance of Book VI, which describes the ground of this indescribable happiness, comes as something of a surprise. The book does contain elaborate accounts of Jean-Jacques's daily routine which emphasize the continuity of his existence rather than eventful moments.[48] The first specific report, however, concerns a renewed attack of illness which convinces him that he is about to die. This attack serves as the background of the rest of Book VI, conditioning Jean-Jacques's daily activities and ultimately leading to a trip away from Maman. The foundation of this brief period of happiness appears at first to be Jean-Jacques's move to the country cottage les Charmettes

47. Rousseau refers to his "cruel imagination" in this context.
48. For a more detailed account of this daily routine, see Chapter 6.

(an almost literal return to nature) required by Maman's finances, but the importance of this move is very quickly replaced by the illness. The major question raised by Book VI is how the prospect of imminent death can serve as the foundation of happiness.[49]

In answering this question, Rousseau addresses two other approaches to the question of death which take fear as their beginning point. One, familiar from Hobbes, is that fear of death is the fundamental human passion and acts as certainly on men's minds as gravity works on their bodies.[50] This fear causes humans to postpone their extinction as long as possible. The second view, typical of religion, is that what is truly horrible is not death but the judgment and punishment that follow it. These very different understandings share the view that the significance of death is primary for humans and that the proper understanding of death is the only solid ground for human happiness. Hobbes attempts to convince his readers that death rather than damnation is truly terrible and that is can be most effectively postponed by submitting to the authority of a sovereign who can give protection from one's fellows.[51] Christianity, one example of the religious alternatives, teaches that damnation is truly terrible and that an excessive attachment to this life stands in the way of eternal life. These positions appear to be opposites, but Rousseau treats them as close relatives. As his criticism of the Sermon on the Mount (discussed in Chapter 2) suggests, both Christianity and some anti-Christian positions agree in focusing people's hopes on future pleasures; they disagree only about the objects of those pleasures. In the context of discussing his own reflections on death, Rousseau changes the subject of his analysis from hope to fear, but he arrives at a similar conclusion about the underlying similarity between Hobbes and Christianity.

In Book VI of the *Confessions* Rousseau is alternately under the sway of each of these views. By dramatizing his own submission to and overcoming of these two views, he attempts to persuade his reader to reject both. He begins by taking the side of Hobbes against Christian hopes for salvation and fear of damnation. He presents these hopes and fears as having their source only in the imagination. Then he turns a similar

---

49. Williams mistakenly finds the sickness inconsistent with the happiness at les Charmettes, *Romantic Autobiography*, p. 142.

50. Thomas Hobbes, *De Cive*, chap. 1.

51. Unless otherwise noted, the quotations from Hobbes are from Thomas Hobbes, *Leviathan*, ed. C. B. Macpherson (Harmondsworth, Middlesex, England: Penguin Books, 1968), pp. 162–201.

attack on Hobbes. He presents fear of death as being as unnatural and imaginary as fear of Hell. In other words, Rousseau accepts a modern philosophic attack on a longing for an imaginary world, but he denies that this attack has done more than replace one imaginary world with another that is at best marginally superior. Rousseau's own understanding of this issue in relation to both modern political philosophy and Christianity can be seen by comparing his presentation of the fear of death with the two outlined above.

The beginning of Hobbes's analysis can be taken to be his assertion that "Life it selfe is but Motion, and can never be without Desire, nor without Feare, no more than without Sense."[52] From this he derives his claim that there is no "perpetual Tranquility of mind" for men on earth. Because life is motion, it consists in alternating inclinations toward (desire) and away from (fear) objects of pleasure and pain. In itself this presentation of life as an alternation between desire and fear implies nothing specific about either death or damnation. A precondition for both of these fears is foresight or anticipation. The anticipation of death and ignorance about what succeeds it cause both fear of death and religious speculation about a future condition.

According to Hobbes, foresight is a great blessing for humans because it contributes to their ability to investigate causes and thereby adds to their power.[53] It is the extent and form of this ability which principally distinguishes humans from beasts. In addition to adding to their power, foresight adds greatly to the anxieties of humans by making them realize how threatened their pleasures are. As a result, even those humans who love peace are prone to regard others as potential enemies who may interfere with their pleasures or even their lives. In Hobbes's presentation this grim picture is relieved because fear of death can be made to lead to a desire to leave the natural condition in which everyone's existence is threatened. Thus fear of death, which at first glance appears to be the bane of human existence, is in the end its salvation.

One thing threatens this neat solution. Some people apparently do not feel their fear of death enough to give allegiance to a community. Some refuse to submit to fear of death out of a sense of honor. In these, anticipation of future reputation is a stronger pleasure than fear of death is a pain. Such people are a constant source of trouble for others,

52. Ibid., p. 130.
53. See the discussion of Condillac in Chapter 3.

but fortunately they are few. Others do not feel the fear of death because they are distracted by fear of God's invisible power. Even though in practice most people fear death more than they fear God, there are enough who fear God more to present difficulties for a community whose foundation is fear of death.

Hobbes has two ways to reconcile these religious people to his community. One is to convince them that their religious beliefs are compatible with and even require allegiance to a sovereign. In taking this approach, Hobbes makes it appear unnecessary to choose between fear of God and fear of death. Both fears lead to the same conclusion.[54] His second, less immediately effective method is to give an analysis of religion which tends to undermine any possible belief in Hell. This analysis proceeds by giving a genetic account of religious belief and distinguishing between those aspects of sound and unsound origins. He argues that, whereas belief in God is the result of sound reasoning, fear of Hell is based on error. For its bearing on the question of damnation, the distinctive feature of the account of religion based on sound reasoning is that it leads to no such fear. This is a striking result in the light of Hobbes's definition of religion as "feare of power invisible, feigned by the mind, or imagined from tales publiquely allowed."[55] In his more thematic discussion of religion, he says, "But the acknowledging of one God Eternall, Infinite, and Omnipotent, may more easily be derived from the desire men have to know the causes of natural bodies, and their severall vertues, and operations; than from the feare of what was to befall them in time to come." It is true that this very desire to know has its source in "anxiety for the future time." Nevertheless, in his discussion of religion Hobbes argues that this originating fear must be put aside because it will hinder the search for causes. The conclusion of this reasoning unobscured by fear is belief in an infinite, omnipotent, eternal, but otherwise incomprehensible God. Because this sort of reasoning leads to no conclusions about God's punishment of humans, it leads to no conflict with the civil law. By the second method, one will obey a sovereign whose punishments are visible in preference to a God whose will is unknown and punishments uncertain.

Hobbes distinguishes this type of reasoning from the faulty opinions he calls "natural seeds of religion." These natural seeds are "opin-

54. For a discussion of this issue, see Clifford Orwin, "On the Sovereign Authorization," *Political Theory* 3,1 (1975): 26–44.
55. Hobbes, *Leviathan*, p. 124.

ion of Ghosts, Ignorance of Second causes, Devotion towards what men fear, and Taking of things Casuall for Prognostiques." Each of these seeds involves either ignorance or error. Those whose opinions of God derive from these sources are likely to be credulous. They are "enclined to suppose and feign unto themselves, severall kinds of Powers Invisible; and to stand in awe of their own imagination." It is then fearful human imagination that causes religious beliefs such as fear of Hell. Generally, Hobbes's treatment of religion is an attempt to calm these imaginary fears and turn attention to the more solid fears that stand behind them. At the very least, he wishes to show that the imaginary fears do not oppose the real fears. For the Enlightenment, imagination is the enemy that must be overcome and knowledge is the means of overcoming it (see Chapter 3).

Rousseau agrees with the substance of Hobbes's analysis of religion. In *Emile* he repeatedly talks about "fantastic imaginings" (*Emile*, 135, 263)—supernatural beings that occur to people under the influence of fear and other distorting passions. The reasoning of the Savoyard vicar about God resembles that of Hobbes in its emphases on a causal chain, the incomprehensibility of God, and lack of knowledge about Hell (*Emile*, 270–75, 284–86).

Rousseau gives a similar presentation in the account of his illness in the *Confessions*. He says that his belief in his imminent death caused him to begin to reflect on the religious matters introduced by Mme de Warens, whose religious opinions closely resemble those of the Savoyard vicar (I, 228–30).[56] Rousseau concludes his account of her instruction by saying, "Finding in her all the maxims of which I had need to guarantee my soul from the terrors of death and what follows it, I drew with security on this source of confidence" (I, 231). Hobbes's reassuring line of argument has its effect. This is not the end of the story, however.

Later Jean-Jacques begins to read Jansenist works, which undermine his confidence. Such religious works produce an effect that Hobbes could have predicted: "The terrors of Hell, which until then I feared very little, troubled my security little by little, and if Maman had not tranquilized my soul, that frightening doctrine would have completely turned me around in the end" (I, 242). Jean-Jacques resolves

56. In the autobiographical section of *Emile* that introduces the "Profession of Faith," Rousseau attributes to the vicar the influence he attributes to Mme de Warens in the *Confessions* (*Emile*, pp. 260–66).

this fear by drawing an omen about his salvation from his ability to hit a large tree with a rock thrown at close range. Rousseau declares that since that moment, "I have never doubted my salvation" (I, 243).[57] Jean-Jacques is able to solve the difficulty once and for all by a childish method.

In sum, Rousseau presents fear of Hell as an imaginary fear founded in faulty reasoning about divinity. Its cure might be found in the calming conclusions of better reasoning, although it is very likely that the imaginary fears are too strong to be overcome by consoling doctrines alone. Rousseau does not recommend the use of omens to assuage religious fears (what if one should miss the tree?), and he calls his own use of such a measure puerile. It works in his case only because his fears are not deeply rooted. He uses this account of a preposterous solution for religious fear to suggest the arbitrary and irrational character of its origin.

While Rousseau is in general agreement with Hobbes's treatment of religion, he differs from Hobbes in applying the same treatment to fear of death. Rousseau insists that fear of death, as distinguished from fear of pain, is not natural to humans. In the *Second Discourse* he argues that "knowledge of death and of its terror is one of the first acquisitions that man has made in moving away from the animal condition" (*Discourses*, 116). Foresight is a necessary condition of this fear. In Rousseau's account, humans naturally lack foresight; their imaginations suggest nothing to them about death (*Discourses*, 117). Civilized humans, however, cannot avoid the acquisition of foresight. That they unavoidably acquire this basis for fear of death suggests that Hobbes's reasoning still applies for all humans one is likely to encounter. His conclusion may not follow for the virtually subhuman ancestors of civilized humans, but it does for all humans in society. Condillac, who agrees with Rousseau that fear of death is not natural, regards this salutary fear as one of the principal benefits humans derive from their imaginations. Rousseau avoids such a concession to Hobbes by arguing that fear of death is neither a desirable nor the necessary consequence of foresight. Emile, for example, has the latter without the former.

In the *Confessions* Rousseau illustrates his position with reference to the effect of reading, just as he does in his discussion of his fear of Hell. During his illness Jean-Jacques begins to study physiology as well as

---

57. Jean-Jacques faces the same dilemma as Max Weber's Protestants, but he shuns worldly commercial success as a means for solving it.

Jansenism. While reading medical texts he believes that he is afflicted with every disease he reads about. "This fatal study" is the source of an even more cruel disease than can be found in any medical book, "the whim [*fantasie*] of a cure" (I, 248). It is not foresight alone that causes the desire for a cure, but foresight joined with the hope of avoiding death.

This hope is encouraged by the promises of doctors. Rousseau argues that extreme, even overwhelming, fear of death occurs only with the imagination that death can be avoided. By nature, even after the acquisition of foresight, humans do not fear death unless they begin to imagine ways to prevent it. Thus, because of their ability to raise imaginary hopes, disciplines like medicine, which seem to be responsive to natural fears, are really prime causes of artificial fears. In the end, although Rousseau is willing to admit that a society could be based on such Hobbesian terms, he denies that this is a necessary or even desirable foundation.[58] Fear of death is no more natural than fear of Hell, and it is less effective for making people just.[59] For individuals, however, both fears can be prevented by sound educations that are not directed by doctors of medicine or theology.

Because these two great causes of torment are unnatural, it is possible to be happy by avoiding or eliminating them. The happiness of the pure state of nature consists largely in the avoidance of tormenting hopes and fears. The same is true of the happiness of the young Emile. Book VI of the *Confessions* shows that Jean-Jacques's happiness is founded in the resignation toward death caused by his acceptance of illness. This resignation temporarily cures him of the civilized desires that torment him, although fears of death and Hell occasionally trouble his calm. He is happy in so far as he is free of these fears.

Rousseau begins his account of this condition of happiness by describing the "sudden and almost inconceivable revolution" in his body at the beginning of his illness (I, 227). His first reaction to this revolution is one of surprise and fear. However, once he becomes convinced (for the moment) that there is no hope of a cure, his fear disappears: "This accident which ought to have killed my body killed only my passions, and I bless heaven each day for the happy effect that it produced on my soul. I am even able to say that I did not begin to live until I regarded myself as a dead man" (I, 228). Thus the result of this

---

58. On the limitations of a society based on fear, see III, 937.
59. Rousseau does argue that the fear of Hell can prevent injustice (*Emile*, 312–14).

physical revolution is to return him to a quasi-natural condition of lack of passion. This revolution is a more radical version of what Maman attempted in her sexual initiation. She tried to control Jean-Jacques's imagination by means of his senses. Now his physical condition succeeds in doing this. To this stage Jean-Jacques has been dominated by the artificial passions of indignation, vanity, and hopes for the future. These civilized passions give way to the stronger force of the unavoidable necessity of death. In effect the belief in imminent death kills the imagination. Jean-Jacques's return to nature can take place only in the absence of those opinions that would make death appear as something other than an absolute necessity. The promises and threats offered by medical science and revealed religion are the primary obstacles to the acceptance of this necessity because both offer hope for an intervention that will secure one's continued existence.

To be sure, this quasi-natural condition differs from the pure natural condition in important respects. Rather than lacking foresight as natural humans do, someone in this new condition requires foresight. When humans in the pure state of nature face the inevitability of death in old age or illness, "they finally die without it being perceived that they cease to be, and almost without perceiving it themselves" (*Discourses*, 109). Civilized humans, like Jean-Jacques, do perceive or imagine their future death. How they respond to this perception depends on their image of death and their ability to see death as unavoidable. In the absence of religiously or medically inspired images of death, the imagination can be directed in a way that approximates the more natural acceptance through ignorance. In such a case, foresight can support the acceptance of death that is necessary to limit the civilized imagination. Rather than natural ignorance or civilized fear, Rousseau says that he felt "less sadness than a peaceful languor which even had its sweetness" (I, 243).

This quasi-natural acceptance of death also leads to a rather different form of happiness than natural ignorance does. Natural humans lead a tranquil existence because they have so few passions. Their happiness consists of satisfying their very limited desires with great ease. When describing this happiness in the *Second Discourse*, Rousseau argues more that it is the opposite of misery than that it is positive pleasure (*Discourses*, 127). The happiness of natural humans is contrasted to the unhappiness of civilized humans tormented by their artificial passions. Natural humans are of course unable to make this comparison between their condition and that of the civilized humans who form

Rousseau's readership. Thus natural humans have no notion of their own relative happiness. After his revolution, Jean-Jacques is conscious of his newly found detachment from "all the vain cares of life" (I, 232). As a result he has both the natural lack of tormenting passions and a consciousness of the significance of this lack. Jean-Jacques's happiness is based on comparison, like that of Wolmar or Socrates, but it need not involve amour-propre because he compares himself only with his own past. In sum, one might say that a natural human's pleasure is largely an absence of pain, whereas Jean-Jacques's is both an absence of pain and a still sweeter awareness of this absence. In this respect his happiness could be considered an improvement on that of someone in the pure state of nature.

This impression is reinforced if one turns from this rather abstract account of happiness to the substance of Jean-Jacques's activity during this period. Rousseau says that he attempted to distribute his time with "as much pleasantness and utility as possible" (I, 235). He engages in light physical activity, raises pigeons, and reads. Most of all, he follows a daily routine filled with pleasures "too simple to be described" (I, 236). He says, "I can say that this time during which I lived in retreat and always ill was that of my life in which I was least idle and least bored" (I, 235). Natural humans are never bored either, but they are idle. Most civilized humans are either bored or tormented, whether they are idle or not. Rousseau presents his own return to a quasi-natural condition as making possible a life of constant but leisurely activity, most of which is positively pleasurable.

To the social picture of happiness in the little circle, then, Rousseau has added an outline of another sort of happiness, one in principle accessible to civilized humans who are not citizens. This happiness can be understood in comparison to that of a natural human. As in his account of the little circle and his earlier description of the departure from nature, the key element in Rousseau's description here is imagination. In the state of nature there is a complete harmony between desires and abilities, or imagination and power. A natural human is a unity because his imagination is reduced to a single point. "His soul, agitated by nothing, is given over to the sole sentiment of its present existence" (*Discourses*, 117). Civilized imagination causes this point to expand. Both desires and abilities expand along with the imagination, but rarely in proportion to each other. In citizens the imagination expands into the self-contained sphere of the community. Citizens' desires are carefully limited by their identification with the community and are satisfied by the community's power. This represents an expansion of the imagination beyond its natural state, but it also includes a careful limitation. A similar, if smaller, expansion and limitation takes place in the imagination of the members of domestic circles. In fact, the flexibility of relations in these circles may even allow a greater degree of imaginative activity than does the rigidity of cities. For the majority of civilized humans, the expansion of the imagination is unlimited. They live within no circumscribed horizon to limit their hopes and fears. They desire unlimited wealth, unlimited recognition from others, unlimited love. One can say that, on one hand, the undefined limits of civilized imagination create constant tensions between desires and abilities. Civilized humans can always imagine receiving more money or honor than they have at present. The limits on their satisfaction are felt as imposed from outside and they rebel against this imposition. On the other hand, the circumscribed imaginations of natural humans, citizens, and members of a family never let this opposition between desires and abilities arise. These people imagine only those things with which their physical abilities, cities, and families can supply them. The limits on their capacities are not felt because they are imposed from inside by limited imaginations. Even when such people feel the sting of external necessity, they do not rebel against it because their imaginations suggest no ways to avoid necessity.

In Book VI of the *Confessions* Rousseau shows a restoration of natural unity for a civilized human even outside the limits of a community. An accident or physical revolution can cut off the imaginative possibilities open to one and return one to a carefully limited sphere or circle. It is a striking feature of this section of the *Confessions* that, while Rousseau emphasizes the amount of time he spends reading, he says nothing about an imaginative projection outside himself except when he reads Jansenist literature and medical books. He never mentions his identification with the characters in the books he reads, nor does he construct new identities for himself.[60] In short, he does not create an imaginary world to live in. His belief in the inevitability of death keeps him from imagining projects for advancement. He lives entirely in the present.

This section of the *Confessions* is important for a number of reasons. It is the first suggestion that external restraint can be placed on the

60. For Rousseau's studies, see "Le Verger de Mme la Baronne de Warens" (II, 1124–29).

imagination, not only before it develops, as with Emile, but also later. Rousseau earlier shows several occasions of Jean-Jacques's imagination becoming focused on a particular object, but never becoming weaker. As a result of this restraint, this is the earliest occasion in which Jean-Jacques can legitimately be regarded as a natural man living in society. Even the early states of Book I, which are presented as paradises, are strongly influenced by the boy's imagination. Finally, by presenting Jean-Jacques in a condition resembling natural happiness, Book VI opens the possibility of a return to a quasi-natural condition for all civilized humans. It suggests that there is a way out of civilized corruption and misery.

The section also raises a number of questions about the practicality and durability of such a return to natural wholeness. The practical difficulty is easy to see. A return to the presumably healthy natural condition which requires sickness and a threat of imminent death is very unattractive to someone who fears death or Hell, as most civilized humans do. Furthermore, the calm pleasures of tranquil imagination are so alien to an inflamed imagination that they are very unlikely to be sought even if their price can be made less stiff.[61] Earlier we saw the problem facing civilized humans who seek to know nature. They are so transformed by civilization that they are incapable of recognizing what is natural. A similar problem arises here. The desires of civilized people are so artificial that, even if they could recognize other desires as natural, they would not wish to renounce their pleasures in pursuit of them. The sort of return to nature shown in Book VI must be inflicted from outside; it is an accident.

A specific version of this difficulty is preserved in Book VI itself. Rousseau argues that fear of death and fear of Hell are artificial fears constructed by the imagination. Even the realization that these fears are imaginary does not dispose of them. On the contrary, disposing of them seems to require a decline in the power of the imagination which cannot occur as long as these imaginary opinions are present. Rousseau suggests that consoling lessons can eliminate the fear of Hell and that at a certain point death must be accepted as inevitable. Nevertheless, he shows the fragility of these measures. He presents himself as intermittently tormented by these imaginary fears after he initially accepts the inevitability of death and the impossibility of a cure.

---

61. Socrates gives a similar account of the unattractiveness of philosophy. Theages became a philosopher only because he was sickly; see *Republic*, 496b-c.

This consideration settles the issue of the durability of this condition of happiness even if it can be attained. Rousseau argues that the acceptance of death and the accompanying deadening of the imagination are possible only if death is regarded as inevitable and near. Its inevitability is easy to accept in general for the indefinite future. But such an acceptance can lead to attempts to postpone the inevitable indefinitely. The precondition of a real acceptance of the inevitability of death is its nearness. However, if death is truly near, the condition of quasi-natural happiness and independence is quite literally short-lived. If death is mistakenly thought to be near, the illusion is eventually exposed and dangerous hopes and fears may arise again.

Rousseau poses one other problem for the durability of this condition. This problem arises from the happiness itself rather than an external source. He says that in the midst of his happiness he was afflicted with a series of peculiar physical symptoms that he traces to a mental cause. Thus, while it may be possible to control the imagination by means of the senses, it should not be forgotten that the imagination can also reverse this condition. After describing his symptoms, Rousseau says, "It is certain that much of the vapors was mixed in all of this. The vapors are the malady of happy people; it was mine" (I, 247). Lest the reader be distracted by what was considered a very quaint term even when Rousseau wrote it, he makes his meaning precise: The symptoms of the vapors "mark that boredom of well-being which makes the sensitivity extravagate so to speak." These physical (as well as mental) symptoms have a nonphysical cause. The state of happiness itself gives birth to an emotional restlessness manifesting itself in physical symptoms. A developed imagination is apparently incapable of remaining at rest under any circumstances. If it has no object at hand it will create one. If it is prevented from creating, it will manifest itself in the restlessness of boredom and the vapors. The condition of happiness attained by acceptance of death is a precarious state indeed.[62]

By speaking of the vapors, humors, and sensitivity here, Rousseau hints at the intimate relation between the soul and the body. He sums up his discussion of his vapors by saying, "We are so little made for being happy here below that it must necessarily happen that the soul or the body suffers when they are not both suffering, and that the good state of one almost always causes harm to the other." The "we" in this statement clearly refers to civilized humans. Natural humans have both

---

62. These symptoms should be compared with those of Julie (II, 689).

healthy souls and healthy bodies, and they have the second in part because they have the first. It is only in the case of a sensitized imagination that a harmony between the two is virtually unattainable. Thus, when the imagination has been calmed by an unhealthy body, it revenges itself, so to speak, by heightening the body's sensitivity. As a result the imagination itself receives a stimulus that causes it to desire a cure for the body.[63]

The Loss of Happiness

The remainder of Book VI, and Part One, traces the dissolution of this quasi-natural state of happiness. As a result of his attack of the vapors and his desire to be cured, Jean-Jacques leaves Maman to seek medical advice at the spa in Montpellier. The predominant feature of this trip is a constant shifting of identity on Jean-Jacques's part as he moves from vanity to sensuality to pride. These changes are a sure sign that he has lost natural wholeness. The first shift takes place when he becomes acquainted with a group of travelers on the road to Montpellier. Jean-Jacques adopts the "bizarre" expedient of pretending to be an English Jacobite named Dudding to present a more dashing appearance than that of a sickly, pious convert. As in his earlier masquerade as the French musician Vaussore, he attempts to gain a reputation by fabricating a new identity. He has relapsed into an unhealthy civilized vanity and is obsessed with how he appears to other people.

This masquerade is more successful than the earlier one, and its consequences lead to a second transformation in Jean-Jacques. One of the travelers, Mme de Larnage, makes sexual overtures to him and succeeds in overcoming his vapors. Rousseau says, "I was no longer the same man" (I, 253). In this instance he is not transformed into someone else, he merely ceases to be the "poor Jean-Jacques" who suffered from vapors and worried about his reputation. This transformation is in part a reattainment of his natural wholeness in that it is accomplished by what Rousseau calls the intoxication of his senses rather than by his imagination. The relative lack of participation of the imagination in this affair is indicated by Rousseau's admission that he did not love his companion. He says of the relationship that "it was a sensuality so burning with pleasure and an intimacy so sweet in conversation that it

---

63. Hartle implies that the fear of death is easier to avoid than Rousseau's presentation suggests; see *Modern Self*, pp. 49–51.

had all the charms of passions without having the delirium which turns one's head and makes one not know how to enjoy." There is an element of vanity in this sexual conquest (I, 254), but on the whole it represents a calming of the imagination and an end of the internal divisions caused by vanity.

Because of a third shift in Jean-Jacques's identity, this intoxication of the senses does not last. After leaving Mme de Larnage with plans to reunite, Jean-Jacques sees his first Roman monument, the Pont du Gard.[64] The spectacle sets his imagination in motion—"The object surpassed my expectation for the only time in my life" (I, 255)—and causes a reverie that culminates in the exclamation, "If only I had been born a Roman" (I, 256). This reverie is distinctly unfavorable to Mme de Larnage. Jean-Jacques's image of himself as a Roman reminds him of his duty to Mme de Warens, and he resolves to return to les Charmettes to assist her in her precarious financial position. He says, "As soon as I had taken my resolution I became another man, or rather I became again the one that I was before, whom this moment of intoxication had caused to disappear" (I, 260). This apparent return to himself is not a return to either vanity or natural wholeness. It is a return to the Jean-Jacques of Book I who identifies himself with Scaevola and Brutus.

That this transformation does not return Jean-Jacques to the state of harmony between his inclinations and his situation is shown by his claim that for the first time in his life he is able to say to himself, "I deserve my own esteem, I know how to prefer my duty to my pleasure." In his period of natural wholeness a choice between the two was unnecessary. The unnaturalness of his new condition is further emphasized by Rousseau's addition that "pride perhaps had as much a part in my resolution as virtue: but if this pride is not virtue it has such similar effects that it is pardonable to be fooled by it." Thus, in the space of a short journey, Jean-Jacques has moved from vanity to sensuality to pride and adopted a persona suited to each.

On his return from Montpellier, Jean-Jacques finds his Roman pride or virtue put to a series of tests. First he finds his place with Maman taken by another man. Jean-Jacques resolves to serve Maman while forgoing sexual relations, a step Rousseau claims begins the growth of "the virtue whose seed is at the bottom of [his] soul" (I, 264). This germinating virtue is put to another test when Jean-Jacques ac-

---

64. The sight of an aqueduct recalls Jean-Jacques's construction of an aqueduct in Book I.

cepts a position as tutor of the children of M. de Mably. Now his virtue is unable to stand the disproportion between his duty and his inclinations, and he reverts to the habit of stealing he acquired during his apprenticeship. At les Charmettes he had never been tempted to steal, because everything was his. Once out of this quasi-natural condition, his Roman virtue does not come to his aid. The identification with Romans cannot be maintained for long in circumstances that do not reinforce it. When outside Rome, it is difficult to do as the Romans do.

This failure of virtue and Jean-Jacques's dismissal as a tutor leads to the close of Part One of the *Confessions*. At the end of Book VI Jean-Jacques sets out for Paris with his new system of musical notation that he hopes will make his fortune. He has fallen back to his extreme hopes for the future and his vanity. This collapse of his virtue merely completes the pattern of Books V and VI. Jean-Jacques lays a foundation for the resolution of the problems caused by his early education only to see it collapse. In these books Rousseau outlines what is required to maintain a domestic community, individual happiness, and individual virtue outside a community. In each case he outlines an alternative to corruption which is available to civilized humans. In each instance he shows that the alternative cannot be maintained in his own case. Because he presents himself as such a singular example of the extreme development of civilized passions and imagination, his own failure at domestic relations, happiness, and virtue leaves open the possibility of a successful adoption of one of these alternatives by less exceptional people. This is true in particular of domestic relations. It would be difficult for anyone to maintain a purely independent virtue in the modern environment, and the preconditions of a quasi-natural happiness are very rarely to be found and unlikely even to be sought. A domestic community that reconstitutes natural wholeness on a different level without demanding the sacrifices of virtue from its members seems a real possibility. In this respect Rousseau presents his own experience as a model for others. He arouses an identification and hopes to be able to inspire imitation where he was successful and better fortune where he failed.

The project of Part Two of the *Confessions* is to take up these same themes again and reevaluate them at a higher level. In Part One Rousseau presents his original departure from natural independence and wholeness, the particular direction taken by his developing artificial sentiments, and his failed attempts to resolve this development through domestic relations, individual happiness, and virtue. Part Two shows a further working through of the artificial passions, vanity in particular. It also shows new attempts to achieve virtue, new domestic relations, and finally a new quasi-natural state of personal happiness.

The Jean-Jacques of Part One of the *Confessions* is by no means a natural man. He does preserve some natural characteristics that most civilized humans lose. More important, he shows his character to be largely unfixed and subject to change. As a result he is open to a wide variety of experiments to restore natural wholeness or to manufacture a social whole. Thus the Jean-Jacques of Part One reveals much about nature and about different aspects of denatured civilization. The completion of the account of his development and his attempt to return to naturalness comes in Part Two.

[5]

The Rediscovery of Nature
(Books VII and VIII)

The Theme and Structure of Part Two of the *Confessions*

Rousseau consistently presents the entirety of his life after leaving les Charmettes as a series of attempts to recapture his brief period of happiness. His experience has given him a glimpse of happiness, but his attempts at reestablishing the conditions in which this happiness took place force him more and more into a world opposed to the peaceful life in the country. At the beginning of Book VII Rousseau extends the period of happiness to include all his life prior to his arrival at Paris. He says, "My peaceful youth has been seen to slip away in a smooth life sweet enough, without great reverses or great prosperity" (I, 277). The stormy course of the narrative of Part One would seem to belie this characterization, but Rousseau's statement can be taken to warn that, however turbulent his early life may have been, it was calm in relation to what follows. He proceeds to compare the two periods directly: "The chance which favored my penchants for thirty years opposed them for the thirty others, and enormous faults, unheard of misfortunes and all the virtues which can honor adversity except force will be seen to be born from this continual opposition between my situation and my inclinations"[1] (I, 277). If Part One is the story of the

---

1. Rousseau's admission that he lacked the virtue of force should be considered in relation to his claim that "force of soul" is the virtue most necessary for heroes (II, 1272). In *Emile* Rousseau identifies force and virtue (*Emile*, 444). Thus Rousseau's statement that he acquired all the virtues but force can be read to imply that he acquired no real virtues.

harmony of situation and inclinations and how it is lost, Part Two is the story of the consequences of this loss and how they can be overcome.[2]

This picture of the difference between the first thirty years of Jean-Jacques's life and the second is complicated by two issues. First, Rousseau's formulation here refers only to the contradiction between his situation and his inclinations. It says nothing about the internal conflict among his inclinations. Jean-Jacques's problem is not simply to find a situation in which his natural inclinations can be satisfied, he must also find a way to cure his unnatural inclinations. Jean-Jacques has longings that lead him in the direction of a natural life, but he also has more powerful longings that lead him away from this life. The conditions at les Charmettes satisfied his desires only because these desires were limited by his illness and his belief about the nearness of death. No purely external condition can bring about this quasi-natural harmony by itself. Second, even if it were granted that Jean-Jacques's experience of happiness formed a pure and unambiguous longing for wholeness and resolution of his contradictions, it would not be clear that this was a longing for what is natural. Jean-Jacques's longings have so far led to flights to imaginary worlds in which his desires are satisfied and his contradictions dissolved. It would be consistent to argue that Jean-Jacques's education, which like that of all civilized humans has removed him from direct experience of natural desires, has also made it possible for him to have longings only for imaginary worlds. The question is whether his longing to return to the condition of les Charmettes is a longing for something truly natural or a longing for another imaginary world. He needs to present some criteria by which a civilized human can distinguish between his own imagination and what is truly natural. This epistemological issue and its psychological accompaniment reveal the decisive questions for Part Two of the *Confessions*. In this half of the work Rousseau shows how or if a return to nature is possible and how he can account for his own claim to understand what is natural.

A look at the structure of Part Two gives some guidance about how Rousseau addresses these questions. Part Two is preceded by a repetition of the epigraph to the entire work, *"Intus et in cute."* This repetition underscores both the break and the continuity between Parts One and Two. The break in the narrative is announced at the end of Book VI with the abrupt remark "But I must stop here" (I, 272) and with the

---

2. On the resolution of oppositions as Rousseau's fundamental project, see Shklar, *Men and Citizens*, p. 64.

equally abrupt beginning of Book VII, "After two years of silence and of patience, in spite of my resolution, I take up my pen again" (I, 277). The gap in the composition of the parts could be taken as an indication that the two are different works, and most commentators have emphasized the stylistic differences between the two.[3] The shared epigraph implies that, however opposed in style and time of composition the two parts may be, they share the same theme.

Of Part One, only Book I uses the device of numbering paragraphs to show different sections of the narrative. Rousseau employs this device again at the beginning of Book VII. This parallel between the introductory books of the two parts is striking but not altogether surprising. What is surprising is that Rousseau takes up the technique again at the beginning of Book IX. There are numerous unresolved (and given the variations in the manuscripts, apparently unresolvable) questions about the precise significance of this technique. There can be little doubt, however, that Rousseau uses it to signal a beginning. Book I, of course, begins Jean-Jacques's life and Rousseau's narrative. Book VII announces the division of his life into two parts, his peaceful youth and his turbulent adulthood. Book IX, which begins with Jean-Jacques's departure from Paris and the public life of that city, divides his adult life into two parts: one in which he seeks a public career and another in which he shuns this career.[4]

It cannot be denied that there are other indications of sharp breaks, divisions, and numerous beginnings of one sort or another in Part Two. This preliminary overview can end, however, with a note of the new beginning announced in Book XII. Rousseau says, "Here begins the work of shadows in which for the last eight years I find myself shrouded" (I, 589). This remark seems to indicate a distinct break with the rest of the work that parallels the break in Book VI from the rest of Part One. Book VI is isolated as the "age of happiness" and Book XII is isolated as the "abyss of evils."[5] After announcing that Book XII marks the beginning of a "work of shadows," Rousseau goes on to say, "Its primitive causes are all marked in the three preceding books," that is, Books IX–XI.[6] Thus

---

3. See, for example, Saussure, *Manuscrits*, pp. 17, 259.

4. Hartle divides the book differently, claiming that Rousseau's division is merely an accident of composition; see *Modern Self*, p. 27.

5. The sharpness of the parallel between Books VI and XII is reduced by the presence of an epigraph for Book VI and the absence of one for Book XII.

6. In the Paris manuscript Rousseau first wrote "two" and then changed it to "three." His first thought would support Hartle's division (see note 4 above).

the true beginnings of the process that culminates in Book XII are to be found in Book IX. Again, this confirms the division of Part Two into two subsections, Books VII–VIII and Books IX–XII. Each of these subsections centers around what Rousseau calls a "revolution," comparable to the revolution in his physical condition at les Charmettes. The first of the revolutions of Part Two is Jean-Jacques's discovery of his system, his understanding of nature; the second is his return to a quasi-natural condition. The movement of Books VII–VIII is toward the first of these revolutions. Book IX reports the second and Books X–XII show its consequences. The first revolution is the subject of this chapter and the second, the subject of Chapter 6.

Book VII: Amour-propre and Knowledge

The departure from nature completed in Part One does not make Jean-Jacques appear to be a very good candidate for the discoverer of a true account of nature. His one advantage is a range of experiences that acquaint him with a wide variety of human feelings, most of which are artificial rather than natural. In Book VII Rousseau shows, first, the extent to which his own artificial passions lead him to pursue knowledge and, second, how the opposition between some of these passions and his social condition helps to predispose him to the discovery of the difference between nature and convention.

In its action Book VII is the account of Jean-Jacques's hopes for fame and fortune in the world of Parisian high society and his brief career as secretary to the French ambassador to Venice. When he reviews this period, Rousseau contrasts it to his life at les Charmettes:

> I felt myself made for retreat and the country, it was impossible for me to live happily elsewhere. At Venice in the train of public affairs, in the dignity of a sort of representation, in the pride [orgueil] of projects of advancement; at Paris in the whirl of high society, in the sensuality of dinners, in the glow of spectacles, in the fumes of vainglory [gloriole], my groves, my streams, my solitary promenades always came to distract me by their memories, to sadden me, to extract sighs and desires from me. (I, 401)[7]

Rousseau characterizes his diplomatic service by pride and the life in high society by vainglory, but he opposes both equally to the life of

---

7. It is possible to read the reference to vainglory as a description of Paris, but it also applies to Jean-Jacques during his life in Paris.

retreat. Both pride and vainglory are derived from unnatural amour-propre. It is this fundamental artificial passion that stands in the way of both a return to naturalness and the knowledge of nature. The guiding motif of Jean-Jacques's sentiments during this period is amour-propre and the modifications it undergoes in different circumstances.

In Part One pride is shown to be the most primitive manifestation of amour-propre. Pride is shown in Jean-Jacques's early ability to identify himself with Plutarch's heroes, which gives birth to his strong feelings of citizenship. This strong sense of pride is also at the root of his experience of indignation. The final manifestation of pride in Part One is his temporary achievement of virtue founded on an identification with the Romans. Throughout Part One, two other elements alternate with and temper this citizenlike pride. The first of these, romantic sensuality, begins with his reading of novels, develops through his relations with Mlles Lambercier, Goton, and de Vulson, and ends after several turns with the intoxication of his senses in his affair with Mme de Larnage.[8] The second element is his vanity, the first "well-marked movement" of which also takes place at Bossey. This vanity arises intermittently in Part One during Jean-Jacques's efforts at achieving advancement and esteem; his masquerade as Vaussore de Villeneuve, the Parisian music teacher, is an example. Pride, romanticism, and vanity are the key features of Jean-Jacques's development into an artificial human.

The importance of vanity for the beginning of Part Two is prepared at the close of Part One, with Jean-Jacques setting off for Paris filled with great hopes for advancement. These hopes are founded on his invention of a new system of musical notation. Rousseau says, "I persisted in wishing to make a revolution in this art through it, and in this way to reach a celebrity which in the fine arts is always joined with fortune at Paris" (I, 286). Jean-Jacques's motive for attempting this "revolution" is his desire for celebrity and fortune; his principle of action is "whoever excels in something is always sure of being sought after" (I, 288). Vanity, or even vainglory, predominates over both romance and pride at this stage of the *Confessions*.

Associated with Jean-Jacques's desire for celebrity are his first account of himself as possessing unique knowledge and his first account of serious artistic activity. Part One is very quiet about Jean-Jacques as a

---

8. The turns include his relations with Mme Basile and Mlles de Graffenried and Galley.

knower,[9] whereas Part Two begins with his first theoretical accomplishment. The connection between this accomplishment and his desire for celebrity poses the general question, discussed in Chapter 1, of the relation between artificial passions and knowledge. Part Two is the beginning of Rousseau's account of his own knowledge.

At first there at least appears to be a potential harmony between Jean-Jacques's theoretical and artistic activities and his desire for celebrity. The invention of a new and useful technique can bring about the celebrity and wealth he desires. His motives, which have nothing to do with disinterested love of knowledge, do not interfere with his activity as a knower. In fact they provide a very strong impetus to succeed at inventing.[10] According to this picture there is no lack of harmony between unnatural civilized desires and knowledge. On the contrary, it is only when artificial characteristics such as foresight and vanity arise that there is any motive for knowing. Natural humans are ignorant precisely because they have no such motive. Neither natural nor civilized humans love contemplation or thinking for its own sake, but civilized humans will think in order to satisfy their desires. Whether they apply themselves to useful arts or useless ones depends on the conditions in which they find themselves.

Rousseau shows that this apparent harmony between selfish motives and the desire for knowledge can be disrupted in two ways. First, although Jean-Jacques's system of music is both new and useful, it is rejected by the Academy. Rousseau's explanation of the rejection is that "if sometimes learned people have fewer prejudices than other men, they hold, on the other hand, even more tightly to those they have" (I, 284). A desire for celebrity may inspire one to discover new truths, but the same desire makes one refuse to recognize the discoveries of a competitor. Vanity may spur individual learning, but competing vanity can be an obstacle to a general acceptance of new discoveries. In the case of useful technological developments, the problem of envy of rivals can be overcome, although not without difficulty, by a public appeal to the utility of a discovery. The public's desire for wealth and preservation makes it open to discoveries that satisfy these desires. In those arts in which the results are less tangible, vanity and prejudice can simply prevent new discoveries from being accepted.

---

9. Book VI does discuss his studies (I, 237); see Hartle, *Modern Self*, pp. 64–65, 89.
10. On the subject of gaining fame by inventing, see Francis Bacon, *Novum Organum*, I, cxxix.

The second cause of the disruption of the harmony between knowledge and artificial desires results from the first. If new and useful truths fail to gain public acclaim, other methods must be tried. As Rousseau says, "whoever excels at anything is always sure of being sought after." This is true even if the excellence in question is in a purely frivolous subject such as memorization or playing a game.[11] Such experts can be considered knowers in some sense, but even a completely sham knowledge can be equally valuable for attaining celebrity. The desire for celebrity requires a greater attention to what is socially acceptable than to what is true. Consequently, the desires of civilized humans lead at most to technological knowledge and false claims of expertise for the sake of celebrity. Rousseau's argument is that civilized humans have desires that lead to either narrow or fraudulent knowledge, whereas natural humans have neither real desires nor real knowledge. In this light, the account of Jean-Jacques's theoretical activity inspired by vanity provides little ground for optimism about the possibility of a successful understanding of the principles of human nature, an understanding that is neither technically useful nor likely to lead to acclaim.

While desire for celebrity hinders the theoretical life, it does not prevent artistic or creative activity. In fact, such a desire is very likely to stimulate the imagination. Because composing involves making a fiction, it is not opposed to the activity of the imagination. In Part One Rousseau consistently describes the exercise of his creative imagination as inspired by his desire for celebrity, but he never shows it leading to any production outside his imagination. This now changes in Book VII, where he discusses his first major artistic composition, the opera *Les Muses galantes*.[12] The subject of this opera, the relation between poets and their critics, derives directly from its author's desire for celebrity. Jean-Jacques finds it easy to identify with his characters. In describing the composition of his first act, which was about Tasso, Rousseau says, "I was Tasso for the moment" (I, 294). It is the "sublime and proud sentiments" of Tasso that inspire him to create, but it is also noteworthy that his desire for celebrity makes him imitate a famous poet.[13]

The desire for celebrity may be a motive for artistic composition, but

11. Rousseau refers to playing chess and memorizing poetry as his activities during this period (I, 287–88).

12. Rousseau had already written *Narcisse*, but he gives no account of its composition (I, 120).

13. In the final version Rousseau replaces the Tasso section with one on Hesiod, under whose guise he presents himself (I, 334–35).

it does not guarantee success. Vanity and greed always entail thinking about oneself, one's interest, and how one appears to others; at least this particular act of composing requires Jean-Jacques to forget about himself temporarily and to project himself into Tasso. Although his artistic activity has the aim of securing celebrity, Jean-Jacques's acts of composition take place while he is absorbed in his work rather than while he is calculating how to please others. The exclusive attention to winning fame would stifle the absorption in an imaginary world necessary for creativity. Both the *Letter to d'Alembert* and the *First Discourse* argue that the dependence of an artist on his audience has a corrupting effect, not only on the audience, whose taste is pandered to rather than improved, but also on the work of art, which is formed by a calculating desire for success. That Rousseau argues that almost all contemporary arts suffer from this debasement and that all art encounters this danger does not mean that no other sort of art is possible. The popular success of art that can avoid this danger, however, is dependent on a chance correspondence with public taste.

This sort of artistic composition does not, however, require the extraordinary conditions that make knowledge possible. Imitative art requires no recapturing of what is natural, because imitation is the characteristic of social humans. The creative imagination and the ability to transport oneself into another are both civilized acquisitions. It would not be too much of an exaggeration to say that, by virtue of their departure from natural wholeness and self-sufficiency, all civilized humans are creative artists to a small degree; that is, they all live in worlds formed by their imaginations. Rousseau claims that they differ from artistic composers only by the relative weakness of their imaginative gifts. They do not create images so much as recombine images given to them by others, and they produce no work of art.[14] Thus, while Rousseau argues against any natural or artificial ground for a theoretical life, he shows a basis in the psychology of civilized humans for a life of artistic creation.[15]

This discussion begins to illustrate that Rousseau's presentation of human nature can cause a profound skepticism about the possibility of anything like the traditional account of the philosophic life as repre-

14. This account should be compared with Rousseau's description of the composition of *Julie* in Book IX.

15. Rousseau does make one statement that is compatible with the idea that knowledge comes from imitation (II, 1128). He refers to his studies "with" Leibniz, Newton, Locke, and others.

sented by Socrates. At the same time, this presentation raises the status of the artistic life by demonstrating both the ways in which imaginative activity is a universal characteristic of civilized humans and the ways in which great artists carry this imaginative ability to an extreme degree of development. It must be kept in mind, however, that Rousseau's presentation of human nature claims to be rationally justifiable or philosophic. Therefore, to substantiate his claim about the near impossibility of a theoretical understanding unwarped by vanity or interest, he must show that this near impossibility is nevertheless realizable in his own case; that is, he must show that his own artificial imagination and amour-propre do not stand in the way of his acquisition of knowledge.

Imagination, the Political Order, and Nature

Jean-Jacques begins his discovery of nature during his stay in Venice, which is also reported in Book VII. Because he becomes wrapped up in his pride at this point, he begins to make this discovery largely in spite of himself. One might say that it is forced on him or occurs by accident. It is forced on him in the sense that his ambition obliges him to encounter the injustice of the existing political order. By itself, however, this encounter would lead to resentment rather than to the discovery of nature, unless an unpredictable event made Jean-Jacques confront quite directly the problem of nature and convention. In this sense his discovery is an accident. Even at the conclusion of this stage, nature is only a problem for Jean-Jacques. Yet another accident is required before he can discover the solution.

Jean-Jacques unwittingly begins his encounter with the political order when he interrupts his composing to take on the more lucrative position of secretary to M. de Montaigu, the French ambassador to Venice. Even in making this career change, he is still concerned with wealth and celebrity. He begins with extensive bargaining over salary. And once he arrives in Venice, he does not "flee occasions to make [himself] known" (I, 307). In short, he leaves for Venice with the same vanity he had in Paris.

Although Rousseau admits that the desire for fortune and celebrity enter into the choice of this position, on the whole he contends that pride takes over in the performance of his duty. Jean-Jacques's citizenlike pride comes from the fact that as secretary he is attending to someone else's concerns rather than his own. He participates "in the dignity of a sort of representation" (I, 301). He is not Jean-Jacques

Rousseau but Jean-Jacques Rousseau, representative of the sovereignty of France. It is the identification with the sovereignty of France that allows him to reacquire his uncharacteristic boldness.[16] For example, he is obliged to confront a Venetian theater owner in the matter of a contract dispute over the services of some performers. He gains entrance to the home of the theater owner by appearing as a masked lady (I, 302). Dropping the disguise, he names himself representative of his sovereign majesty and demands justice, which is quickly given.[17] In this instance, unlike his earlier impostures, Jean-Jacques is successful, because even behind his disguise he is the representative of someone other than himself. His own vanity and interest are not at stake here, although his pride is. He says that when he removed his mask he named himself, but the self he named is identical to his representative function. The necessity or possibility of speaking for someone else appears to grant a freedom and boldness lacking when Jean-Jacques speaks for himself.

Jean-Jacques's skill as a representative brings him the prospect of rising in the diplomatic corps. His talents and pride in performing his duties point to a political order in which his merit will find its true place. Yet Rousseau presents his relationship with his superior, the corrupt, tyrannical, and foolish M. de Montaigu, as destroying the harmony between him and the sovereign he represents. Montaigu persistently attempts to control Jean-Jacques's actions and his composition of dispatches to the French foreign ministry. In itself this is unexceptionable; Montaigu's position as ambassador obviously makes him more directly the representative of the king than a mere secretary could be. Montaigu's interference, however, is always motivated by greed and petty vanity. Thus the harmony between a sovereign and his dutiful representative is destroyed by the self-interest of a corrupt official.

Jean-Jacques is confronted by an opposition between the conventional political order and the order justified by natural talents, as he was at the beginning of his stay at the Gouvon household. After concluding his description of M. de Montaigu's unjust treatment, Rousseau says,

> The justice and uselessness of my complaint left in my soul a germ of indignation against our foolish institutions in which the true public

16. Jean-Jacques has a similar boldness when he represents the so-called Archimandrite of Jerusalem (I, 155–56).

17. On Jean-Jacques as a representative, see Williams, *Romantic Autobiography*, pp. 190–94.

good and true justice are always sacrificed to I know not what apparent
order, destructive in effect of all order, and which only adds the sanc-
tion of public authority to the oppression of the feeble and to the
iniquity of the strong. (I, 327)[18]

This description of the social order lies clearly at the base of Rousseau's
lessons, which teach that humans are naturally good but corrupted by
society. At this stage Jean-Jacques has not yet gained this understanding. He has only the germ of the understanding. In his experience with
the Gouvon household it was his imaginary hopes that prevented him
from overcoming the opposition between his conventional place and
the one warranted by his talents. Before arriving at his understanding
of nature, Jean-Jacques must come to terms with the various oppositions among nature, convention, and his own imagination.

   Jean-Jacques's attempt to grapple with these issues is the theme of
a long digression about "the celebrated amusements" of Venice, music
and women (I, 313). This part of Book VII is given special significance
by Rousseau's use of the term *"confession,"* a term that appears only
rarely in the book as a whole (I, 316).[19] This is his fourth and final
specific confession or admission. At the beginning of one part of this
confession he says, "Whoever you may be who wishes to know a man,
dare to read the two or three pages that follow, you will know J. J.
Rousseau to the full" (I, 320). With this Rousseau asserts that this
section most clearly reveals the subject of the *Confessions* as a whole.
This section of two or three pages and its surrounding context should
be considered the heart of the *Confessions*.

   The digression as a whole contains five different steps or incidents.
The first step calls attention to Jean-Jacques's imagination; the second
shows the ability of his imagination to transform the world; the third
(which begins the "confession") begins to show conflicts among imagination, a natural desire, and a social institution; the fourth brings this
conflict to a crisis; and the fifth (which concludes the "confession")
shows a very tentative resolution of the conflict. Together these steps
present the crux of the conflict between nature and a corrupt society
and the imagination's reponse to this conflict. Because of its centrality
to the major issues of the *Confessions*, this very short section must be
examined in great detail.

----

18. Critics often attribute the origin of Rousseau's career as a thinker to his resentment over this experience; see, for example, I, 1404–5. Rousseau himself presents his
anger as a barrier to his thought.
   19. See "Confession and Rousseau's Autobiographical Project" in Chapter 1.

The first step in the digression is a brief account of Jean-Jacques's friends, which quickly turns to the subject of their common enjoyment of Italian music. Rousseau begins his discussion of Italian music by admitting that he arrived in Venice with a prejudice in favor of French music. He is capable of being cured of this prejudice, he says, because he has "received from nature that sensitivity of tact against which prejudices do not hold" (I, 314). In Book I this same sensitivity to music was one of the earliest signs of his aroused imagination. It is this sensitivity of tact that makes him susceptible to all forms of stimulation and therefore leaves him open to the charms of the particularly stimulating Italian music. He describes the ability of Italian music to stimulate his imagination by telling the story of his falling asleep at a concert and being awakened by a beautiful song. He exclaims, "What an awakening! What rapture! My first idea was to believe myself in paradise" (I, 314). Melody leads his imagination out of this world into paradise. He indicates the necessity for unreflective listening for this effect when he says that he acquired the score of the piece that awakened him "but it was not on my paper as in my memory." Rousseau goes even farther, however, by concluding, "Never can this divine air be executed except in my head, as it was in effect the day that it awakened me." A repeat performance of the piece would be unable to reproduce its initial effect. The mediation by a performance or, worse, by a printed score would spoil the effect because it would interfere with the immediacy of Jean-Jacques's recollection of his images.[20]

This first step in Rousseau's digression prepares for the second. The opening lines of the song, *"Conservami la bella/Che si m'accende il cor"* (the beautiful one protected me who thus inflames my heart), reveal a connection between his ideas of paradise and love. The second step in his account concerns music sung by young girls from the Venetian *scuole* (houses of charity) with whose voices Jean-Jacques falls in love. Rousseau now argues that the music performed by these girls is much superior to that found in the opera. Thus this second step presents the same theme of music and love at a higher level.

Paradise itself is not missing from this step. Rousseau says that while listening to the singing he imagines the concealed singers to be "angels of beauty" (I, 315). On meeting the angels he finds that each has a "notable flaw"; one is horrible, another one-eyed (*borgne*), a third disfigured by smallpox. Soon, however, Jean-Jacques recalls their singing and declares, "In the end, my manner of seeing them changed so well,

20. See the discussion of imitation in Chapter 1.

that I left almost in love with all these ugly girls." The music in his head restores the image of paradise. As a result, when he hears them sing again he perseveres "in finding them beautiful in spite of [his] eyes." In this case, unlike the preceding one, a real performance does not spoil the effect of the imagination. It is not the real singing, however, that plays the crucial role in restoring the illusion; it is Jean-Jacques's memory of his original image of the girls that allows him to forget their ugliness even when they are not singing. Again music stimulates the imagination, but once stimulated it is the imagination itself rather than music which guides the way Jean-Jacques sees the world.

In the first step, nothing outside the music counters its effect. In the second step, Jean-Jacques's imagination uses music to transform natural ugliness and deformity into celestial beauty. Once stimulated, his imagination is set back only temporarily by an opposition between the illusion it creates and the world. It is stimulated by the initial sensory perception of the sound of music but then breaks free of the senses. Consequently, his imagination can give an agreeable form to the naturally deformed. In the first step, nature is absent. In the second, it is decidedly inferior to imagination.

The third step in the digression begins the so-called confession. This three-part confession is the final and most revealing of the specific confessions in the work. Each of its three parts concerns Jean-Jacques's relations with women, but not with wards of society like the orphans of the *scuole*. Instead, these parts are about his involvement with social outcasts, prostitutes and kept women. With the first two parts Rousseau moves from the natural ugliness of the choirgirls to a conventional and moral ugliness that overcomes natural beauty. Jean-Jacques begins to observe, with the first glimmerings of understanding, the way the political order can corrupt nature. Specifically, he sees one of the ways sexual relations, the only natural relations between humans, can be transformed by social life.

The first incident in this confession is Jean-Jacques's reluctant visit to a prostitute at the urging of Montaigu's lackeys. Rousseau mentions that his own low position as a humble secretary places girls of reputable families out of his reach. Because he is at the bottom rung of the social ladder, he can be badgered into seeking his pleasure among those who live within society but as social outcasts. In a way, prostitution promises to reduce sexual desire to its purely physical or natural component. It severs the senses from the imagination. Certainly Jean-Jacques's imagination is not romantically engaged during his visit to la Padoana. Although she is beautiful, her beauty fails to stimulate Jean-Jacques's imagination. Even her singing has no effect on him. His fear of venereal disease and distaste for prostitutes are enough to calm the most romantic imagination. The same fear and distaste also destroy his more natural physical sexual desire (*Emile*, 231). After some halfhearted preliminaries, Jean-Jacques attempts to leave, paying la Padoana for her time, "but she had the singular scruple of not wanting what she had not earned" (I, 317). With this intrusion of business concerns, Rousseau indicates that prostitution not only reduces sex to a physical act but also turns the physical act into a business transaction. He shows that the promise of a simple and straightforward satisfaction of a natural need is a fraud. Natural sexuality satisfies physical needs immediately without the intervention of money. The purely artificial intervention complicates even the natural need. In this instance, the reader is obliged to picture an act of intercourse between la Padoana, satisfying her scruples and congratulating herself for being an honest tradeswoman, and Jean-Jacques, timidly obeying her and already believing that he feels the onset of disease. Jean-Jacques has descended far from the imaginary paradise elicited by Italian music. The picture of love in this story is the antithesis of the picture in the previous story. The choirgirls show the triumph of the imagination over the senses. La Padoana offers the triumph of money over both the imagination and the senses.[21] In the final analysis, the social institution of prostitution is the enemy of both the rarefied pleasures of the imagination and the simple pleasures of nature.

The fourth and most important step in the digression, the central part of the confession, is Rousseau's account of his encounter with the lovely courtesan Zulietta.[22] It is a part of this story that Rousseau says will allow the reader to know him to the full. This story also exposes the contradictions among nature, convention, and imagination to the greatest degree. In the earlier steps, imagination is presented in a favorable light, both as an opponent of corrupt social institutions and as an embellisher of imperfect nature. Now Rousseau reveals the imagination as a co-conspirator with society against nature. This revelation, to repeat, is only dimly perceived by Jean-Jacques. Nevertheless, it later serves as the precondition of the discovery of his philosophic system.

21. On the opposition of prostitution and masturbation, see *Emile*, 333–34.
22. Rousseau connects this incident with the first one in the digression by referring to paradise. He connects it with the second incident by searching for a "secret flaw" (I, 321) corresponding to the "notable flaws" of the girls in the choir.

In spite of the similarity in theme to the visit to la Padoana, Jean-Jacques's adventure with Zulietta is "of a very different sort both as to its origin and as to its effects" (I, 317–18). He does not visit her reluctantly; rather, he is introduced to her in return for a service rendered to a French ship captain. In addition, in spite of sharing some of la Padoana's well-developed sense of business ethics, Zulietta does not behave at all like a prostitute. In fact, she insists that she is paid less for her services as a prostitute than for the boredom she suffers at having to be tender to people she does not love. "Nothing is more just" than such compensation (I, 319). Moreover, she proudly declares that she will accept none of the insults that prostitutes must endure. She explains her habit of keeping pistols on her dressing table by saying, "I will not miss the first one who lacks respect for me" (*je ne manquerai pas le premier qui me manquera*). Her pride coexists with a sort of vanity, but she is not moved at all by avarice. In short, because she so thoroughly avoids the appearance of a prostitute, Zulietta is capable of entrancing Jean-Jacques with her extraordinary charms.[23]

The form that Jean-Jacques's infatuation takes shows the power of his imagination even more than does his episode with the choirgirls: "The young virgins of the cloister are less fresh, the beauties of the seraglio are less lovely, the houris of paradise are less piquant. Never has such sweet enjoyment offered itself to the heart and senses of a mortal" (I, 320). Zulietta appeals both to the heart, or imagination, and to the senses. She combines the appeal to the imagination found in Italian music with the appeal to the senses offered by Mme de Larnage. Jean-Jacques imagined the girls of the *scuole* as angels and he saw Mme de Larnage as a passionate woman, but he combines the two in Zulietta by seeing her as even more than a houri of paradise. Rousseau emphasizes the harmony between his senses and his imagination by warning the reader not to attempt to imagine her charms because "you would remain too far from the truth." It may be Jean-Jacques's unusually powerful imagination that makes her surpass virgins, beauties of the seraglio, and houris, but it is nature that has made her more beautiful than the reader's more feeble imagination can conceive.[24]

After portraying the agreement between his heart and his senses,[25]

<hr />

23. Jean-Jacques's uncharacteristic freedom in the beginning of his relations with Zulietta can be explained by her identification of him as her former lover M. de Brémond (I, 318–19).

24. There is external confirmation of Rousseau's description; see I, 1320.

25. Zulietta thus combines the attractions of Mlles Goton and de Vulson (I, 27, 1247).

Rousseau introduces the disharmonious element of his head. He is unable to taste "fully and completely" the happiness offered by Zulietta: nature "has put into my wretched head the poison of this ineffable happiness, the appetite for which she has put in my heart" (I, 320). His senses are by no means the source of his problem. His heart, or imagination, has the appetite for paradise. It is his head, or intelligence, that poisons the happiness his imagination seeks.[26] It is the understanding of the oppositions among his head, his senses, and his heart which Rousseau says is the key to the knowledge of his nature. This is the point at which he says, "Whoever you may be who wishes to know a man, dare to read the two or three pages that follow, you will know J. J. Rousseau to the full." These pages are the ones that most completely fulfill the purpose of the *Confessions* as a whole.

Those who dare to proceed find that the poisoning observation made by Jean-Jacques's "head" concerns Zulietta's social status as a prostitute. This status conflicts with "the divinity" Jean-Jacques believes he sees in her person. This opposition between image and reality can be compared to a similar opposition in Jean-Jacques's experience with the girls of the *scuole*. His image of these girls as angels clashes with their natural ugliness and deformity. Rousseau emphasizes that the girls are not simply unattractive to him; their flaws are the result of illness and disfigurement. Their imperfections are natural imperfections. Thus this opposition is between Jean-Jacques's image and nature. In the case of Zulietta, the opposition is between his image of her beauty and her social standing.

The mature Rousseau who wrote the *First Discourse* and *Second Discourse* might be expected to resolve this contradiction by indicting the social institutions that so degrade nature. The thirty-two-year-old Jean-Jacques is unaware of the political character of the contradiction. He has not yet left his diplomatic post and still hopes to advance in the world. He believes that, although Zulietta cannot be aware of his merit, his talents will secure him the place he deserves. Because he is not yet cured of his ambitions, Jean-Jacques's observations throw him into confusion instead of leading directly to an indictment of society: "Suddenly in spite of the flames that devoured me, I feel a mortal cold running through my veins, my legs tremble, and ready to faint, I sit down and cry like a child" (I, 320).

---

26. For a good discussion of this opposition in relation to Rousseau's influence on later writers, see Duffy, *Rousseau in England*, p. 136.

Jean-Jacques's head forces him to reflect on the paradox of how "the masterpiece of nature and love" can be simultaneously "a miserable trollop given up to the public" (I, 321). Two alternative explanations occur to him. One is that his heart has fascinated his senses. According to this explanation the imagination is at fault, for it conceals the truth that Zulietta is "an unworthy slut." Unlike Rousseau, who emphasizes the harmony between Zulietta's natural charms and his image of her, Jean-Jacques considers the possibility of a complete rupture between his imagination and nature. The other possible explanation is that Zulietta possesses a "secret flaw" that belies her appearance. According to this explanation Jean-Jacques's senses are at fault—they are unable to detect the truth behind the appearances. In neither of these explanations does Jean-Jacques consider the possibility that Zulietta does not deserve to be a prostitute, that she is what she appears to be but has been degraded by an unjust political order.

Faced with the alternative of blaming either his imagination or his senses, Jean-Jacques decides that the fault is in his senses. In spite of his experience with the choirgirls, he does not believe that his imagination deceives his senses in this case. Therefore his senses must have led his imagination astray. If his imagination is wrong, it must be because Zulietta has deceived him. As a result of his decision to blame his senses, Jean-Jacques begins to search for the secret flaw with "a singular application of mind." Zulietta is not oblivious to this novel spectacle of tears and intense scrutiny. To reassure herself she looks in the mirror, which reflects only her appearance and reveals no secret flaw. Having reassured herself, she reassures Jean-Jacques. Just as his senses are about to triumph over his reason, he notices, or thinks he notices, that one of her breasts has a malformed nipple (*elle avait un téton borgne*).[27] After closer examination he decides that this flaw "pertains to some notable natural vice." Thus he finds a natural justification for Zulietta's social position. Zulietta's appearance may have temporarily deceived him, but social convention has relegated her to her proper place.

In his experience with la Padoana, Jean-Jacques's imagination failed to transform reality into a romantic image. Her open commercial concern disengaged his imagination completely. With Zulietta, Jean-

27. The term "*borgne*" links this incident to that of the girls of the *scuole*, one of whom was one-eyed (I, 315). The meaning of the term as applied to Zulietta is somewhat unclear. Rousseau's description emphasizes the inconspicuousness of the flaw. To the best of my knowledge only one critic claims to understand how Zulietta acquired this deformity; see Huizinga, *Self-Made Saint*, p. 85.

Jacques thinks that he has also "disenchanted" the romantic image, but Rousseau shows that he has merely replaced one image with another.[28] Describing his impression at the time, Rousseau says, "I saw as clear as day that, in the most charming person whose image I could form, I held in my arms only a sort of monster, the outcast of nature, of men and of love" (I, 321–22). Zulietta had earlier appeared to be the masterpiece of nature; now she appears to be its outcast. Jean-Jacques has restored the harmony of nature, convention, and imagination by seeing Zulietta as a monster. He sees this "as clear as day," but Rousseau refers to this judgment as a "stupidity" and an "extravagance." To disenchant Zulietta is to see her as an attractive woman with a slight deformity. It is only Jean-Jacques's imagination that turns her into a monster, just as it earlier turned her into something more than a houri. The difference between the two cases is only that in the latter his imagination is pulled into the service of the social order that degrades Zulietta.

When Jean-Jacques adds to his earlier spectacle by seeking to discuss the secret flaw with Zulietta, she responds by making an appointment for a later date which she has no intention of keeping. She is disdainful of her unique client, but her failure to shoot him on the spot shows that she does not find his behavior insulting. That she does not find him boring is indicated by Rousseau's failure to mention paying her.[29] She dismisses him with the remark, "Zanetto, give up the ladies and study mathematics." She thereby shows her judgment of the proper study for a lover who is apparently obsessed with the careful measurement of the symmetry of her body. Like Rousseau himself she regards Jean-Jacques's head as the cause of his failure.

Zulietta is correct in her diagnosis, although perhaps less perceptive about the proper cure. It is Jean-Jacques's head that has turned his imagination in the wrong direction. He has failed to find the proper solution to the riddle posed by Zulietta's station. These pages reveal Jean-Jacques's character to the fullest because they show him attempting to understand the operation of his imagination and its relation to the world. Rousseau repeatedly refers to his efforts at reasoning in this section—to "what passed in [his] head at the moment," to his "reflections," to his "searching in [his] head," to "turning and returning the

28. For two alternative interpretations of Zulietta which develop this point, see Schwartz, *Sexual Politics*, pp. 103–6. For a discussion of the whole of Book VII, see Madeleine B. Ellis, *Rousseau's Venetian Story* (Baltimore, Md.: Johns Hopkins University Press, 1966).

29. It is possible that Zulietta had already been paid by the ship captain.

idea." Unlike earlier presentations of mental activity in the *Confessions*, this section reveals Jean-Jacques attempting to understand the world instead of flying to an imaginary world. That he fails to avoid such a flight in this case is an indication of the depth of the problem of self-understanding. The inability to understand oneself is a serious obstacle to a correct understanding of the world, and of politics in particular.

Rousseau's presentation of this scene encourages the reader to draw the political conclusions that Jean-Jacques fails to reach; that is, it encourages the reader to blame society for the degradation of Zulietta. The sole positive step made by Jean-Jacques himself is represented by his confusion after the encounter. Days later he is still "uneasy in spite of what [he] had done to reconcile the perfection of the adorable girl with the indignity of her station" (I, 322). What is distinctive and important about this event is that it forces Jean-Jacques to reflect on his fantastic image of the world and leaves him troubled by doubts. Rousseau's "confession" does not teach Jean-Jacques the truth it teaches the reader, but it does leave him more open to learning.

The final story of both the digression as a whole and the confessions about women concerns what Rousseau calls a "simple project" he undertakes with his friend Carrio. The two men enter a partnership to purchase an eleven-to-twelve-year-old girl being sold by her mother. Jean-Jacques seems on the verge of collaborating in the social corruption he failed to understand in Zulietta's case. The object of this project is to rear the girl to serve as their mistress. They propose to educate her to be accomplished and charming. In effect, they propose to overcome the disproportion between image and reality, to force reality to correspond to their image of perfection. Their plans are disrupted by two things: Jean-Jacques's rupture with M. de Montaigu forces him to leave Venice, and, more fundamental, the men find that their images of little Anzoletta change faster than she does: "Insensibly my heart became attached to the little Anzoletta, but with a paternal attachment, with which the senses have so little part that to the degree that it increased it would have been less possible for me to make them enter, and I felt that I would have horror at approaching this girl after she became nubile, as an abominable incest" (I, 323). This naive attempt to force the world to suit imaginary desires is doomed to failure because the possession of the desire does not stand outside the world. The imagination cannot find a resting place or fulcrum to act on the world without being acted on. Jean-Jacques's desires shift because of his efforts to realize them. He begins by attempting to unite his senses and his heart, but in the end his heart overcomes his senses altogether.

Considered in its entirety, this digression reveals the problem of the *Confessions* as a whole: Rousseau portrays civilized humans as prisoners of images created by their own imaginations, which have been stimulated and directed by their communities; but this picture does not show how one can free oneself from the enslaving images to the point of understanding the enslavement. Rousseau's account excludes the possibility of any natural desire to know or ability to recognize the truth that could remedy this situation. To use a Platonic image, Rousseau presents civilized humans as living in caves constituted by the imagination. Citizens of good regimes and corrupt humans alike live in caves. What Rousseau needs to explain is the accessibility of the natural world outside the cave to those inside. The narrative of Zulietta shows the problem as clearly as one could desire. The Jean-Jacques within the narrative is trapped by his imagination and can find no way out. He seems totally lacking in knowledge of how institutions (in the broad sense of education) distort his own perception of things. To use the language of the *First Discourse*, he lacks a criterion to distinguish the natural from the conventional particularly in his own case. Without this criterion he is doomed to move from image to image, from houri to monster, in his attempt to explain the disharmony in what he sees. On the other hand, Rousseau the narrator clearly understands the complex relations among the imagination, nature, and convention. He constructs the stories in the digression, as he constructs the *Confessions* as a whole, to reveal these relations to the reader, to allow the reader to distinguish the natural from the acquired. But what is his criterion for distinguishing and how does he acquire it? What is the connection between the Jean-Jacques within the narrative and the Rousseau who constructs the narrative? How does one move from the former to the latter? These questions indicate that Rousseau is beginning to close in on the major issue of the *Confessions*. He is about to explain how someone as thoroughly denatured as Jean-Jacques can return to a stable quasi-natural condition or, failing this, to explain how he can attain an understanding of a natural condition.

Book VIII: "I Saw Another Universe"

Book VIII presents, among other things, Jean-Jacques's discovery of his system. It shows the beginning of both his life as a thinker and his fame. Both beginnings represent remarkable changes in his life. The sudden transformation of a minor music teacher and failed diplomat into an important thinker must come as a great surprise, and Rousseau emphasizes the suddenness and the completeness of this transformation. It would be a mistake to think that the earlier events in the *Confessions* show the transformation to be inevitable. Nevertheless, these events do set the stage for Jean-Jacques's discovery. Accordingly, we can summarize one thread of his development to this point and then move on to the precise nature of his discovery.

In the *Letter to Beaumont* Rousseau gives an important indication of how his early life contributed to the discovery of his system by describing what he calls "the history of my ideas" (IV, 966). This history gives both less and more information than the *Confessions*. It gives less in that it ignores the most important aspect of the *Confessions*, his history of feelings. It gives more in that it provides a lucid account of the development of a certain line of thought in Rousseau's life. He says,

> As soon as I was in a condition to observe men, I watched them act, and I heard them speak; then, seeing that their actions did not resemble their discourses at all, I sought the reason for this dissimilarity, and I found that for them being and appearance, being two things as different as acting and speaking, this second difference was the cause of the other, and itself had a cause which remained for me to seek. (IV, 966)[30]

This "history" identifies three stages: the observation of a contradiction, the discovery of an underlying contradiction, and the beginning of a search for a still deeper cause. Rousseau goes on to say that he found this cause in the opposition between "our social order" and nature over which it tyrannizes.

Within the history of feelings given by the *Confessions*, Jean-Jacques's discovery of the dissimilarity between action and speech begins with the Lamberciers' mistaken punishment of him while they claim to be benevolent (see Chapter 3). This "discovery," as we have seen, is based on a mistake on Jean-Jacques's part, but it opens him to the possibility of dissimulation. He has discovered the underlying split between being and appearance by the time he makes himself appear to be innocent during his false accusation of Marion. He begins his search for the deeper cause of this split after his confrontation with the disproportion between Zulietta's being and her appearance. He could have learned about the opposition between nature and the tyrannical social order from this confrontation, but he fails to do so, apparently because his ambition

---

30. I am indebted to Arthur Melzer for calling this passage to my attention.

continues to tie him to the social order. Even his quarrel with M. de Montaigu fails to open his eyes. In this instance his anger is directed toward a single injustice, and one connected with his own private interest. His ambition has met a check; it has not been cured.

Rousseau gives a precise description of his ideas at this time in a passage in the *Dialogues*. The character Rousseau says of Jean-Jacques, "He glimpsed a secret opposition between the constitution of man and that of our societies, but it was rather a dumb feeling, a confused notion than a clear and developed judgment. Public opinion had subjugated him too much for him to dare object against such unanimous decisions" (I, 828). It is this dumb feeling that is clarified and developed in Book VIII. For Jean-Jacques to make the discovery, it is first necessary for his amour-propre to become less subjugated to public opinion.

Book VII concludes with Jean-Jacques's return from his life of proud service at Venice to his life in the world of vainglory at Paris. In this context Rousseau refers to his "extinguished ambition" (I, 331). It might seem from this that the disappointment of ambition had been sufficient to cure his amour-propre.[31] Rousseau's elaboration shows, however, that civilized desires cannot be reformed entirely by disillusionment of this sort and that this extinguishing of ambition represents at best a small step toward naturalness. He concludes that his "projects of ambition" failed because of his dependence on other people (I, 329), but the rejection of dependence does not in itself entail a rejection of ambition. Rousseau continues, "I resolved no longer to attach myself to anyone, but to remain in independence by relying upon my talents." Jean-Jacques is still interested in celebrity but wishes to gain a celebrity less dependent on the whims of others.[32] Rousseau also claims to have required "a lively sentiment which refilled [his] heart" to replace his ambition. To the irritable sensitivity of a civilized human, the extinguishing of one passion merely calls forth another. In this case, affection is meant to take the place of ambition and Jean-Jacques begins his long relationship with Thérèse le Vasseur.[33] Thérèse is meant to be a new Mme de Warens; Rousseau says, "I found in Thérèse the supple-

31. Socrates seems to present such disappointments as sufficient at *Republic*, 496a-e.

32. In terms of the argument of the *Second Discourse*, success based on talents is closer to natural equality than is success based on convention alone. This success nevertheless is "the first step toward inequality and, at the same time, toward vice" (*Discourses*, 149).

33. This relationship with Thérèse also resembles the habitual preromantic ties of the first families described in the *Second Discourse*. See also Schwartz, *Sexual Politics*, pp. 104–7.

ment which I needed" (I, 332). A supplement is a substitute for what is
desired, it is not equal to the thing itself. While he here insists on the
completeness he receives from this supplement, he later gives reason to
modify this assessment.

Even in the present context Rousseau does not claim that his affection for Thérèse caused him to abandon his quest for success based on
talents. Immediately after describing their meeting, he says that their
"retired life" was very advantageous for his work (I, 333). This work
consists of completing the opera begun before his trip to Venice and
then entering into an uneasy collaboration with Voltaire and Rameau
on their *Fêtes de Ramire*.[34] In both activities Jean-Jacques finds the success deserved by his talents thwarted by Rameau. Thus he learns that,
in a social context in which success depends on personal dependence, it
is impossible for talent to make its way alone. He concludes, "I abandoned every project of advancement and of glory, and no longer
dreaming about the true or false talents by which I prospered so little, I
consecrated my time and my cares to providing my subsistence and that
of my Thérèse" (I, 342). Jean-Jacques sees that even true talents depend on recognition. There is no fair competition between true and
false talents. Now the rejection of ambition seems complete.

After his return from Venice, Jean-Jacques's passions seem to develop in stages that move him closer to nature quite against his will. After
losing his desire to advance through influential people, his first resort is
to attempt to advance by talent alone. When this is shown to be impossible, he rejects ambition altogether. This rejection is based more on Jean-
Jacques's experience of failures than on his understanding. His ambition
persists in looking for an avenue to success only to be thwarted by social
institutions. His rejection of ambition does not occur because persistent
natural desires win out in a struggle against artificial desires. On the
contrary, the artificial desires simply exhaust themselves in a struggle
with social institutions. Jean-Jacques now understands that ambition can
lead to dependence and failure, but he does not yet understand that it is
an unnatural passion.

That the rejection of ambition does not lead immediately to a real
independence is shown by Jean-Jacques's formation of two new friend-
ships. Diderot and Grimm, his new friends, are intimately connected
with Jean-Jacques's discovery of nature and his attempt at personal

---

34. It is the hostility of Rameau that Rousseau depicts in his autobiographical Hesi-
odic act of *Les Muses galantes* (I, 334).

reform. Diderot instigates Jean-Jacques's literary career and Grimm leads a conspiracy that determines Jean-Jacques's personal fate. In both instances friendship complicates Jean-Jacques's relations with the social order. His desire for friends catches him in a web of dependence. The conspiracy is one of the themes of Chapter 6. The beginning of Jean-Jacques's literary career can be discussed here.

Diderot is the occasional cause of Jean-Jacques's philosophic and literary career in two ways: he precipitates the event that gives Jean-Jacques something to write about and he encourages him to begin writing. While walking to visit Diderot imprisoned at Vincennes, Jean-Jacques reads the question posed for a prize by the Academy of Dijon: "Has the restoration of the sciences and arts tended to purify morals?"[35] On reading the question Jean-Jacques experiences a "sudden inspiration" (I, 1135): "I saw another universe and I became another man" (I, 351). On his arrival at Vincennes he reports his discovery to Diderot, who encourages him to enter the essay contest.[36] It is this inspiration that at last gives Jean-Jacques the solution to the split between appearance and being which troubled him with Zulietta.

Rousseau's assertion that he saw another universe and became another man raises two questions: What was the universe he saw? Who did he become? Another pair of questions complement these: What was the universe that he had seen before? Who was he before he changed? The questions about the two universes concern the relation between the world of the imagination and the natural world. The questions about his identity concern Jean-Jacques's ability to transform himself into another person; that is, it concerns his amour-propre rather than his imagination simply.

That Jean-Jacques sees another universe is nothing new within the *Confessions*. In the course of his life he has seen many "universes," some of his own making and some made by his education. Each has been the product of either his consciously directed or his unconsciously active imagination. He saw a universe in which he was Scaevola or Hannibal. He saw a universe in which his teachers were willful torturers. He saw a universe in which Zulietta was a divinity, and then another in which she was a monster. Rousseau's use of the term "universe" here marks a distinction between this more consistent and comprehensive analysis

---

35. On Rousseau's alteration of this question, see *Discourses*, 66–67.
36. For a balanced account of Diderot's contribution to the *First Discourse*, see Trousson, *Socrate*, pp. 105–24.

and his earlier descriptions of imaginative activity. In the early cases
Jean-Jacques is torn between conflicting images of the world, between
his romanticism and his Romanness. Later, he is simply confused about
the disproportion between Zulietta's appearance and her real condition. With this "sudden inspiration," the contradictions, both within
Jean-Jacques and outside him, disappear. In the "Letters to Malesherbes" Rousseau says,

> If I had ever been able to write one quarter of what I saw under that tree
> with what clarity I would have made all the contradictions of the social
> system seen, with what force I would have exposed all the abuses of our
> institutions, with what simplicity I would have demonstrated that man is
> naturally good and that it is by these institutions that men become bad.
> (I, 1135–36)

Jean-Jacques is now able to give precisely the sort of explanation that
eluded him in Zulietta's chamber. There he called nature and his imagination into question to explain the conflict between Zulietta's appearance and station. Now he realizes that if Zulietta is a monster it is
not because she is the outcast of nature but because she is the outcast of
society. In this new universe Jean-Jacques sees things as they are for the
first time.[37]

Comprehensiveness and consistency alone do not prove that the new
universe is the true one. It could be another imaginative creation like
those Rousseau objects to in the systems of other philosophers who are
frequently led astray precisely by their mania for comprehensiveness
and consistency, their *esprit de système*. Alternatively, the new universe
could be like the ones made by lovers whose imagination transforms the
appearance of both each other and the world.[38] The philosopher and the

37. Rousseau's inspiration on the road to Vincennes should be compared with Paul's
experience on the road to Damascus; see Acts IX. Two important differences should be
considered: Rousseau presents his experience as accidental rather than miraculous, and
his sudden clarity of vision contrasts with Paul's blindness.

38. The discovery of "another universe" repeats a formulation that Rousseau uses
elsewhere in his works. In the second preface of *Julie* Rousseau says, "Love is nothing but
an illusion, it makes for itself, so to speak, another universe" (II, 15). The sort of universe
made by love is nothing like a true picture of the world: "When it is at its peak, it sees its
object as perfect, it then makes it its idol; it places it in Heaven; and as the enthusiasm of
devotion borrows the language of love, then enthusiasm of love also borrows the language of devotion. It sees only paradise, angels, the virtues of the saints, the delights of
the celestial region" (II, 15–16). This passage connects the ways the imagination makes a
universe for itself when inspired by love or devotion. It also raises a question about the
nature of the relation between those universes made by enthusiasm and the other universe that Jean-Jacques sees in his inspiration.

lover make universes for themselves rather than seeing the real one. In short, the possibility of a comprehensive and consistent, but nevertheless false, view of the universe raises the question of whether this particular new universe is discovered by Jean-Jacques or made by him. This new universe is presented as having resolved Jean-Jacques's contradictory understanding of the world by dispelling his illusions. It is now necessary for Rousseau to show that he has not simply replaced one set of illusions with a more consistent set.[39]

This issue recurs later in Book VIII when Rousseau describes the composition of the *Second Discourse*, a major part in the gradual unfolding of his principles:

> In the forest, I sought, I found the image of the first times whose history I proudly traced; I made a clean sweep of the petty falsehoods of men, I dared to unveil to the nude their nature, to follow the progress of time and of the things which disfigured it, and comparing the man of man with the natural man, to show in its pretended perfection the true source of its miseries. (I, 388)

Rousseau begins by saying that he found the "image" of the first times, and continues by saying that he "unveiled" human nature. Unveiling to the nude suggests a direct contact with what is natural, but finding an image calls into question the directness of this contact. His claim seems to be that, in this discovery of an image, his imagination makes possible direct contact with human nature. This makes the truth of his understanding of nature depend on the accuracy of an image. For certainty, one would prefer the discovery to be derived from the direct contact with nature. In sum, Jean-Jacques's system stands in the same situation as the philosophic systems Rousseau attacks. It appears to be a rationally constructed image of the world, but neither its rationality nor its comprehensiveness proves that it is a correct image of the world. As I argued in Chapter 1, the personal character of the *Confessions*, compared, for example, to the general character of Hegel's *Phenomenology of Mind*, leaves Rousseau vulnerable to the charge that his system is radically dependent on the existence of a unique individual.

Although the accidental character of this discovery does pose a problem for the foundation of Rousseau's system, it is nevertheless required by the system itself. Unlike Hegel, Rousseau presents the

---

39. For interpretations that stress the role of the imagination in this discovery, see Eigeldinger, *Réalité*, pp. 146–47; Hartle, *Modern Self*, p. 118; Starobinski, *L'Oeil*, pp. 135–42; and Williams, *Romantic Autobiography*, pp. 2–3.

initial departure from the primitive stage (which Hegel calls sense-certainty and Rousseau calls the state of nature) as an accident that need not have occurred. This fateful accident is the cause of a radical gulf between naturalness and social life. Rousseau's system is devoted to demonstrating the barriers to bridging that gulf as much as it is to building the bridge. Because of its radicalness, the gulf can be crossed only by an accidental occurrence, a sudden inspiration. Although it does not provide the certainty promised by the *Phenomenology of Mind*, the accidental character of the inspiration is consistent with Rousseau's system as a whole. If the system is true, Rousseau can convince others of its truthfulness only by combining rational demonstration with attempts to set off sudden inspiration in his readers. Such a system is incapable of completely bridging the gap between plausibility and certainty. It must be, in some sense, "shot out of a pistol."[40]

A more decisive mark of the truth of Jean-Jacques's system would be its ability to return him to a natural or quasi-natural condition like the "age of happiness" described in Book VI. The attempt at such a return is the theme of the next chapter, but two events shortly after the inspiration dramatize how Jean-Jacques's discovery cures him of some of his imaginary views of the world. The first occurs during a visit from the now impoverished Mme de Warens. Rousseau asks, "Was this the same Mme de Warens formerly so brilliant to whom the Curé Pontverre had sent me? How my heart was broken!" (I, 391). It is true that Maman's condition had seriously deteriorated, but it is more important to note that Jean-Jacques's imagination now ceases to adorn her. His heart, the source of his imagination, breaks rather than transforming what his eyes show him. He sees the wretchedness of her position, makes some offers of assistance, and leaves never to see her again. The second incident is the unexpected appearance of his old friend Venture de Villeneuve, whose romantic image had fascinated the young Jean-Jacques. Now Rousseau says, "How changed he appeared to me. Instead of his ancient graces I found in him only a crapulous air, which kept me from brightening up with him. Either my eyes were no longer the same, or debauchery had brutalized his mind, or all his first luster pertained to youth which he no longer had" (I, 398). Jean-Jacques's eyes have changed in that he now sees the truth rather than what his heart dictates to him. Again, there may be real changes in Venture, but

---

40. This is not to deny that criteria such as comprehensiveness, consistency, and correspondence to observed facts could not help to close the gap between plausibility and certainty; see "The Necessity of Philosophic Autobiography" in Chapter 1.

Jean-Jacques's imagination remains inactive. He sees both Venture and Maman as they are without adornment. It is only after Venture's departure that Jean-Jacques recalls "all those ravishing deliriums of a young heart" which made up his youth. He now sees his delirium for what it was; rather than returning to his illusions, he merely regrets their passing. Now he has disenchanted his past. These incidents form one sort of evidence about the change brought about in Jean-Jacques by his sight of another universe.

"I Became Another Man"

That substantial changes are brought about in Jean-Jacques by the discovery is also indicated by his phrase "I became another man." To determine the nature and extent of his disenchantment, it is necessary to subject this other man to the same scrutiny that was applied to the other universe. The simplest implication to draw from Rousseau's statement "I became another man" is that he is no longer what he was before. To this point, Part Two has shown Jean-Jacques to be under the influence of one or another form of amour-propre. First he has a desire for celebrity of any sort. He suffers from the tendency of vanity to look for success by manipulating and being manipulated by opinions. Then he has a desire for advancement as the representative of a sovereign. He experiences the proud characteristic of identifying with a community. Finally, he now glimpses the defects of social institutions and forms a desire for success based on talent alone. This appears to be a desire for celebrity and independence at the same time. Jean-Jacques wishes celebrity without bowing to opinion. To see who Jean-Jacques becomes after his illumination, it is necessary to explore what happens to his amour-propre.

The disenchantment, indicated by Jean-Jacques's new ability to see Maman and Venture as they are, points to a condition in which the imagination ceases to cause illusions. It also seems to point to an overcoming of the unnatural amour-propre that is the source of many of these illusions. One of Rousseau's earliest accounts of the illumination, a fragment written years before the *Confessions*, appears to confirm such an overcoming: "I believed that I felt myself animated by a more beautiful zeal than that of amour-propre" (I, 1113). Of course, believing that one is animated by something other than amour-propre does not prove that one is so animated. In the *Confessions* itself Rousseau indicates that his amour-propre was modified, but not that it disappeared completely:

> Until then I had been good, afterwards I became virtuous, or at least drunk with virtue. This drunkenness had begun in my head, but it had passed into my heart. The most noble pride germinated there on the debris of uprooted vanity. I pretended nothing; I became in effect what I seemed, and during the at least four years that the effervescence lasted with all its force, nothing great and beautiful could enter into the heart of a man, of which I was not capable between Heaven and myself. (I, 416)

According to this statement, Jean-Jacques's vanity has been uprooted, but it has been replaced by the "most noble pride." This newly identified pride determines the sort of man Jean-Jacques has become as the result of his discovery. This most noble pride is a complex passion with at least three separate attributes that appear in combination or alternation.

The first attribute is revealed by a very simple answer to the question of who Jean-Jacques becomes on the road to Vincennes. Rousseau says that the one thing he wrote at the time of the inspiration was the part of the *First Discourse* called the "prosopopoeia of Fabricius" (I, 351). Here Rousseau resurrects the great Roman citizen to comment on the corruption of Rome in the centuries after his death (*Discourses*, 45–46). This speech is written in the first person and thus presents a clear example of Jean-Jacques becoming a character about whom he is thinking. While agitated by the inspiration, he becomes not a natural man but Fabricius, the citizen of Rome. When he writes the rest of the *Discourse*, he ceases to be Fabricius but retains the identification—he refers to himself as Jean-Jacques Rousseau, "Citizen of Geneva."

This aspect of the most noble pride identifies this passion as a simple repetition of Jean-Jacques's early experience of identification with Scaevola or Brutus. It is the passion whose representative par excellence is Cato. Rousseau connects his new experience of this passion with his first experience when he says that the victory of the *First Discourse* in the contest "put into fermentation in my heart the first lessons of heroism and virtue that my father and my country and Plutarch put there during my infancy" (I, 356). The major difference between this identification and the earlier ones is duration. Rousseau specifies how much longer the effervescence lasted: "If you recall one of the short moments in my life in which I became another and ceased to be me, one finds it again in the time about which I speak, but instead of lasting six days, six weeks, it lasted almost six years" (I, 417). Another distinctive feature of this identification is that it does not turn Jean-Jacques into an ordinary citizen. The identification with Roman virtue is an identification with citizen virtue as such rather than with a particular version such as Genevan virtue. Rome is the "model of all free peoples." Jean-Jacques's writings and conduct attempt to make the "Citizen of Geneva" a model of citizen virtue as such. This first aspect of Jean-Jacques's new pride is not directly dependent on his new understanding of nature. An identification with Fabricius is an imitation and therefore stands at the opposite pole from philosophy.

Another aspect of this pride is more easily compatible with a philosophic understanding of the world. In "My Portrait" Rousseau says, "A proof that I have less amour-propre than other men or that mine is made in another manner, is the facility that I have at living alone" (I, 1124). In this statement Rousseau does not deny that amour-propre is compatible with a sort of independence, he merely asserts that such an amour-propre is uncommon. In the *Confessions*, immediately after referring to his attachment to citizenship, he declares his attachment to living "above fortune and opinion and to suffice to oneself" (I, 356). This desire for independence resembles the Socratic independence discussed in Chapter 2. There it is argued that in Rousseau's view Wolmar and Socrates are examples of a refined sort of amour-propre that takes the form of pride in the independence one has from the illusions suffered by other people. This form of pride requires clear-sightedness far beyond that required of a citizen.

Finally, the *First Discourse*, the work written under the immediate influence of the inspiration, reveals one more form of noble pride. Rousseau begins the *First Discourse* with a statement showing that he is one of those who "wants to live beyond one's century" (*Discourses*, 33). He makes a similar claim in the "Letters to Malesherbes" (I, 1145). Rousseau explains, "The wise man does not chase after riches, but he is not insensitive to glory" (*Discourses*, 58). These statements imply that amour-propre and wisdom need not conflict with each other. Ordinary vanity, the desire for contemporary celebrity that is uprooted in Jean-Jacques by the inspiration, leads to a slavish following of public opinion or an equally slavish departure from it (*Discourses*, 33, 50). A desire for recognition from posterity can liberate one from obsessive concern with changing fashions of the day. Future glory can be acquired only by the discovery of useful truth. This form of noble pride is compatible with the desire to cause "a revolution in the universe" which Rousseau attributes to Jesus.

It is not easy to see how these three versions of amour-propre—love

of citizen virtue, desire for independence, and wish for future glory—
can coexist. Nevertheless, Rousseau does give clear indications that he
is affected by all of them. He reveals a triple effect of the inspiration
compatible with these three types of amour-propre: "My feelings as-
cended with the most inconceivable rapidity to the tone of my ideas. All
my little passions were stifled by the enthusiasm for *truth*, for *liberty*, for
virtue" (I, 351, emphasis added). Enthusiasm for virtue is the quality of
the citizen; for liberty, that of the independent person; and for truth,
that of someone who rejects the fashions of the age in quest of a knowledge that will change future generations. The period of effervescence,
enthusiasm, or drunkenness is one in which Jean-Jacques attempts to
combine the excellences of the greatest exemplary figures. He attempts
to incorporate all the noblest human aspirations.

Effervescence and Intoxication

The coexistence or alternation of these incompatible elements of
the most noble pride keeps Jean-Jacques in "effervescence" for the six-
year period beginning with the illumination. This effervescence is
caused by the effect his ideas have on his feelings. During this period
Jean-Jacques makes continuous efforts to reform his personal life to
make it compatible with these new ideas and feelings. His continued
affliction with amour-propre in whatever form it may take is an indication that the discovery of nature does not return his feelings to a natural state.

The distance Jean-Jacques stands from naturalness is shown by his
response to another bout of illness, which reinforces his decision to
renounce the goal of celebrity. Once again Jean-Jacques believes that
he is about to die. When this first happened, in Book VI, his belief in
the nearness of death returned him to a condition of quasi-natural
wholeness by checking his imaginative flights into the future. At that
time his only remaining concerns for the future were his fear for his
soul, which was easily calmed, and his desire for a cure, which troubled
him intermittently. One might expect that the discovery of the system
of nature and the belief in the nearness of death would now restore
Jean-Jacques to this state of tranquil resignation. But his intoxication
with virtue and his desire for glory in future generations prevent this.
The possibility of posthumous glory is not affected by the necessity of
death.

Jean-Jacques's current project begins to resemble that of a political founder or legislator. He seeks to "give an example by [his] conduct" (I, 362). Rousseau says that his "design" of breaking the chain of opinion and setting an example of virtue is "possibly the greatest or at least the most useful to virtue that a mortal had ever conceived."[41] This language is impossible to misinterpret. Jean-Jacques has set out to make himself into an exemplary figure to rival those of the past.

The significance of this great and useful project can be seen by comparing it with Rousseau's analysis of earlier great projects. Because the inspiration has unveiled civilized corruption, Jean-Jacques's situation can be compared to those of Socrates, Cato, and Jesus, each of whom also found himself living in a corrupt society. Socrates' response is to live independent of the corruption. Cato's response is to attempt to reform his society by the example of his virtue. Jesus's response after realizing the impossibility of reforming his own community is to cause a revolution in the universe. Jean-Jacques's project resembles Socrates' in that it attempts to establish independence from corrupt public opinion. Unlike Socrates, however, Jean-Jacques actively sets an example for others to follow. According to the standard set in the "Discourse on the Virtue for a Hero" (written shortly after the inspiration), his design is heroic rather than philosophic because it is concerned with public utility. In this respect it resembles Cato's project. Jean-Jacques, like Cato, wishes to be a model of civic virtue. Unlike Cato, his example is not intended for the citizens of only one community. The universal applicability he intends recalls the revolution in the universe undertaken by Jesus. Jean-Jacques's design differs from Jesus's in that the example he proposes is more compatible with the demands of earthly life. Jean-Jacques's revolution is not precisely political; he sets out to model in his private life virtuous living in corrupt times.

This personal reform requires a visible form that can inspire emulation. Jean-Jacques's status as a celebrity is secured by the publication of the *First Discourse*. He begins to make his reform visible by renouncing an offer of lucrative employment from the Dupin family and resolving to live on the small income of a music copyist. He adopts a simple style of dress—and is assisted in this resolution by the theft of his fine linen by Thérèse's brother. These conspicuous displays of independence and simplicity are intended to demonstrate to the world the possibility of renouncing the tangible benefits of celebrity in the name of independence and virtue.

41. On Rousseau as an example, see Starobinski, *Transparence*, p. 50.

The one flaw in this attempt comes with Jean-Jacques's unwillingness to dissolve his relations with his friends. He shakes off the yoke of
public opinion but not that of friendship. His project of personal reform is incompatible with relations with men of letters. Rousseau says
that his example of independence caused the jealousy of his "so-called
friends," who also felt his reform to be a reproach directed at them.
Grimm, Diderot, and the other men of letters pursued contemporary
fame and were not indifferent to the rewards of celebrity.[42] Thus Jean-
Jacques remains on intimate terms with people who envy his success
and resent his virtue.

The success of his opera also reveals a flaw in Jean-Jacques's intoxication with virtue. His Roman virtue has not entirely subjugated his
romantic imagination. Rousseau presents himself as torn between his
"Roman tone" and a nervous desire to please an audience (I, 376).[43] He
attributes his pleasure at the success of the opera to the voluptuousness
of pleasing women who "seemed as beautiful as angels" (I, 379) more
than to vanity. The true test of his Roman principles comes with the
offer of a pension from the king, who is pleased with the opera. Rousseau argues that the acceptance of this pension would end any possibility of independence and disinterestedness, but he does not attribute
his refusal to a desire to maintain these preconditions of virtue. Rather,
he attributes it to his illness and his inability to deliver an impromptu
speech. Rousseau shows himself here to be cured of the simple desire
for celebrity and money which he had felt earlier, but he also shows the
difficulty of maintaining a stance of citizen virtue while composing
operas for a king. It is easier to maintain the combination of severe
republicanism and respect for a king while disputing with the King of
Poland over the effects of the arts on morals than it is to maintain this
combination while accepting a reward for a musical composition.[44]

The public furor caused by the success of the *First Discourse* further
intensifies the difficulty of maintaining the life of independence. *Le
Devin du village*, written in the Italian style, precipitates a violent dispute
over the relative merits of French and Italian music. The ensuing pam-

---

42. In this context Rousseau calls particular attention to Grimm's calculating attempts
to become fashionable. He also says that Grimm and Diderot were jealous of the success
of his opera (I, 369–70).

43. The substance of the opera does forward the purpose of Jean-Jacques's moral
reform in its praise of simple country life.

44. In discussing his defense against the King of Poland, Rousseau distinguishes
between vanity and desire for the esteem of worthy people (I, 399).

phlet war, known as the Guerre des Buffons, leads to threats against Jean-Jacques's life. Rousseau evaluates the entire period after the publication of the *First Discourse*: "I felt then that it is not always as easy as one imagines to be poor and independent" (I, 379).

The controversies and encounters with celebrity seekers lead Jean-Jacques to a new resolution to carry out his personal reform. He decides that it is necessary to leave Paris altogether. His first choice of refuge is Geneva, where he expects to be able to live as a true citizen. He takes the first step by traveling to Geneva to renounce Catholicism and regain his citizenship. At the time of the publication of the *First Discourse*, in fact, the "Citizen of Geneva" was not a legitimate citizen of any place; he had forfeited his citizenship at the time of his conversion.

The prospect of a return to Geneva opens the possibility of the sort of life Rousseau discusses at the end of Book I. There he suggests that he could have lived happily in the limited sphere offered by Geneva because his powerful imagination could satisfy him. The course of Part One of the *Confessions* shows that it is precisely this powerful imagination that makes it impossible for Jean-Jacques to live within such a limited sphere. The inspiration on the road to Vincennes, however, has altered his imagination. It has cured him, to some extent, of his tendency toward romantic fantasy. Furthermore, his intoxication with virtue restricts his imagination to the concerns of citizenship. What remains in doubt is the compatibility of the demands of life in Geneva with his project of setting an example for general emulation. Is Geneva compatible with Jean-Jacques's great and useful project, or is it too corrupt to tolerate his brand of citizenship?

These possibilities are not brought to the test. Jean-Jacques decides that Voltaire's recent move to the vicinity of Geneva would lead to quarrels. In addition, the poor reception given to the *Second Discourse* at Geneva indicates that he will not be welcome. He therefore agrees to Mme d'Epinay's proposal that he accept a home in the country outside Paris. It is this move that Rousseau says cures him of the effects of the intoxication with virtue and causes a new revolution in his soul.

The earlier revolution, caused by Jean-Jacques's rediscovery of nature, does not lead directly to a return to naturalness. That seeing another universe turns him into another man means that he is less natural than he had been before. Thus Rousseau accomplishes one of the philosophic aims of the *Confessions*: he shows how he discovers his system. It remains to be seen whether the new revolution accomplishes the second aim of showing a return to naturalness by a civilized human.

[6]

The Return to Nature?
(Books IX–XII)

The Problem of a Return to Nature

The *Confessions* contains a series of what Rousseau calls "revolutions." Each of these revolutions in some way relates to the possibility of a return to nature from civilized corruption. The physical revolution of Book VI restores Jean-Jacques to a quasi-natural state. The mental revolution of Book VIII, his sudden inspiration, allows him to discover nature. Book IX contains two more revolutions, one that takes place when Jean-Jacques moves to the country and a final one that Rousseau calls "the great revolution of my destiny" (I, 474). Both the revolutions in Book IX concern the effect of the inspiration about human nature and its ability to change Jean-Jacques's character. They set in motion the chain of events that brings the *Confessions* to a conclusion.

Whether any "revolution" can restore natural wholeness is a problematic issue in Rousseau's thought. Whether anyone as thoroughly denatured as Jean-Jacques can be restored is even more problematic. That his discovery of nature causes an intoxication with virtue indicates that there is no necessary relation between knowing what nature is and living according to it. That there should be a disproportion between what one knows and the way one lives is simply the straightforward conclusion of Rousseau's system. The naturalness of the humans described in the first part of the *Second Discourse* is virtually defined by the absence of all reflective knowledge. After making his case for the advantages of this condition of ignorance, Rousseau concludes, "I almost dare affirm that the state of reflection is a state contrary to nature and that the man who meditates is a depraved animal" (*Discourses*, 110). This statement makes no distinction between those whose meditations are true and those whose meditations are false; it applies equally to all who meditate. If this conclusion were true without qualification, one's discovery of nature would entail the knowledge that one is doomed to live unnaturally. Rousseau's statement, however, does have a qualification: he does not quite dare to affirm that all humans who meditate are depraved. The possibility, however slight, remains that someone who has discovered nature can use this knowledge to become more natural.

In Book IX Rousseau gives an account of an unfinished book that was intended to show how knowledge of nature can be used to change one's character. Rousseau's description of this project, the *morale sensitive*,[1] is particularly useful for understanding the *Confessions* because Rousseau says that his conclusions are owed to "observations made on myself" (I, 408). The work is meant to describe how it happens that "most men are in the course of their life often unlike themselves and seem to be transformed into completely different men." It is also meant to show how these apparently random and arbitrary revolutions can be controlled. Rousseau's discovery is that "these diverse manners of being . . . depended in great part on the anterior impression of exterior objects" (I, 409). When elaborated, this discovery would allow one to discover "an exterior regimen which, varied according to circumstances, could put or maintain the soul in the state most favorable to virtue." As Rousseau describes it here, his plan is to enable others to make themselves virtuous (or to put themselves in a state favorable to virtue) through this regimen. The person who undergoes the regimen must either be virtuous already or wish to become virtuous. In the first case, the existing virtue precedes and is independent of knowledge of the regimen. It has been imposed by accident or a teacher. In the second, the knowledge precedes the imposition of the regimen. Thus, one begins by being either ignorant but virtuous or knowledgeable but lacking in virtue. The knowledge of the regimen, accordingly, can be used to maintain or change one's present character.

Although the object of the regimen is described here as the attainment of virtue, Rousseau's description of the principles involved implies that the regimen can be used to induce naturalness instead of virtue. This change of object means adopting as one's goal the transfor-

---

1. One might translate this title loosely as "the moral philosophy of feeling."

mation of oneself into a naturally whole person. For example, just as virtue can be encouraged through an identification with and emulation of a virtuous man like Cato, naturalness can be encouraged by preventing any identification with or concern about anyone else. Something like the regimen of the *morale sensitive* is used by Emile's tutor to maintain the boy's naturalness as long as possible. The physical revolution of Book VI accidentally imposes a regimen that restores Jean-Jacques to naturalness. The *Confessions* now turns to the question of whether one can impose such a regimen on oneself. The revolution of Book VIII gives Jean-Jacques the knowledge of the exterior regimen, or at least the understanding of nature from which it can be derived. Possessing this knowledge, however, is not the same as undergoing the regimen. Rousseau says that the purpose of the *morale sensitive* is to assist people who, "sincerely loving virtue, distrust their feebleness," but these people must wish to apply the regimen, or be fortunate enough to have someone else apply it to them, if it is to succeed. Jean-Jacques's discovery of nature in Book VIII would entail a return to nature only if it gave him the desire to impose an exterior regimen comparable to that in Book VI; that is, if it made him love naturalness while distrusting his feebleness.

There is always the possibility of this regimen being imposed on Jean-Jacques by an accident comparable to that in Book VI. His condition at the beginning of Boox IX should, however, be understood in contrast to his condition in Book VI. The earlier book shows a temporary reversal in the denaturing that begins in Book I and continues through Part One. For this brief interval, Jean-Jacques's illness counters his civilized passions and returns him to a quasi-natural condition of psychological, if not physical, self-sufficiency. The revolution in his body (I, 227) returns his soul to a condition like that of a natural man (see *S.C.*, 70–71). Although Jean-Jacques does undertake a routine of study and Rousseau says, "I have never been so close to wisdom as during that happy epoch" (I, 244), his description of wisdom in this context has little to do with self-conscious understanding.[2] Rather, his wisdom consists in an unreflective submission to the pleasures of the moment. This wisdom has its source in the accident that affects the internal workings of his soul by an external and physical change in his condition.

The discovery of nature described in Book VIII is similarly the

2. For a different view of this declaration, see Hartle, *Modern Self*, pp. 64–65.

result of an "accident" (I, 1135) and is the cause of a "revolution" (I, 418). This revolution is not a revolution in the body, however, it is a revolution in the soul and has no externally imposed physical cause. In the physical revolution of Book VI, Jean-Jacques returns to a quasi-natural condition but has no understanding of the basis of this condition. In the mental revolution of Book VIII, he acquires the understanding of nature he lacked earlier, but his passions do not return to the quasi-natural condition of Book VI. Instead of living in the present, he has plans for glory that will be acquired in future ages. Instead of an unreflective enjoyment of the present without thought of others, he feels pride in his independence of others and in his citizenlike devotion to the good of others.

In Book VI the key to the exterior regimen is the belief in the nearness of death. Jean-Jacques's illness restores him to natural unity, and when this unity breaks down he knows no way to recapture it. The issue of Books IX–XII is whether the discovery of nature can reproduce this earlier return to nature. In these books Jean-Jacques attempts to establish a social unity for himself (Book IX), experiences the collapse of all his hopes for happiness based on civilized desires (Books X and XI), and finally achieves a sort of return to natural wholeness (Book XII).

Book IX: "My Soul in Motion": The Failure of Social Wholeness

The possibility for a return to naturalness based on a regimen like that promised by the *morale sensitive* depends on either the imposition of the regimen from outside or the desire to impose it on oneself; that is, it depends on the existence of either external conditions or internal conditions. Jean-Jacques's attempt in Book VIII to combine love of virtue, wisdom, and freedom show that his desires do not lead him toward a return to nature. In Book IX his move to the country gives him one of the external conditions for such a return, but his unnatural, social desires lead him into a series of failed attempts to achieve social rather than natural wholeness.

In Book VI Jean-Jacques's accidental achievement of a return to natural wholeness is preceded by his short-lived participation in a social whole, the circle of three composed of himself, Maman, and Claude Anet. Similarly, in Part Two, one further attempt at social wholeness precedes Jean-Jacques's final effort to recapture natural wholeness.

The story of this attempt to form a new little circle is given in Book IX. This is the book that describes the effects of the "second revolution" following the inspiration on the road to Vincennes.

The setting and course of the lengthy Book IX can be summarized briefly. Rousseau presents the lack of fulfillment in his relations with Thérèse as leading to his desire for friendship. His so-called friends encourage him to begin a literary career, which in turn causes him to undertake the personal reform that estranges his friends. His move to the country, undertaken in the name of this reform, further estranges his friends. This move subsequently turns him away from virtue to life in an imaginary world and ultimately to love. Inspired by love, he wishes to establish a small self-sufficient society, which in the end leads to the final break with his friends. In all these events the moving force is Jean-Jacques's desire for social wholeness. It is this artificial desire that leads, with the assistance of accidents and outside malevolence, to the concluding disaster of Book IX.

The book begins with Jean-Jacques's departure from Paris to live in the country, the result of his decision to undertake a complete moral reform. This move brings about an external regimen that transforms Jean-Jacques's feelings. Rousseau says that he has been "out of [his] element for fifteen years" and refers explicitly to his existence at les Charmettes (I, 401). He emphasizes the self-sufficiency of his new condition by saying, "in sum my resources, proportioned to my needs and to my desires, could reasonably promise me a happy and durable life in this one which my inclination had chosen for me" (I, 402). This formulation of the proportion between resources and needs is also used to describe natural wholeness and self-sufficiency in *Emile* (*Emile*, 80). Rousseau concludes his account of the plan for his new life by referring to his "agreeable and solitary asylum" and "this independent, equal, and peaceful life" (I, 413). These terms similarly evoke the solitude and independence of the state of nature and again suggest that Jean-Jacques's new condition will entail a return to natural wholeness.

In still another parallel with Book VI, Rousseau gives a picture of the daily routine that is the product of this independence, but in the development of this parallel an important difference emerges. In Book VI Jean-Jacques's routine consisted largely of studying, motivated by the desire to prepare himself for death. Now, beyond the pleasant activities of copying music and taking walks, he sets out to compose a series of works "which . . . ought to put the cap on [his] reputation" (I, 404). These works include his planned *Political Institutions*, but they also comprise the editing of the works of the Abbé de St. Pierre, the *morale sensitive*, a system of education that becomes *Emile*, and a musical dictionary. Thus Jean-Jacques begins with exterior conditions conducive to natural wholeness but is still intoxicated with virtue and hope for future glory. Book IX sets out to show the effect of this exterior regimen on Jean-Jacques's interior condition to see if it accomplishes the same result as the illness in Book VI.

Rousseau gives an account of his inner condition at the time of the move in a summary of the events covered in Books VII and VIII beginning with his return to Paris from Venice. He explains the necessity for this repetition: "Before telling the effect this state, so new for me, had on my heart, it is convenient to recapitulate its secret affections, so that one can follow better the progress of these new modifications in its causes" (I, 413).[3] By focusing exclusively on the secret affections of his heart, Rousseau reveals the desire that keeps him from wishing to return to nature.

The secret affection that dominates this discussion appears at first glance to be a natural desire. It is a desire for wholeness or unity. Rousseau indicates the depth of this desire for unity by saying, "the thirst for happiness is not extinguished in the heart of man" (I, 412). This formulation makes it appear that this thirst is natural, but Rousseau traces his own only to his relationship with Maman. Jean-Jacques's thirst for happiness does not manifest itself as a desire for complete natural independence. Rousseau does not say that he wished to be a numerical unity, entirely for himself. Rather, he attributes to himself a specifically civilized version of the desire for wholeness:

> The first of my needs, the greatest, the strongest, the most inextinguishable, was entirely in my heart: it was the need for an intimate society and one as intimate as it could be: it was above all for this that I needed a woman more than a man, a lover more than a friend. This singular need was such that the closest union of bodies would still not suffice for it. I would have needed two souls in the same body, without that I would always feel the void. (I, 414)[4]

In certain respects this passage shows perfectly the dilemma of any civilized human as Rousseau understands it. His reference to the need

3. This is similar to the terminology Rousseau uses in the Neuchâtel preface to describe the goal of the *Confessions* as a whole (I, 1149).
4. This description should be compared to the speech of Aristophanes in Plato's *Symposium*. For Rousseau's judgment of the *Symposium*, see *Emile*, 344.

in his "heart," a term he usually employs as a synonym for the imagination, distinguishes this form of the need for wholeness from the form that might be felt by a natural human. Once one's imagination has carried one away from natural wholeness and independence, the natural numerical unity or wholeness changes into an artificial fraction in search of a complementary fraction. The part seeks to be a part of a whole, but the separateness of bodies means that the void will always be felt. A supplement will always be needed to fill the void. As Rousseau says here, his need is entirely in his heart. Because the desire for wholeness Rousseau emphatically attributes to himself is not a true or natural need, this longing for happiness cannot be a natural longing. Far from being a sign of an enduring attraction for the natural, this particular form of the desire for wholeness is an obstacle to the attainment of natural independence. Thus, when Rousseau calls this the first of his needs and says that it is inextinguishable, he is showing the depth of his departure from nature and not his persistent attachment to natural wholeness.

Rousseau describes his relations with Thérèse as the attempt to reconstitute the wholeness he had come close to with Maman. He says, "I have always regarded the day which united me to my Thérèse as that which fixed my moral being" (I, 413). This is similar to his earlier statement that his life with Maman fixed his character (I, 179). In this case, it even seems that his relations with Thérèse approach natural relations: "The needs of the senses that I have satisfied with her have been uniquely for me those of sex, without having anything pertaining to the individual." This could easily be the description of the relations of a natural man and a natural woman.[5] If Jean-Jacques were returned to a quasi-natural condition, this relationship with Thérèse would be exactly what he would require to satisfy his desires. The restriction of satisfaction to the senses would be the mark of its naturalness. In this context, however, Rousseau presents this very naturalness as the source of his lack of satisfaction. Because his desire for wholeness is a desire of the heart rather than a physical desire, "the void of the heart was, however, never well fulfilled" (I, 415). Thus, if his union with Thérèse fixes Jean-Jacques's moral being, it fixes it in a condition that lacks wholeness, a condition that feels a void and demands a supplement to fill it.

This inability to find fulfillment with Thérèse is exacerbated by the

5. See Schwartz, *Sexual Politics*, pp. 104–6.

presence of her family, who constantly attempt to drive a wedge between the two. The birth of children might have united the pair more closely, but Jean-Jacques's decision to abandon them adds to the estrangement. As a result, Rousseau says, "not being able to taste in its plenitude that intimate society for which I felt the need, I sought some supplements which might not fill the void but which would make me feel it less" (I, 416). As this remark shows, supplements are not adequate substitutions for wholeness. As Book IX progresses, it shows the tendency of successive supplements to reveal a new void and consequently a need for yet another supplement. Rousseau's term "supplement" is carefully chosen from mathematics to illustrate the emphasis on unity and completeness. The analogy should not be pushed too far, however. This sort of supplement, unlike a supplementary angle, always leaves a minute void that tends to widen. It is the source of only a false satisfaction. The need for more and more such supplements is the fate of those civilized humans who are complete neither in themselves nor in their participation in a community.[6]

The first supplement Jean-Jacques resorts to in trying to fill the void in his relations with Thérèse is friendship with Diderot and Grimm. This type of friendship is a supplement rather than a source of wholeness for two reasons. First, Diderot encourages Jean-Jacques in his literary career, that is, in a pursuit of fame which is incompatible with wholeness. Second, Grimm uses Jean-Jacques as an instrument for the satisfaction of his own desire to advance in the world. The intimacy he offers is a sham. Thus these two relationships offer only a temporary or illusory satisfaction. The void, or gap, between Jean-Jacques and his friends becomes manifest during his intoxication with virtue, which they regard as a reproach. Far from filling the void, this supplementary friendship intensifies it. In sum, prior to his move to the country, Jean-Jacques is plagued by an unfilled desire for social wholeness. He manifests no interest in natural wholeness.

The return to the country begins to change his desires first by eliminating his feelings of pride and independence. Rousseau says that the absence of the spectacle of the vices of Paris "restored [him] to nature above which [he] had wished to elevate [himself]" (I, 417). The exterior regimen imposed by the sight of Parisian vice had fueled his indignation and kept him as another man. The external regimen of the coun-

6. For a useful discussion of supplements in Rousseau's works, see Derrida, *Of Grammatology*, pp. 141–64.

try, however, returns him to himself. Rousseau's claim that this second revolution returned him to nature might suggest that the exterior regimen of the country returned Jean-Jacques to a quasi-natural condition in need of no supplement. Yet he quickly makes it clear that the "nature" to which he was restored is the corrupt civilized nature. He says, "I became fearful, complaisant, timid, in a word the same Jean-Jacques that I had been before." Rousseau concludes this section by adding that in one respect this second revolution does not simply return him to his old condition. Instead it carries him "rapidly to the other extreme." He says, "Since then my soul in motion has done no more than pass through the line of repose, and its always renewed oscillations have never permitted it to stay there" (I, 417). The nature of these oscillations has been shown from the beginning of the *Confessions*. Jean-Jacques's earliest reading formed the romantic Jean-Jacques, who was succeeded by the Roman Jean-Jacques. In Book VI his intoxication with the sensuality of Mme de Larnage was reversed by his virtuous resolutions inspired by Roman ruins. Now his intoxication with virtue is replaced, not by nature, but by a romantic longing. Rousseau mourns his failure to achieve a peaceful social wholeness here by saying, "this is again one of the short moments of my life in which I have seen happiness close up without being able to attain it" (I, 420).

To show the effects of his continuing desire for social wholeness and the frustration of this desire, Rousseau focuses on the curious ties between his friends and Thérèse's mother. His household in the country consists of himself, Thérèse, and Mme le Vasseur. Rousseau says, "Being only three in our retreat, leisure and solitude ought naturally to tighten our intimacy" (I, 418). However, Diderot and Grimm disrupt this intimacy by enlisting Mme le Vasseur in their attempt to get Jean-Jacques to return to Paris. Because Thérèse keeps the secret of this league, she also maintains a less than complete intimacy with Jean-Jacques. Furthermore, the isolation in the country reveals their lack of harmony in pleasures and thoughts. Hence for both external and internal reasons this new society of three is incapable of matching the short-lived one of Book VI. As Rousseau says, "the situation in which I was, was precisely that in which all my desires joined: I had no more to wish for and I still had an empty heart" (I, 424).

At this point, one might well wonder what has happened to the imagination, which Rousseau asserts at the close of Book I can adorn any situation and take him outside himself. What he insists would have secured his happiness in Geneva should be sufficient to do the same in his new domestic arrangement. Now Jean-Jacques finds himself in a pleasant country setting, living on his trade of copying music. Rousseau anticipates precisely this question from the reader and even demands it: "What did I do on this occasion? Already my reader has divined it if only he has followed me to this point. The impossibility of attaining [happiness] with real beings, threw me into the land of chimeras" (I, 427). The imagination itself is Jean-Jacques's final supplement after his failure to be fulfilled by more limited ones. He attempts to reconstitute wholeness in an ideal world of the imagination. His intoxication with virtue is replaced by an opposite intoxication.

This new intoxication is more transient than the earlier intoxication with virtue. This brief imaginative flight nevertheless shows the most complete development and liberation of the imagination in the *Confessions*. Jean-Jacques's discovery of nature and social corruption makes him cease the search for an imaginary perfection in the real, social world. Consequently, his imagination is all the more free to create another world. Rather than adorning what exists, or generating additions to it, the creative imagination makes a completely new world for itself. At this point Jean-Jacques's new understanding of how civilized imagination deforms nature leads to an intensification of his imagination instead of a return to nature.

Nature, however, reexerts itself against the imaginative flight: "At the height of my greatest exaltation I was pulled back by the cord all at once like a kite and put back in my place by nature, with the aid of a lively attack of my illness" (I, 428). As happened in Book VI, illness has the effect of curbing the imagination, although in this instance only enough to make it "a little less exalted" (I, 430). In the end, the imagination cannot offer a complete escape from nature.

The limitation is enough to pull Jean-Jacques back into a contradictory relation with the real world. The first consequence of this return is that Jean-Jacques draws on his less-exalted images to write *Julie*.[7] The second consequence is that he falls in love with Sophie d'Houdetot by attributing to her the imagined qualities of his fictional Julie—much as Emile falls in love with his Sophie by applying a preconceived image to her. Thus Jean-Jacques's attempt to acquire wholeness and independence through an imaginary flight ultimately leads to another attempt to gain wholeness through domestic relations. Unlike his failed rela-

---

7. As in his account of the composition of *Les Muses galantes*, Rousseau here emphasizes his identification with his character (I, 430).

tions with Thérèse, these new ones promise to achieve wholeness by combining images with the real world.

As is shown in Book V, Jean-Jacques's imagination requires something less orthodox than the domestic relations of a normal family. Rather than wishing to be married to his Sophie, Jean-Jacques sees himself as the confidant of both Sophie and her lover, St. Lambert. Thus he again wishes to reestablish something like the society of three he claims to have shared with Maman and Claude Anet. In describing this new project he says, "We formed the charming project of a close society among us three, and we could hope that the execution of the project would be durable seeing that all the feelings which can unite sensitive and upright hearts formed its base, and that we assembled in the three of us enough talents and knowledge for us to suffice unto ourselves and to have need of no foreign supplement" (I, 479; see 440). This projected intimate society promises to solve the problem of Jean-Jacques's civilized imagination. It represents a solution that involves being on the fringes of society, not radically apart, but out of its mainstream. Rousseau's description identifies three crucial features of this unconventional attempt to reconstitute some form of wholeness. First, he argues that it will be durable. Second, its durability stems from its self-sufficiency; it requires no supplements from outside. Finally, this self-sufficiency stems from the variety of talents and knowledge of its members. It is a small community that maximizes outlets for the imagination while endeavoring to satisfy it.

The apolitical character of this little circle constitutes its charm, but it also leads to a certain vulnerability. This sort of community of complementary, imaginative friends can exist only outside the demands of normal domestic and political life. These demands of what one might call foreign policy are very real, however. Entanglements outside the society of three constantly threaten to intrude. Rousseau's argument for the durability of such a society refers only to its internal relations. In its external relations it proves to be very fragile indeed. Mme d'Epinay becomes enraged at the transparent attachment between Jean-Jacques and Mme d'Houdetot. The destruction of this little society begins even before it can come into being.

Rousseau calls his subsequent rupture with Mme d'Epinay "the great revolution of my destiny" (I, 474). The jealousy of Grimm and Diderot was the germ of his misfortune, but this germ required a precipitating incident to turn it into a real misfortune. The rage of Mme d'Epinay serves as this precipitating incident. The remainder of Book

IX shows the abandonment of the plan for the society of three because of the intrigue against Mme d'Houdetot and Jean-Jacques's trouble with each of his friends in turn. After his account of the rage of Mme d'Epinay, Rousseau discusses his stormy relations with Diderot following the appearance of the latter's attack on the solitary life in the *Fils naturel*. From this, Rousseau turns to his uneasy reconciliation with St. Lambert and Mme d'Houdetot, then to Grimm's various efforts to discredit him. These troubles end with no definitive rupture and even a further touching reconciliation with Sophie and St. Lambert in which the three renew their plans for their little society (I, 479). But a complete break with Mme d'Epinay shatters all attempts at reconciliation.

In Book IX Rousseau uncovers the greatest hopes for a creative, imaginative life of withdrawal from both nature and society. He also prophesies the inevitable disappointment of such hopes. With this book it is possible to delineate the final form of Rousseau's "topography" of the imaginary world. In the first position is the pure state of nature. Natural humans have virtually no imagination, they form images only of real objects, and their rational faculties are not sufficiently developed to cause serious misinterpretations. The few images they do form do not conflict with their experience of the world. The second position is the civilized world, which begins even prior to the establishment of civil society with the first departure from the pure state of nature. From this first departure, civilized humans are almost by definition divided beings; that is, they imagine things that do not correspond to what is. It is only the rare young Emile whose ability to live in the world remains unaffected by imaginative distortions. The majority of civilized humans are divided in numerous ways; their imagination pulls them outside themselves in the hopes and fears of foresight, it makes them seek recognition from others by vanity, and it gives them contradictory understandings of the world. Frequently the images in terms of which they live are at odds with their experiences. A third position is that of citizens, who are made to "see objects as they are, or sometimes as they should appear to be" (*S.C.*, 67). For them the contradictions within the imaginary world are resolved. Even so, citizens still live in an artificial world. Their communities mask the illusions, but sufficient shocks inflicted on the community can return citizens into the second position of ordinary civilized humans. A Cato must end his life when his community ceases to live up to his image of it. A fourth position can be found in the lives of the lovers whose view of the world revolves around their image of each other. In Book IX Rousseau presents one more position: life in an entirely imaginary world rather than in the non-imaginary world of the state of nature or the mixed world of civilization. This position is possible for someone with a completely developed imagination. If, as it seems, civilized humans cannot shed their imaginations, they can attempt to use them to the fullest degree, to take the greatest advantage of their ability to enchant. Once one discovers that the miseries of civilized humans are caused by the contradictions between the real world and the imaginary world and within the imaginary world itself, one can try to resolve these contradictions by an imaginative flight from the real world. In such a condition, a freedom resembling that of the state of nature can be reattained. The imaginative person, like the natural person, can live a life of wholeness and lack of contradiction (I, 1135).

This picture is appealing because it promises a way out of dividedness for civilized humans. Taking this route, they can regain wholeness without sacrificing the undeniable charms of the imagination. Although this solution is attempted by Jean-Jacques, Rousseau claims that, however free it may seem and however far it may fly, the imagination can easily crash back to earth. What Book IX leaves open is whether the disillusionment of Jean-Jacques's hopes either for a wholly imaginative life or for relations with others cures him of these hopes or leaves them simply unfulfilled. This question begins to be answered with the account of the effects of the new "revolution" caused by the rupture with his friends.

Books X and XI: Social Dependence

The conspiracy against Jean-Jacques is the predominant theme of Books X and XI. Rousseau's apparent obsession with this alleged conspiracy manifested here and in other works is the basis for the widespread view of his insanity.[8] As a rule Rousseau's assertions on this matter are seen as an embarrassment by those who wish to take him seriously as a thinker. This embarrassment is an important part of the attempt to separate the autobiographical writings, in which the conspiracy is an issue, from the theoretical writings, in which it is not. Similarly, those who wish to discredit Rousseau as a thinker are pleased to find evidence that allows them to attack his thought without having to confront his arguments. Such critics attempt to link the autobiographical

8. For the variety of these interpretations, see Starobinski, *Transparence*, pp. 430–44.

and theoretical works in order to implicate the latter in the madness of the former. Both sides share the view that Rousseau's presentation of the conspiracy cannot be a part of any rational view of the world. His supporters therefore attempt to divide him into rational and irrational parts, while his detractors regard him as an irrational whole. Any attempt to argue for the philosophic importance of the *Confessions* must confront these opposing camps.

Perhaps the most interesting scholarly account of the significance of the conspiracy is provided by Ann Hartle. Hartle notes the difficulties confronted by those interpreters who take a psychological approach when they are confronted by Rousseau's lucid analysis of an imaginary Jesuit plot. She says that such interpreters must have recourse to "a marvellous struggle between understanding and madness" in which first one and then the other gains the upper hand within the space of a single paragraph.[9] In their more sophisticated versions such interpreters have recourse to different "zones" of Rousseau's consciousness, one in which he is lucid and another in which he is blind.[10] Such interpreters characteristically begin by presenting their approach as the straightforward way to solve the problem of interpreting Rousseau, but the claims of straightforwardness very quickly give way to ad hoc constructions of wrestling matches and zones of consciousness. In contrast to these interpreters, Hartle insists that Rousseau's deliberateness be taken seriously.

The key to Hartle's interpretation is Rousseau's presentation of his temporary belief in a different plot against him. In Book XI Jean-Jacques is confronted with unexplained delays in the publication of *Emile*. He hears that a certain Jesuit has referred to the book. Immediately "my imagination went off like a flash and unveiled to me the whole mystery of iniquity: I saw its progress as clearly, as surely as if it had been revealed to me" (I, 566). One might say that he sees it as clearly as he had seen that Zulietta was a monster. In this instance his mind is comparably active. He considers a "crowd of facts and circumstances" and assembles "the evidence and the demonstration." As before, his imagination fashions a false view of the world, although instead of seeing a monster he "sees nothing but Jesuits everywhere" (I, 567). He believes that the Society is delaying the publication of *Emile* in order to falsify it after his death.

9. See Hartle, *Modern Self,* pp. 172–73.
10. Ibid., p. 172; cf. Starobinski, *L'Oeil,* pp. 163–64.

Just as he did earlier, Rousseau calls this understanding an "extravagance" (I, 568), which he contrasts with his current understanding: "Today even though I see the most frightening plot which had ever been woven against the memory of a man proceeding without obstacle to its blackest execution, I will die much more tranquilly, certain of leaving in my writings a witness for me, which sooner or later will triumph over the plots of men." This conjunction of his admittedly deluded belief in one conspiracy and his subsequent belief in another must astonish the least careful reader. Such conjunctions are the evidence cited to prove the existence of the different zones of Rousseau's consciousness.

It is this apparent tension between lucidity and blindness that Hartle seeks to resolve. She says, "The characterization of his construction of the Jesuit plot as 'mad' points to the character of the Great Plot as a figment of his imagination."[11] Other interpreters agree that the "Great Plot" is a figment of Rousseau's imagination, but Hartle claims that Rousseau deliberately juxtaposes the two plots "so that we may see their madness." Thus she implies that Rousseau no more believes in the "Great Plot" than he does in the Jesuit conspiracy.[12]

Hartle's interpretation has a number of strengths. In the first place, by arguing for Rousseau's self-consciousness in his presentation of the conspiracy she excapes the unavoidable arbitrariness of those interpreters who attempt to separate Rousseau's lucid sentences from his supposed deluded ones, a separation that can be made only on the basis of an understanding of Rousseau that claims to be independent of what Rousseau himself says.[13] In the second place, Hartle's approach maintains the connection between Rousseau's presentation of the plot and his presentation of himself in the *Confessions*. She is able to show the crucial role of the imagination in both presentations.

Hartle's interpretation faces some obstacles, however. First, the *Confessions* is not the only place Rousseau expresses a belief in the conspiracy. Not only does he refer to it in other works, such as the *Dialogues* and *Reveries*, it also fills his private correspondence. Rousseau did adapt

---

11. Hartle, *Modern Self*, p. 122.

12. Hartle suggests that Rousseau's presentation of the plot is essentially a parody of the Christian notion of Providence: whereas Rousseau pretends that he believes that his life is controlled by a malevolent personal force outside himself, Christians believe that their lives are controlled by a benevolent personal force outside themselves; see Hartle *Modern Self*, pp. 122–25.

13. See ibid., p. 125.

his way of life in order to demonstrate some of his principles, but there is little ground for disputing the sincerity of his belief in the conspiracy. The most that one can say is that he was also well aware that his imagination made him prone to mistaken judgments on such matters. Second, within the *Confessions* the conspiracy is one instance in which it is difficult to distinguish between the opinions of Jean-Jacques the character and those of Rousseau the narrator. Rousseau repeatedly refers to his present belief in the conspiracy as well as to his earlier beliefs. If there is a difference it is that Rousseau blames himself for not having been more aware of the conspiracy at an early date. Hartle's interpretation would have more support if Rousseau emphasized Jean-Jacques's belief in the conspiracy rather than his own.

The implication of Hartle's interpretation becomes apparent when it is extended beyond the presentation of Jean-Jacques's personality in the *Confessions* to Rousseau's entire philosophic teaching. When discussing the illumination on the road to Vincennes, Hartle correctly draws attention to its accidental character. As she says, "the recovery, or uncovering, of nature is an accident because one does not know that the recovery has to be made until it has been made."[14] Rousseau presents the domination of civilized humans by the imagination as being so complete that only an accident can free them or even make them aware of their enslavement. Hartle also seems to claim that the accident does not lead to a systematic understanding of nature. She says, "Nature has room for chance; all-inclusive 'systems' are madness."[15] What Rousseau sees in the illumination is his "timelessly substantial inner self." Thus Hartle's interpretation requires the dismissal of Rousseau's often repeated claims of the truth of his own system. According to Hartle, what distinguishes him from other thinkers is his discovery of this inner self. His constructions beyond this are mere exercises of the creative imagination with no validity. In the end, Hartle's interpretation must dispose of Rousseau's "great and sad system" as completely, or more so, than any of the psychological interpretations. In disposing of the system, she does not reject, rather she insists on, Rousseau's depth as a thinker. Although Hartle ends by suggesting a connection between the *Confessions* and the political writings,[16] it seems necessary to conclude that, to the extent that Rousseau asserts that he has a system, he is in the

14. Ibid., p. 138. Hartle's account does slight the importance of Zulietta.
15. Ibid., p. 138.
16. Ibid., pp. 155–57.

same position as when he asserts that he sees the systematic plot formed
against him by Grimm and the others.

Hartle's approach and the psychological approach lead to complementary difficulties. Hartle saves Rousseau's self-consciousness as a
thinker at the expense of his system. Critics with a psychological approach as a rule care little about either his self-consciousness or his
system. In so far as they wish to rescue his system, they do so only by
asserting Rousseau's lucidity during his philosophic activity and his
delirium at other times. This position may be tenable, but it hardly
inspires confidence in the system. At the very least this approach requires the dismissal of the last few books of the *Confessions* and most of
Rousseau's subsequent writings.

There are then three alternative approaches to the conspiracy: one
can ignore it and attempt to preserve Rousseau's systematic understanding, one can take it seriously and ignore Rousseau's system, or one
can claim that Rousseau took neither the conspiracy nor his system
seriously. Perhaps one of the most remarkable features of Rousseau's
presentation and analysis of the conspiracy is that it in effect predicts
the first two interpretations and attempts to overcome them in advance.
This prediction of the critic's dilemma is shown most clearly in *Dialogues: Rousseau Judges Jean-Jacques*, but it is also apparent in the *Confessions*. A brief look at Rousseau's procedure in the *Dialogues* helps to
illustrate how he presents the relation between the conspiracy and his
system.

The *Dialogues* is by all accounts a curious work, and at first glance a
baffling one. It consists of three dialogues between two characters, one of
whom is identified simply as a Frenchman, the other as Rousseau. This
seems to be straightforward enough, but it quickly appears that the
character Rousseau both is and is not Rousseau himself. The character is
not the author of *Emile*, the *Social Contract*, or the *First* and *Second
Discourses*. He is meant to be a characterization of Rousseau as he would
be if he had read but not written these works. He is presented as a
foreigner who knows nothing of the author's reputation or character.
The Frenchman, on the other hand, has never read the works because he
has accepted the public characterization of the author, who is called
Jean-Jacques, as a moral monster. Thus, at the beginning of the *Dialogues*, one character is impressed with Jean-Jacques's system but has
paid no attention to the author's personality, and the other dismisses the
system because he is convinced of the unsoundness of Jean-Jacques's
personality. The *Dialogues* proceeds by showing the disproportion be-

tween the image of Jean-Jacques as a monster and the greatness of his work. It resolves the contradiction by first presenting an alternative account of his personality and then showing the systematic character of his works.

The positions of modern critics are reflected in those of Rousseau and the Frenchman at the beginning of their discussions.[17] To be sure, Rousseau's critics more generally characterize him as a madman rather than as a moral monster. As a result they can adopt a tone of conde-scension rather than outright hostility, although the two reactions can go together.[18] Like the Frenchman, they are distracted from giving his work serious attention because their view of the personality of the author makes it inconceivable to them that the works could be pro-found or true. The *Dialogues* forces a confrontation between these two sorts of interpreters and attempts to establish the unity of Jean-Jacques, the man and his system. Clearly it is the hostile Frenchman whose opinions must be altered the most, but even the opinions of Rousseau or his ability to support them change in the course of the work.

In the *Dialogues* the great obstacle that Rousseau and the French-man must overcome to arrive at an accurate appraisal of the author and his work is the public opinion of Jean-Jacques as a monster. Here the conspiracy enters the picture, and it becomes useful to turn back to the *Confessions*. What is important to note in the brief summary above is that Rousseau presents the conspiracy largely as an attempt to prevent serious attention to his writings. Thus it has a close connection to the success of the project those writings embody.

While the *Dialogues* is primarily concerned with the conspiracy as an obstacle to those who wish to understand the character Jean-Jacques and his writings, the *Confessions* is primarily concerned with the effects of the conspiracy on Jean-Jacques himself. Reflection on the relation between these two perspectives reveals several dimensions of Rous-seau's presentation. The first issue the *Confessions* addresses is the na-ture of the conspiracy against Jean-Jacques; the second is the effect of the conspiracy on him.

One of the keys to understanding the conspiracy is the character of its author, Grimm. "Grimm alone formed the plan in his head, and showed the other two [Diderot and d'Holbach] only what they needed

---

17. Paul de Man suggests that modern critics have fulfilled Rousseau's fantasy of a conspiracy directed against him; see *Blindness and Insight* (New York: Oxford University Press, 1971), p. 112.

18. A notable example of this is Huizinga, *Self-Made Saint*.

to see to join in the execution" (I, 492). From his first appearance in the *Confessions*, Grimm exemplifies the worst forms of amour-propre, a characteristic he shares with the other conspirators.[19] Rousseau constantly emphasizes Grimm's falseness, whether he is speaking about his affectation of sentiment (I, 370) or his use of cosmetics (I, 417–18). Grimm is the great manipulator of appearances. Beneath his deceptive appearance lies his "interior doctrine," which teaches that the "unique duty of man is to follow the penchants of his heart in everything." The penchants of Grimm's heart are far from those of a natural human.

Like Jean-Jacques, Grimm is the author of an "obscure and profound system," but his system is the artificial conspiracy rather than an understanding of nature. Rousseau says that the object of this system is "to reverse my reputation from top to bottom" and that its first step is "to abuse the whole public" (I, 493). Unlike the system of nature, this one exists entirely in opinions. Grimm wishes to influence public opinion and does so by presenting the public with an image that can capture its imagination. The "social contract" that enlists the public against Jean-Jacques is based on a shared image for execration rather than emulation. It is based on an appeal to vanity rather than pride. In this case the legislator's model is a negative one, that of Jean-Jacques the monster.

Just as Jean-Jacques is the discoverer of the system of nature, he is also the discoverer of the system invented by Grimm. Although there is a relation between these two discoveries, there are also differences between the types of knowledge required for each. The relation between the two is seen in the structure of the causal chain Rousseau attributes to each. He describes his knowledge of the conspiracy, saying, "I feel the shock of the blows inflicted on me, I perceive the immediate instrument, but I am unable to see either the hand which directs them, or the means that it puts to work" (I, 589). With this statement Rousseau divides the causal chain into two sections. He refers, first, to what is accessible to him through direct experience, what he feels or perceives, and second, to what is inaccessible, to what he cannot see. With regard to the second section he says that he is unable to "trace back to the moving hand, and to assign causes in stating facts." Although he has no immediate access to it, he knows that the moving hand is Grimm's. Thus his ignorance is restricted to the intermediate cause, about which

19. Most of the references to amour-propre in Part Two are to the conspirators or their allies (I, 281, 405, 407, 429, 502, 537, 554).

he cannot even conjecture. The structure of this chain of knowledge is similar to the structure of the *Second Discourse*. The first section corresponds to the condition of civilized humans, which is accessible to everyone's experience; the intermediate causes, to the hypothetical history of governments; and the moving hand, to the basic principles of human nature.

In spite of the similarity of structure of these two chains, there are two important differences. First, Rousseau claims that the intermediate causes in the conspiracy are even harder to know than is the hypothetical history. Second, the primitive cause of the conspiracy is less comprehensible than "the first and simplest operations of the human soul" (*Discourses*, 95); that is, Grimm's motives are much more complex than those of a natural human. These differences are of great importance for assessing the certainty Rousseau claims about the conspiracy. No one denies that Rousseau suffered persecution. Indeed, few defend completely the motives of many of those whom he regarded as participants in the conspiracy. There is no question that Grimm, Diderot, Mme d'Epinay, Voltaire, and a host of others wished Rousseau ill and acted accordingly. The issue is about the nature of the connection between these motives and the particular events involved in Rousseau's persecution. The only things that can combine the two elements into a "system" are the intermediate causes about which Jean-Jacques can see only "horrible mystery" (I, 622). Rousseau's own account of the system raised against him is unclear about its systematic character. That Rousseau (and Jean-Jacques) believe in the existence of the system is clear; that Rousseau claims to know that it exists in the same sense as he knows the system of nature is doubtful. The knowledge of nature is certain, whereas the belief in the conspiracy is conjectural.

To these questions concerning the existence of a conspiracy and the depth of Rousseau's belief in it can be added the question of whether the belief is a sign of madness. None of these questions can be conclusively settled on the basis of the *Confessions* alone. Rousseau argues that the reader must use information outside the text to settle these questions (I, 589–90, 656). What the *Confessions* does describe is the effect of the belief in the conspiracy on Jean-Jacques. For an interpretation of the *Confessions*, the real issue raised by the conspiracy is what it means that Jean-Jacques is susceptible to such a belief.

Rousseau says that Jean-Jacques was vulnerable to the intrigues of the conspirators because he "had preserved the simplicity of [his] first tastes" (I, 492). Compared to Grimm and the others, Jean-Jacques may be uncomplicated, but his relative innocence should not be confused with naturalness. A natural human would be as powerless as Jean-Jacques is against a conspiracy, but he would also be invulnerable to harm from a conspiracy against his reputation. The young Emile is so indifferent to his reputation that he would behave and feel the same whether he were alone or "if the whole universe were watching" (*Emile*, 132). It is only someone concerned with reputation who can be injured by such a conspiracy. Until Jean-Jacques overcomes this civilized passion he cannot be considered a natural human.

Throughout the period covered in Book X Rousseau does portray himself as immune to the hostility of his former friends. First he was distracted from his initial grief: "objects presented themselves that were sufficiently interesting to my heart to cause a salutary diversion from those which occupied me in spite of myself" (I, 494). These objects are his books, the *Letter to d'Alembert* and *Julie*. He further claims that the rupture in fact freed him from the constraints imposed by his demanding friends (I, 503). His lack of concern with his reputation is shown by his resolve: "[I was determined] to close myself up for the rest of my days in the narrow and peaceful sphere for which I felt myself born" (I, 515). Jean-Jacques shows evidence of being on the verge of a return to natural independence.[20]

This "project of complete retreat" is at first complicated but then aided by Jean-Jacques's new relationship with M. le Maréchal Duc de Luxembourg and his wife. The Maréchal's offer of refuge appears as the fulfillment of the plan for a retreat. Of his new home at Montmorency Rousseau says, "I was there in the terrestrial paradise; I lived there with as much innocence, and I tasted the same pleasures" (I, 521). This echoes his remark in Book I that after the false accusation by the Lamberciers he was "as the first man is represented to us still in the terrestrial paradise, but having ceased to enjoy it" (I, 20). At the close of Book X Rousseau even presents himself as being partially cured of his tendency to fall in love (I, 544). Thus his indifference to public opinion and his freedom from his former friends has apparently returned Jean-Jacques to his state prior to the formation of his artificial passions.[21]

His establishment in a quasi-natural condition seems as complete as can be reasonably expected. Nevertheless, unlike the description of

20. Note the reference to the "narrow and peaceful sphere." See Chapter 4, note 40.
21. Of the passions aroused in Book I, Jean-Jacques seems to be fairly well cured of simple vanity and sexual desire.

happiness in Book VI, the account of terrestrial paradise is pervaded by a tone of imminent doom. Immediately after a glowing description of his accommodations, Rousseau says, "In the bosom of this transient prosperity the catastrophe which should mark its end was prepared from afar" (I, 528). And, whereas Book VI stands in isolation from the surrounding books, Rousseau makes a special effort to connect Book X with the quarrel which begins in Book IX and its effects shown in Book XI. The peace of Book X seems a passing stage, one to be overwhelmed by the conspiracy already in operation out of Jean-Jacques's view.

Book XI almost immediately shows that the terrestrial paradise at Montmorency has distracted Jean-Jacques's lively imagination, not destroyed it. Rousseau shows the beginning of the effect of the conspiracy on him coinciding with a period of illness. In Book VI an illness was the foundation of his happiness; now it is its destruction: "Augmented by a thousand inquietudes, the physical illness rendered me still more sensitive to them" (I, 564). In Book VI the only sources of inquietude were fears of death and damnation. Jean-Jacques's condition in Book XI can be compared to the earlier period during which he feared Hell. He is no longer concerned with salvation, but he is concerned with reputation after death. Far from being calmed by the prospect of an early death, the hopes for posthumous fame are augmented by illness. Accepting the necessity of death does not eliminate the hope for glory as it eliminates ordinary vanity. It aggravates this hope and turns it into fear that glory is not yet secure. This is the civilized passion by which the conspiracy can gain a hold on Jean-Jacques.

Because Jean-Jacques's hopes for glory are centered on his books, his fears focus on the publication of *Emile*, his "last and best work" (I, 566). This fear inspires his belief in the Jesuit plot. Rousseau describes the role of his imagination in aggravating his fears: "The aspect of the most hideous monster would frighten me little, but if I saw in the night a figure under a white sheet, I would be afraid. This then is my imagination which being lit up by this long silence occupied itself by tracing phantoms for me" (I, 566). Although uncertainty has little or no effect on someone lacking imagination, it awakens a peaceful imagination and can cause it to construct a false interpretation of the world. Rousseau's account reveals that his imagination allows the belief in a conspiracy to have an affect on his happiness whether or not that belief is mistaken.

Whether Jean-Jacques is deluded in his belief or not, his concern about other people's intentions and the judgment of future generations

is the mark of a complete denaturing. From the perspective of Rousseau's understanding of the difference between natural and social humans, it makes little difference whether the belief in the plot is accurate.
The distinction between real persecution and paranoia is secondary to
the distinction between being concerned with others' intentions and
opinions and not being so concerned.

As long as Jean-Jacques keeps his hopes for future recognition, he is
vulnerable to fears based on the uncertainty of the future. During the
course of Book XI these fears disappear only intermittently. At one
point he is calmed with a reassurance that he is not about to die: "My
imagination, repressed by this knowledge, no longer made me see a
cruel death in the pain of the stone. . . . Delivered from imaginary ills
more cruel for me than real ones, I endured the latter more peacefully"
(I, 572). As long as he is alive, he is still able to take steps to secure his
reputation. The eventual appearance of *Emile* gives another respite
from worry. Although warned about the danger of publishing the
work, "I remained tranquil" (I, 576). The satisfaction at setting the
keystone of his reputation is stronger than any fear of present persecution.

Typically for Part Two of the *Confessions*, Book XI ends on a dis-
quieting note. After recounting his flight from France to avoid arrest,
Rousseau says, "It is thus that blind and confident in my hopes, I am
always impassioned for what ought to cause my misfortune" (I, 587).
The specific blind hope referred to here is his belief in his security on
Bernese territory, but it can be extended to include his hope for glory
now that his major work has appeared. Shortly after his departure from
France, Jean-Jacques undertakes a new series of works that attempt to
justify and explain *Emile* and the *Social Contract*.[22] He seems to concede
or realize that his books can be misinterpreted, and the possibility of
misrepresentation reopens the prospect of the ultimate success of the
conspiracy. The conspirators can control Jean-Jacques's reputation
among future generations if they can successfully distort his doctrines.
Jean-Jacques faces an endless need to explain and justify himself that
can never guarantee what must always be an uncertain fortune.

These events reveal the precariousness of an independence from
the present generation founded on the hope of posthumous glory. This
hope is created entirely by the imagination. Because it depends entirely
on the future opinions of other people, it combines artificial foresight

22. The works are the *Letter to Beaumont* and the *Letters Written from the Mountain*.

and amour-propre. It can be enjoyed only in anticipation. It is perhaps the least natural of all possible pleasures, although it can be one of the most powerful. This desire can give a partial immunity to the desire for contemporary celebrity and to other artificial desires, but it demands constant reassurance that the glory will be achieved. At the end of Book XI Jean-Jacques may be cured of his imaginary love, but not of his love of the imaginary. Book XII shows the effects of the final revolution on Jean-Jacques. It addresses the questions of whether the vulnerable desire for glory can be abandoned and whether it can be replaced by a better foundation for happiness and independence.

Book XII: A Second "Age of Happiness"

Jean-Jacques's vulnerability to the conspiracy stems from two sources. First, his active imagination allows or forces him to see connections between events whether these connections exist or not. In short, his imagination makes him see a "system" of conspiracy. Second, his desire for glory from future generations can be frustrated by the actions of other people. In short, this modification of amour-propre places him in a position of troubling uncertainty. If Jean-Jacques is to be happy in spite of the conspiracy, he must cure one or both of these artificial characteristics. He must either find a way to distract or limit his imagination or end his quest for an uncertain dependent pleasure. Accomplishing one or the other of these goals can give temporary respite; a more durable happiness depends on accomplishing both.

Within the *Confessions* the model for such an accomplishment is the "age of happiness" described in Book VI. There Jean-Jacques's imagination is both distracted and limited by his belief in the nearness of death. He abandons the uncertain and dependent pleasures of vanity because of a stronger certainty, that of his imminent death. This certainty eliminates all possibility of attaining artificial pleasures, and Jean-Jacques's submission allows his imagination to be distracted to other pleasures. The key to this "age of happiness" is the recognition of necessity, the abolition of uncertainty.

The desire for glory after death cannot be overcome by belief in the nearness of death; therefore the necessity to which it must bend must come from another source. There are two ways Jean-Jacques's uncertainty about his reputation could come to an end. For one, he could become convinced that his efforts have succeeded in securing his reputation against all attempts to damage it. The variety of his efforts to secure his reputation is a sign that complete certainty on this matter is impossible in the long run. Or he could become convinced that the conspiracy is so powerful that it can frustrate all his efforts. An omnipotent and inexorable conspiracy would kill his desire for future glory by destroying the hope that it could be fulfilled, just as the necessity of death kills other desires by destroying the hope that they can be satisfied. For the remainder of the *Confessions* Jean-Jacques fluctuates between these two methods of ending uncertainty. To the extent that he follows the first, he remains uncured of his artificial desire. To the extent that he accepts the second, he does accomplish something like a return to natural wholeness.

The external facts reported in Book XII represent an unbroken chain of triumphs for the conspiracy. The friendly reception at Bern is very brief, and Jean-Jacques is forced to seek refuge at Môtiers under the protection of Frederick the Great. He is then driven from Môtiers to St. Peter's Island and finally to England.

In addition to severing Jean-Jacques's attachment to any particular place, the events of Book XII cut his remaining attachments to his fellows. The first break with his contemporaries is revealed in one of the recurring motifs of the *Confessions*, a descriptive catalog of Jean-Jacques's acquaintances in his new surroundings.[23] The catalog begins with Marshal Keith, Frederick's governor of Neuchâtel. Rousseau insists that the friendship established between himself and Keith is perfect, claiming it is the source of "[his] last happy memories" (I, 599). This friendship contrasts with the deepening estrangement from Thérèse (I, 594), but at the same time it quickly leads to another disappointment. Rousseau concludes this section of the book by listing a series of losses. The first of these is the death of M. de Luxembourg, the second the death of Maman, and the third Keith's departure for Scotland and subsequent rupture with Jean-Jacques. To these three losses he tentatively adds the death of the Abbé de Mably. On reflection, Rousseau says that their bad relations in recent years means that Mably's death cannot precisely be considered a loss to Jean-Jacques. This reference, tentative though it may be, shows the significance of the list of losses. Mably's inclusion on the list makes it an unbroken chain of Jean-Jacques's relationships. Jean-Jacques left Maman to be a tutor with the

---

23. Other catalogs occur at I, 6–7, 139–43, 280–81, and 349–50. The function of these descriptions is to illustrate the social environment in which Jean-Jacques finds himself.

Mably family. The abbé and his brother, Condillac, facilitated Jean-Jacques's absorption into the Parisian world of letters. His rupture with this world was immediately succeeded by his friendship with M. de Luxembourg. Finally, the friendship with Keith is Jean-Jacques's final attempt at a tie with a contemporary. These losses, then, coupled with the estrangement from Thérèse, mark the end of the chain of close relationships that begins with Maman. These losses end Jean-Jacques's hopes for friendship and consequently contribute to a cure of the desire for friendship.

The rest of the catalog of acquaintances shows how unpromising Jean-Jacques's new circumstances are for achieving any intimacy. When he moved from Paris to the country, Jean-Jacques found himself besieged by visitors who sought his acquaintance because of his celebrity. At the Hermitage and Montmorency his visitors could allege at least some harmony of "talents, tastes, and maxims" to justify their visits (I, 611). At Môtiers he is plagued by visitors who with a few exceptions are interested solely in his celebrity. Parisians can share Jean-Jacques's talents to some degree and also his tastes even if they only pretend to share his maxims. At Môtiers he finds himself on close terms with people such as a certain M. Laliaud, who claims to want a sculptor to make a bust of Jean-Jacques for his library. Closer acquaintance with M. Laliaud reveals to Jean-Jacques that "none of my writings were in the small number of books that he read in his life" (I, 613). The new visitors lack the good hearts of his earlier provincial friends and are bad imitations of Parisians. Even his one agreeable visitor, the supposed Baron de Sauttern, who appears to combine elegance and "sweetness of character" (I, 616), is revealed as a fraud. The lack of potential friends completes the cure of the desire for friendship begun by the loss of old friends. Because Jean-Jacques owes the position that brings him such acquaintances to the conspiracy, the conspiracy can be said to be successful at depriving him of the possibility of friendship. Rousseau especially blames the conspirators for detaching him from Keith (I, 598). The more successful the conspiracy is at convincing Jean-Jacques of the hopelessness of his desire for friends, the more it tends to cure him of this desire.

The gradual triumph of the conspiracy represents the gradual cure of Jean-Jacques's artificial desires and passions.[24] The conspiracy has

24. The complete success of the conspiracy would mean that the conspirators would cease to be able to torment Jean-Jacques. They could torment only themselves; see I, 586.

not yet had the same effect on his desire for glory, but it is moving in that direction. If it were completely successful, or if Jean-Jacques were to be convinced of its success, it would cure him of virtually all his unnatural desires. One can see this by comparing Jean-Jacques's position as a victim of the conspiracy with that of a natural human in the pure state of nature. The natural human is considered happy largely in being subject to few pains and in accepting those that are necessary or unavoidable. A civilized human is unhappy largely because increased imagination and desires bring anguish from all sides for pains that seem avoidable; that is, the imagination creates hopes by opening horizons of possibilities, and these hopes cause pain when they are unfulfilled, as they must be in large part. As the victim of the conspiracy, Jean-Jacques can still imagine having a lover, a friend, and future glory. In this respect he is like a civilized human rather than a natural one. His belief in the conspiracy, however, can convince him that his desires are hopeless. If this happened he would submit to his pain in the way that a natural human submits to illness, with resignation rather than a prayer or demand for a remedy.

It is not clear how satisfying this condition of resignation is. Natural humans are not really happy when ill or hungry; they merely avoid the additional unhappiness caused by tormenting hope and fear. Their real happiness occurs only with the fulfillment of their natural desires for food and perhaps sex. It is when natural needs are fulfilled that "[the natural human's] soul, agitated by nothing, is given over to the sole sentiment of its present existence" (*Discourses*, 117). The picture of nature involves a more positive pleasure than mere resignation to unavoidable ills.

The more positive pleasures open to Jean-Jacques are described in the next section of Book XII, which almost brings the *Confessions* to a close. The structure of this account is almost identical to that of the account of happiness at les Charmettes in Book VI. In fact Rousseau refers directly to his earlier happiness and its resemblance to his new condition (I, 644). Thus, just as Jean-Jacques's brief moment of happiness was the culmination of Part One, another similar moment is the culmination of Part Two. In Book XII Rousseau has already described the psychological basis for his condition, namely, his belief in a conspiracy devoted to depriving him of his hope for future glory. Accordingly, he turns to a description of the physical setting of his new retreat, the material basis of his condition. The precision in the parallels of these two accounts makes it possible to compare them with a view to identifying the distinctive features of the ultimate happiness.

Each description begins with the material and psychological preconditions or foundations of Jean-Jacques's happiness. Then each gives a general description of his activities, organized around the topic of idleness. Next, each gives a precise account of Jean-Jacques's daily routine. Finally, each concludes by showing the dangers that threaten or destroy the period of happiness. Within the parameters set by this common structure, significant differences emerge.

A general account of the happiness of Book VI is given in Chapter 4. Its outlines can be summarized briefly. The psychological preconditions of Jean-Jacques's happiness are there found in his acceptance of the necessity of death; the physical precondition is les Charmettes, which offers pleasantness and self-sufficiency. The general characterization of activities emphasizes constant light work, such as caring for pigeons or studying. Rousseau says that this period "was the one in my life in which I was the least idle and the least bored" (I, 235).

At les Charmettes, Jean-Jacques's day begins with prayer (I, 236–37). Rousseau emphasizes the contemplative aspect of his prayers and his need for direct contact with nature, but he also mentions that he prayed for "an innocent and tranquil life, exempt from vice, from suffering, from painful need, the death of the just and their lot in the future." That he asks for divine assistance is one small indication of a sense of dependence on divine will or a belief that his happiness can be threatened from outside. After breakfast with Maman, Jean-Jacques studies philosophy, geometry, and Latin to teach himself how to think and to improve his memory. Even when he thinks he is dying, his activities are directed by clear purposes. His feeling of the nearness of death merely turns him away from purposes that serve vanity alone. After studying, he works in the garden, cares for his "friends the pigeons" or "another little family," the bees (I, 239). After lunch he returns to books for "recreation and amusement" rather than study (I, 240). This reading consists of history, geography, and astronomy. He does not read novels or lives, which could turn him into another man. Yet his studies do remove him from himself in a more limited sense. History does so by taking him away from his own experience into the distant past.[25] Geography and astronomy take him to distant places.[26] The account of the daily routine concludes with a reference to country labors, which return Jean-Jacques from these mental journeys.

25. On the dangers of history, see Chapter 1.
26. On geography, see *Emile*, 109–10. On geography and astronomy, see *Emile*, 167–72. The object of Emile's education is to turn the entire earth into his island (*Emile*, 167).

This daily routine contains three elements that somewhat compromise Jean-Jacques's position of quasi-natural wholeness and independence. First, there is his acknowledged dependence on God. His prayers for the continuation of his present condition and a future reward indicate some hopes and fears based on foresight. Second, his studies are guided by a purpose that is of use only in future efforts. Finally, his leisure reading moves Jean-Jacques outside his present condition. It is on these points that the account in Book XII departs from that in Book VI.

As argued above, the psychological precondition of Jean-Jacques's happiness in Book XII is based on his certainty about the future. His account vacillates between assertions that he has secured his reputation by his works and that he no longer feels the "whiffs of vainglory" at all (I, 639–40). He says, "I took leave as it were of my age and of my contemporaries," but it is not entirely clear that he has abandoned the future. In any event, he has given up efforts directed toward future rewards just as he did in accepting death in Book VI.

The physical preconditions of happiness are achieved when Jean-Jacques is forced to move once more. After an attack on his home at Môtiers, he is faced with the choice of what to do next. Rejecting the options of England, Scotland, and Potsdam, he chooses St. Peter's Island in Lake Bienne. It is this island that provides the natural conditions for his happiness. In his description of the island Rousseau calls special attention to its self-sufficiency. The island "furnishes all the principle productions necessary for life" (I, 637). Its description culminates with this assessment:

> It seemed to me that in this island I would be more separated from men, more sheltered from their outrages, more forgotten by them, in a word more given over to pleasures of inaction and of the contemplative life: I would have wished to be so confined in this island that I might have no more commerce with mortals, and it is certain that I took all imaginable means to avoid the necessity of undertaking any. (I, 638)

Although this statement is somewhat tentative, it emphasizes isolation. The island is not only self-sufficient, it is also relatively safe from interference. At least it would be safe if the voluntary nature of his stay could be made compulsory. The security of this island retreat is somewhat threatened from outside.

After the account of the physical conditions for happiness in the isolation and self-sufficiency of the island, Rousseau turns to another material condition, that of his subsistence. He manages to secure himself from want (for the moment) by accepting an assortment of pensions and by arranging at last for the publication of a general edition of his works. Then he says, "Being in repose with respect to subsistence I had no other care" (I, 638).

This account of preconditions is followed by a general account of Jean-Jacques's happiness. Rousseau now refers to his condition as "the great project of the idle life" (I, 646). At first glance this idleness could not be more clearly distinguished from the complete lack of idleness described in Book VI, but Rousseau reduces the implicit contrast by opposing his own activity to that of sophisticated civilized humans in both cases. This shared opposition reveals what idleness and busy activity can have in common. Both states appear natural when compared to the artificiality of civilized life.

In Book XII Rousseau characterizes his idleness simply as "doing nothing." This sort of idleness is directly comparable to the inactivity of natural humans: "To do nothing is the first and strongest passion of man after that of self-preservation" (*Oeuvres*, Geneva, 1782–89, XVI, 221). For a primitive natural human, doing nothing means, "sleeping, vegetating, staying immobile." Rousseau opposes this total indolence to the restlessness, foresight, and activity of civilized humans. Nowhere is this contrast more vivid than in the civilized attempts at idleness of the circles of high society. According to Rousseau, far from being restful, this so-called idleness is comparable to "the labor of a convict" (I, 641). Social idleness requires constant attention to the demands of social behavior, to how one appears to other people. It requires an extraordinary constraint of will. Rousseau complains that at social gatherings he is unable to run, leap, sing, cry, or gesticulate when he wants to. A natural man might not wish to do any of these things, but he would share Rousseau's resistance to being compelled to pay attention to what others are doing and saying. Jean-Jacques's idleness shares the characteristic of natural idleness of freedom, even though it does involve some activity. "It is at the same time that of a child who is ceaselessly in movement to do something, and that of a dotard who combs the countryside while his arms are at rest" (I, 641). For the natural human, freedom takes the form of inactivity, of not doing anything at all; for Jean-Jacques it takes the form of aimless activity, of doing things that are not guided by any goal. Thus, for Jean-Jacques, doing nothing means doing nothing in particular. It is quite compatible with being very busy.

In Book XII there is one particular activity that exemplifies this doing nothing: "Botany, as I have always considered it, and as it began to become a passion for me, was primarily an idle study, fit for filling the void of my leisure, without leaving a place for the delirium of imagination, nor for the boredom of a total inactivity" (I, 641). This statement has enough implications to merit detailed consideration.

Rousseau presents botany as an alternative to the choice between delirium of imagination and boredom of inactivity. The latter two choices represent the ordinary lot of civilized humans. In the first case, their imagination drives them to furious activity guided by foresight and hope. In the second case, it rebels against enforced inactivity. Both alternatives are unintelligible to a natural human, who knows neither delirium nor boredom.[27] Earlier in the *Confessions* Jean-Jacques often tries to avoid these civilized alternatives. He uses numerous "supplements" to attempt to fill the void and return to something like natural wholeness. Each of these supplements, masturbation, Thérèse, friendship, literary career, and others, merely aggravate his imagination rather than calm it. Here Rousseau claims that botany fills the void completely; rather than being a supplement that only conceals the void, it is a complement that completes it. Botany steers the imagination on a course between furious activity and boring inactivity.

Rousseau emphasizes that botany is a sort of study—clearly not the kind of activity that could absorb a natural human. He confirms this point in his description of the charm of botany:

> However elegant, however admirable, however divine the structure of plants may be, it does not strike an ignorant eye enough to interest it. The constant analogy and still the prodigious variety which reigns in their organization transports only those who already have some idea of the vegetal system. Others have only a stupid and monotonous admiration at the aspect of all the treasures of nature. (I, 641)

If an ignorant civilized human is incapable of appreciating botany because of a lack of knowledge, the same must be true for a natural human, who does not feel even a stupid admiration at nature. Wishing only to vegetate, a natural human has no interest in admiring the vegetal system.

That Rousseau presents any study or science as a fulfilling activity is

27. Rousseau's understanding of the imagination is crucial for the development of the significance of boredom. The claim that all the charm of life comes from the imagination makes it necessary to describe the condition of uneasiness in which the imagination fails to do its work.

a remarkable reversal. To this point he has consistently presented quests after knowledge as inextricably linked to imagination and artificial needs. He hints at precisely this issue in his introductory statement on botany. He indicates that it is only by a particular interpretation that botany can be regarded as a study that can fill the void. His reference to botany, "such as I have always considered it, and such as it began to become a passion for me," is somewhat contradictory. Rousseau's more consistent argument is that botany began to become a passion for him when he learned to consider it properly. Two factors earlier kept him from forming this proper understanding: Claude Anet's death prevented Maman from establishing a royal garden of plants, which would have drawn Jean-Jacques to this study, and Maman's combination of medicine with botany kept him from developing an interest. Several times Anet invited Jean-Jacques on botanizing expeditions, but the youth declined with disdain because he "regarded it only as the study of an apothecary" (I, 180). It is this utilitarian interpretation that would make botany indistinguishable from other sciences. Throughout his botanical writings Rousseau decries the tendency toward making botany a branch of medicine. The opening line of his botanical dictionary is "The first misfortune of botany is to have been regarded since its birth as a part of medicine" (IV, 1201). He argues that this view restricts the scope of botany to those plants useful for medicinal purposes and also distracts attention from the "organization" of plants by focusing on their properties. Such botany ignores what plants are by paying attention to what they can do. For botany to become a science in its own right, it is necessary to sever it from utilitarian concerns.

Rousseau offers an alternative notion of a true science of botany in his "Letters on Botany."[28] He is "persuaded that at every age the study of nature dulls the taste for frivolous amusements by forestalling the tumult of passion and carries to the soul a nourishment which profits it by filling it with the most worthy object for its comtemplation" (IV, 1151). Here the usefulness of botany is identified as a distraction from other outlets for the imagination. In the *Confessions* Rousseau similarly presents his own study of botany as a distraction from the delirium of his imagination, the source of his artificial passions.[29]

28. Rousseau's language in the "Letters on Botany" is traditional. He glosses over some of the difficulties of knowing nature in these letters, which were written to a twenty-five-year-old mother for the purpose of training her daughter in botany.

29. For discussions of botany in Rousseau's works, see Eigeldinger, *Réalité*, p. 82, and Lionel Gossman, "The Innocent Art of Confession and Reverie," *Daedalus* 107,3 (1978): 59–78.

According to Rousseau the analogy and variety of plants can "transport" those who have some knowledge of botany. Nevertheless, contrary to what one is led to expect from the "Letters on Botany," beyond a certain point the pleasure of botanizing does not increase in the same proportion that knowledge increases. Rousseau describes his own pleasure as follows:

> To wander nonchalantly in the woods and fields, to take mechanically here and there, sometimes a flower, sometimes a branch, to graze about at random, to observe thousands and thousands of times the same things, and always with the same interest because I always forget them, was enough to pass eternity without being bored for a moment. (I, 641)

Here Rousseau implies that the contemplation of natural things is pleasing only, or especially, when it is novel. According to this presentation, unvarying contemplation of (as opposed to learning) the order of nature would be boring. Such contemplation would be boring because it would provide no distraction for the creative imagination. If it did not find a supply of diverting objects in nature, the imagination would attempt to create them for itself. Rousseau's praise of the study of botany shows some features of the traditional or ancient praise of the contemplation of nature unguided by utilitarian concerns. At the same time, the insistence on the constant recurrence of novelty represents a reaffirmation rather than a rejection of Rousseau's very modern teaching that the greatest charms of a civilized life are in the imagination rather than in reason or nature. Neither utility nor contemplation can fill the void created by the imagination.

Rousseau's transformation of the traditional understanding can be seen in his contrast between the uninformed and the informed understanding of plants. The average person's enjoyment of nature is monotonous. Everywhere one looks, one sees the same thing. The knowledge of plants allows the botanist to see the combination of variety and sameness underneath this monotony.[30] On the traditional understanding, the average person sees only flux, where the botanist finds eternal principles worthy of contemplation. For Rousseau, both the average person and the perfect botanist see different but equally boring uniformity. The informed amateur alone enjoys an endlessly enchanting variety. Rousseau's position is a consequence of his more fundamental position that denies that humans are natural reasoners. For Rousseau,

30. See Starobinski, *Transparence*, p. 279.

the knowledge of permanent principles is a means to enjoying the endless play of variety. The principles themselves are boring.[31]

There is one further implication of Rousseau's statement connecting the pleasure of botany to his lack of memory. Properly speaking, he often rediscovers what he has known before rather than finding something completely new. The only description of a specific botanizing expedition in the *Confessions* extends this combination of forgetting and rediscovery beyond the limits of botanical science. This expedition is described in Book VI, but it takes place shortly before Jean-Jacques moves to the island. In his description of the expedition Rousseau mentions that he astonished his companion, Du Peyrou, by suddenly crying out with joy, "*Ah, here is some periwinkle*" (I, 226, emphasis in original). In this instance Jean-Jacques's joy is based on a sudden recollection or redscovery, but not one based on the principles of botany. Instead of recollecting the application of these principles, he recollects the last time he had seen some periwinkle, about thirty years before (during the period covered in Book VI). That occasion was the first day that he and Maman went to les Charmettes for an overnight stay. On the road Maman had stopped to exclaim, "Here is some periwinkle still in bloom." By stimulating the recollection of the past, botanizing allows Jean-Jacques to recapture his past happiness. Thus botany keeps his thought away from his present problems and worries about the future. Rousseau makes this explicit in the passage in Book VI. He uses the example of the periwinkle to illustrate a transformation in his imaginative faculty: "My imagination, which in my youth always went forward and now retrogrades, compensates with sweet memories, for the hope which I have lost forever. I see nothing in the future which tempts me anymore; only returns to the past can gratify me, and these returns so lively and true in the epoch of which I am speaking often make me live happily in spite of my misfortunes" (I, 226). This recollection is an exercise of the imagination, but not one that projects into the future or embellishes the present. Rousseau insists that he recalls this period "entirely as if it still endured." Most important, such an experience gives birth to no hopes, it is a compensation for having no hopes. In this example botany provides a link between the sort of happiness Jean-Jacques enjoys on the island and his brief period of happiness at les Charmettes. In Book VI he shows himself to be unable to make this

31. The pleasures of botany should be contrasted to the contemplation of nature described in Book II (I, 57–58).

happiness last. In Book XII he can reestablish it almost at will by re-
discovering his happiness in his memory.

In this way, the study of botany is the model of a civilized activity
that carries with it none of the disadvantages of civilization and preserves the advantages of the natural condition. It represents the possibility of a positive pleasure involving the imagination, something unavailable to a primitive human. A simple return to the state of nature is
impossible for any civilized human whose passions and imagination
have developed. Nevertheless, there are activities that fill the void
caused by the development of these faculties. Someone who happens
across one of these activities can satisfy the imagination without letting
it create a view of the world that would inspire tormenting hopes and
fears. Such activities are the highest forms of civilized idleness and
activity.

Rousseau's account of his daily routine elaborates on this picture of
happiness by showing Jean-Jacques's new superiority in independence
and self-sufficiency. Like the description in Book VI, this one also begins with an account of the morning prayer. Now, however, Jean-
Jacques's prayers are purely contemplative. He asks for no divine assistance or favor whatsoever. He has no further hopes that center around
God. His morning activities lack the purposefulness of his study of
philosophy, geometry, and Latin at les Charmettes. He arranges papers
and botanizes, doing both solely for the immediate pleasure they offer.
His afternoon activity is a return to the study of geography, but Jean-
Jacques's study never passes beyond the visible limits of the shore of the
lake. He dreams while floating in his boat and investigates a neighboring island, where he introduces a colony of rabbits. These activities
keep him firmly tied to his actual condition. The final activity in the
daily routine more directly links this period with les Charmettes. Rousseau says, "To these amusements, I joined one which recalled to me the
sweet life of les Charmettes, and to which the scene particularly invited
me" (I, 644). He is referring to the harvest, an activity he finds pleasant
both in itself and for the memories it arouses. Such is the description of
Jean-Jacques's final achievement of happiness.

If these were the only elements of this description and if the *Confessions* ended here, the project of a return to natural wholeness in the
life of an individual would be a dazzling triumph. Some elements
within the account, however, trouble the image of "supreme happiness" (I, 640). Moreover, the *Confessions* does not end here.

The troubling elements can be isolated in the progression of Rousseau's references to the imagination in this section. As might be expected from his crucial assertion that botanizing does not leave room for "the delirium of imagination" (I, 641), such references to the imagination are rare. Rousseau's first discussion of a product of the imagination occurs in his account of his afternoon activities. When discussing his exploration of the neighboring island, he says that he goes there to botanize and "to build for [himself] an imaginary dwelling of this little island like another Robinson" (I, 644). This reference does little to harm the picture of natural wholeness.[32] Rousseau's next reference to the imagination in Book XII confirms the impression of a relatively inactive imagination. Rousseau says that even his occasional visits to the towns in the vicinity "already fatigued [his] imagination" (I, 645). In the immediate context he says, "I acquired such a taste for St. Peter's Island, and the stay suited me so well, that by virtue of inscribing all my desires in that island I formed that of never leaving at all." Inscribing all his desires in the island conforms to the pattern of lack of imaginative activity. Thus the fatigue suffered by his imagination on visits is caused by the use of an unexercised faculty. So far, the imagination poses no threat to natural wholeness.

Rousseau's account of exactly what he means by inscribing his desires in the island gives one final reference to the imagination. This account of an image he forms during his idle activity is the one jarring note in the return to self-sufficiency and wholeness: "I felt a singular pleasure at seeing the waves break at my feet. I made from them the image of the tumult of the world and the peace of my habitation, and sometimes I was moved to the point of feeling the tears falling from my eyes at this sweet idea."[33] This singular pleasure is the sole pleasure experienced on the island that involves a comparison with a worse condition.[34] Because of this comparison with what had been his lot, Jean-Jacques is able to form fears that he can lose his present happiness and hopes that he can keep it. As a result he closes this section as he opened it, by referring to his wish that he could be confined on the island. He wants to change a condition that depends on both his own will and that of his persecutors to one of complete necessity. Only by doing so could he completely calm his hopes and fears.

32. On the identification with Robinson Crusoe, see Chapter 3 and I, 296.
33. Lucretius gives a similar account in *De Rerum Natura* II, 1–61.
34. Rousseau says that the cause of his pleasure is a "secret congratulation at being in this condition out of the grasp of the evil" (I, 643). This explanation is lacking in the Paris manuscript (I, 1604).

This concluding discussion of his desires and fears completes the parallel with Book VI. Rousseau concludes his account of his life at les Charmettes by referring to his fear of damnation, concern for Maman's financial affairs, and hopes for a cure. He is able to resolve the first two fears with little difficulty, but the hopes for a cure strike at the very foundation of his happiness. In both Books VI and XII Jean-Jacques's happiness requires a firm foundation in necessity or certainty, the necessity of death or the necessity of confinement on the island. Both of these apparent certainties turn out to be illusory.

Jean-Jacques's fears for his position on the island are soon realized. He is ordered to leave on very short notice. As a result he becomes convinced that there is no place of exile safe from his persecutors, who have now revealed that they will work either through public opinion or legally sanctioned force according to circumstances. It could well be argued that this demonstration of the implacable power of the conspirators gives a certainty to Jean-Jacques's position that he lacked on the island. Knowing that no asylum is available can be compared to knowing that death is near. Both make one seek one's enjoyment in the past and present rather than in the future. This abandonment of hope for the continuation of the pleasures of the island can lead to a less troubled enjoyment. This is the argument that Rousseau himself makes in the *Reveries*. There he concludes his account of the stay on the island by referring to his inability to return there because of his persecutors. He continues, "But at least they will not prevent me from transporting myself there each day on the wings of imagination, and from tasting for several hours the same pleasure as if I still lived there" (I, 1049). This imaginative recollection is comparable to the one experienced on the island when he regained the immediate experience of the pleasures of les Charmettes. In the *Reveries* Rousseau makes the connection between such pleasure and the imagination more explicit, but he still indicates that it is a very well directed imagination that can restore this pleasure.[35] Thus, in his last word on the subject, Rousseau argues that once hopes and fears have been extinguished, his imaginative recollection can make him immune to the influence of the conspiracy.[36] The imagination is compatible with a whole and independent pleasure.

35. Rousseau claims that his memory of his happiness depends on his imagination (I, 1049).

36. That the account of the stay on the island given in the *Reveries* is so much more elaborate than the one in the *Confessions* is an indication that imaginative recollection also involves embellishment.

Rousseau does not make this argument in the *Confessions*. He is less willing there than he is in the *Reveries* to make an assertion of his own cure from hopes and fears. In the *Reveries* he dates this final cure only from 1776, several years after the completion of the *Confessions* (I, 997). After relating the order expelling him from the island in the *Confessions*, Rousseau turns to the consideration of one final "project" for the future that he has been considering for some time (I, 648). This project is to undertake legislation for Corsica. Rousseau says that only one consideration has previously kept him from this enterprise: "Made to meditate at leisure in solitude, I was not at all made to speak, act, to deal with affairs among men" (I, 650). This suitability for solitude is connected with Jean-Jacques's disposition, and Rousseau says that after "having returned from the chimeras of love and friendship" he was particularly in need of peace. Nevertheless, it is not so much his desires as his appraisal of his talents which stands as an obstacle. He concedes that "the greatness, the beauty, the utility of the object animated my courage." He is still capable of feeling the desire for posthumous glory as a founder.

Thus, in the *Confessions* and unlike the *Reveries*, instead of putting an end to all his hopes, the expulsion from St. Peter's Island serves as the occasion for the arousal of new ones. In the first place Jean-Jacques begins to imagine that his persecutors will be unlikely to pursue him to Corsica. Once there he plans "to renounce, at least in appearance, the work of legislation" (I, 651). Having made this apparent renunciation, he will be free "to undertake without noise the instruction necessary to be more useful to them if [he] saw a time to succeed at doing so." While Jean-Jacques ultimately rejects the project, he does so only because of external inconveniences. He makes it clear that while his experience has succeeded in curing him of his sexual passions and petty vanity and has even been able to impose some limits on his imagination, it has not succeeded in ending his attachment to justice and glory. The return to wholeness is revealed as partial and temporary.

The Conclusion(?) of the *Confessions*

The remainder of the narrative of Book XII reinforces the impression of the incompleteness of Jean-Jacques's reform. He relates the confusing series of events surrounding his departure from the island and then, rather than concluding, he indicates that his story is not at an end: "It will be seen in my third part if ever I have the strength to write it, how believing that I was leaving for Berlin I left for England, and how the two women [Mmes de Verdelin and de Boufflers] who wished to dispose of me after having by virtue of intrigues chased me from Switzerland where I was not sufficiently in their power, succeeded in the end of giving me over to their friend" (I, 656).[37] Thus Rousseau breaks off his narrative on an incomplete and ominous note. This statement of the possibility of a third part has a number of effects on the reader. Most important, it causes uneasiness by giving the impression that one has not read a completed book. At the same time that Rousseau announces this incompleteness he fills it by summarizing the substance of the missing third part. This part promises to be the relation of the complete success of the conspiracy. In this preview, Rousseau says nothing about what he has previously taught his readers to regard as most important, namely, his chain of sentiments. While he broadly hints at the success of the conspiracy, he leaves it to his reader to deduce the effect that this success will have on Jean-Jacques. The reader's ability to judge this matter without being told the result will be the test of the *Confessions'* success at teaching the knowledge of the human heart.

After implicitly imposing this new burden on his reader, Rousseau adds a brief postscript account of the reception of one of the readings he gives of the *Confessions*. Rousseau finished this reading by reaffirming the accuracy of his narrative, the goodness of his character, and the verifiability of this goodness to all who would examine it. Then he concludes, "I finished my reading and the whole world was silent. Mme d'Egmont was the only one who seemed moved; she visibly shuddered; but she recovered very quickly, and kept the silence as did all of the company. Such was the fruit that I obtained from this reading and from my declaration" (I, 656). At first glance this conclusion suggests Rousseau's final admission of the failure of the *Confessions* to elicit the desired response. Most critics have read the passage as Rousseau's rejection of the *Confessions* for the renewed autobiographical attempts in the different forms of the *Dialogues* and *Reveries*.[38] This view has an element of truth. It is certainly the case that Rousseau understood the *Dialogues* and *Reveries* as improvements on the *Confessions*. What he has to say about this matter is examined in Chapter 7. For the moment it suffices

37. The friend is David Hume.
38. A recent statement of this case is by Williams, who argues that all of Rousseau's works follow a dynamic that drives him from one literary form to another; see *Romantic Autobiography*, pp. 3, 63.

to make a precise appraisal of the significance of this conclusion within the terms of the *Confessions* itself.

It should be noted that from a purely literary standpoint Rousseau's abrupt conclusion of the narrative followed by his account of his auditors' response has its advantages.[39] As Georges May points out, autobiographies can never be quite complete. The narrative must end before the story is finished.[40] Even if the autobiographer aims at the revelation of a persisting character rather than a simple chronicle of events, the wholeness of this revelation is threatened by the possibility of a deathbed conversion or renunciation. Rousseau does more consciously and dramatically what all autobiographers are constrained to do.[41] In one respect his nonconclusion mirrors and confirms his procedure at the beginning of the book. In the first book of the *Confessions* Rousseau presents a number of incidents as if each of them were the single radical break from nature that determined his future. Hence he demonstrates the importance of these childhood events while at the same time raising a question about the absolute importance of any one of them. Book I poses in a complex way the difficulty of understanding beginnings or origins and their determining effects on the future. Rousseau's conclusion raises a comparable question about endings. On one hand, he implies that his essential account of his personality is complete and that the reader now should know him so thoroughly that there is no need of further narrative to follow the chain of sentiments to its conclusion; on the other, by alluding to a third part, he opens the possibility of future revolutions in his character.[42] Thus he poses, in an equally complex way, the difficulty of understanding endings or finality in the life of a civilized human whose possibilities are limitless.[43]

It is also important to note that Rousseau's statement of the reaction of his auditors concerns only one small audience. He mentions only the last of his four readings, and there is some evidence that his other listeners were more demonstrative in their responses (I, 1611–14). Rousseau's list makes clear that this particular audience, unlike the others, is made up of titled members. Thus the failure of the *Confessions* before this audience represents its failure only before a certain type of group, one that might be expected to be less receptive than others.

---

39. On the *Confessions* as unfinished, see Saussure, *Manuscrits*, p. 259.
40. See May, *L'Autobiographie*, p. 162; see Hartle, *Modern Self*, pp. 38–39.
41. On a contemporary autobiographer's attempt to come to terms with this dilemma, see Germaine Brée, "Michel Leiris: Marginale," in *Autobiography*, ed. Olney.
42. The beginning of the *Reveries* presents just such a revolution.
43. See Hartle, *Modern Self*, p. 28.

Moreover, Rousseau consistently expresses his lack of hope or concern for success among the generation of his contemporaries. The negative judgment of his contemporaries stands as a challenge to future generations of readers. Rousseau implicitly suggests that people can be judged legitimately by their response to his life.

Finally, even this reading is not a total failure. One out of the five listeners is visibly moved. While this is not an astonishing rate of success, neither is it a total failure. Furthermore, while being visibly moved is one measure of being affected by a book, it is not the only one. Moving or persuading an audience by inspiring certain feelings in them is only one of the purposes of the *Confessions*. Rousseau, as perhaps is fitting, is silent about whether he may have convinced or taught any of his listeners. The practical, moral effect of the *Confessions* is both limited and knowable. Its philosophic effect is harder to grasp.

[7]

The Success of
the *Confessions*

The success of Rousseau's *Confessions* must be judged in relation to each of his objects in writing the work. Rousseau's treatment of the genre of lives and his explicit statements about the *Confessions* reveal three different goals. First, Rousseau presents a moral fable. This image of human experience is meant to form certain feelings in readers in order to change the way they experience their lives. Second, Rousseau gives a philosophic account of human nature by showing its modifications in a uniquely revealing example. Third, Rousseau reveals the epistemological underpinnings for his "system" by showing how it is possible for a civilized human to acquire knowledge of human nature. To these goals of Rousseau, the author of the *Confessions*, can be added the goal of Jean-Jacques, the protagonist of the *Confessions*—to cure his civilized corruption and to return to a quasi-natural condition of wholeness.

Jean-Jacques's project shows the way to evaluate Rousseau's goals. One can address the epistemological issue by considering how Jean-Jacques acquires his knowledge of nature and how this knowledge affects him. One can arrive at the account of human nature by seeing how naturalness is lost in an individual and whether some approximation of naturalness can be recovered by an extraordinary individual in unusual circumstances. One can identify the substance of Rousseau's moral fable by reflecting on the general image of human experience given in the account of Jean-Jacques's life.

Rousseau's Judgment of the *Confessions*

Before appraising the *Confessions* on these issues, we should consider Rousseau's own testimony. In the preceding chapter I argue that the enigmatic conclusion of the work does not, in itself, prove that Rousseau considered the *Confessions* a failure. To that argument, based largely on evidence within the text, can be added the evidence of Rousseau's efforts to preserve the work by depositing copies with several guardians.[1] In addition, Rousseau writes his last work, the *Reveries*, as if the reader is familiar with the contents of the *Confessions* (I, 999–1001, 1035–38). It is indisputable that Rousseau regarded the *Confessions* as worthy of preservation, if not as a complete success.

It must be admitted, however, that the existence of the subsequent autobiographical works and the absence of the promised Part Three of the *Confessions* testify to reservations on Rousseau's part. In both the *Dialogues* and *Reveries* he discusses the reasons for these new excursions in autobiography and for his use of very different formats. In his preface to the *Dialogues*, "On the Subject and Form of This Writing," Rousseau distinguishes between his new work and the *Confessions*: "As for those who wish only an agreeable and rapid reading, those who have sought, who have found only that in my *Confessions*, who cannot suffer a little fatigue, or sustain a coherent attention for the interest of justice and truth, they will do well to spare themselves the boredom of this reading. Far from seeking to please them, I will avoid at least this final indignity that the tableau of the miseries of my life might be an object of amusement for anyone" (I, 666). This statement is more a criticism of some readers of the *Confessions* than it is of the work itself. Rousseau argues that those who read the *Confessions* only as an agreeable work have missed its point. To the extent that this is a criticism of the *Confessions* itself, it implies that Rousseau made it too easy for the reader to read for pleasure rather than understanding. The very title of the *Dialogues*, *Rousseau Judges Jean-Jacques*, shows his disappointment in the audience of the *Confessions*. The title implies that rather than playing the role of subservient confessor to an audience of judges, Rousseau now undertakes to educate his audience about how they should act as his judges. Thus the *Dialogues* can be regarded as a manual for the readers of the *Confessions*. Once they have learned from Rousseau how to judge Jean-Jacques, readers can read the *Confessions* properly. What-

---

1. On the history of the manuscripts of the *Confessions*, see Saussure, *Manuscrits*.

ever defects the *Confessions* may have from being too agreeable can be overcome by the more fatiguing *Dialogues*.

The criticism of the *Confessions* found in the *Reveries* is more damaging. The first reference to the *Confessions* occurs in the First Walk. After describing his hopes for the *Dialogues* and the shattering of these hopes, Rousseau describes his new position: "Nothing remains for me to hope or to fear any longer in this world, and here I am tranquil at the bottom of the abyss, a poor unfortunate mortal, but impassive like God himself" (I, 999). This description represents the attainment of the condition Jean-Jacques strives for in the *Confessions*. Thus it is fitting that Rousseau continues, "It is in this state that I again take up the continuation of the severe and sincere examination that I previously called my *Confessions*." This statement shows the continuity between the *Confessions* and the *Reveries*. The latter work is the continuation or sequel (*suite*) of the former. This statement, however, also reveals an important change. Although there is a continuity between the two works in that each is a "severe and sincere" self-examination, the continuation is no longer called a confession. It is not a confession because it is not directed at a divine or human judge. Rousseau's assessment of the failure of the *Dialogues* entails the judgment that it is impossible to educate the public about how to judge him. Thus the position of the audience moves from judge (or confessor) in the *Confessions*, to pupil in the *Dialogues*, and then to nothing in the *Reveries*. Rousseau says that he will converse with his soul rather than with any particular audience of other people. This is the necessary result of the abandonment of hope and fear. He ceases to have any relations with others. The *Confessions* begins by asking God to assemble an audience for Rousseau. The *Reveries* begins by declaring quasi-divine independence from his audience.

From the perspective of this argument, the *Confessions* is simultaneously necessary and dispensable for the *Reveries*. It is necessary in that Rousseau could not achieve the position of divine impassivity without having gone through the experiences of the *Confessions*. The *Confessions* is dispensable because once these experiences have been undergone and transcended they need not be repeated or remembered. Among the dispensable aspects of the *Confessions* is its author's desire to write for, or confess to, an audience. To the extent that the *Reveries* is the goal toward which the *Confessions* moves, it is a continuation of the earlier work, but as a goal that has been attained, it transcends that work altogether. Thus, after explaining the difference between the two books, Rousseau loosens the connection between them. Instead of calling the *Reveries* a continuation of the *Confessions*, he finally decides, "These pages can be regarded then as an appendix of my *Confessions*" (I, 1000). An appendix both is and is not a part of the book it accompanies.

Thus, in the *Reveries*, although he expresses certain reservations about the *Confessions*, Rousseau does not precisely reject the earlier work.[2] From the perspective of his new state of impassivity, the *Confessions* has lost much of its importance for him. The earlier work retains, however, its importance for the reader of the *Reveries* who wishes to understand Rousseau's progress toward that state. The same point can be put somewhat differently in terms of structure. The *Confessions* proceeds chronologically, the *Reveries* does not. In the *Confessions* Rousseau wishes to reveal an ordered chain of sentiments. In the *Reveries* he wishes to "apply the barometer" to his soul at different distinct moments (I, 1000–1001). These projects can be approached in their own terms without the second constituting a rejection of the first.

Rousseau turns his attention to the *Confessions* at one other place in the *Reveries*—the discussion of truthfulness, lying, and moral fables in the Fourth Walk. In Chapter 1, I argue that Rousseau both qualifies his claim that the *Confessions* is a simply factual report and substitutes the standards of general and moral truth for factual truth. In the Fourth Walk Rousseau refers to three sorts of lies he might be accused of committing in the *Confessions*: lies in interpreting the significance of facts, lies in adding to the facts, and lies of omission (I, 1035–36). His ultimate evaluation of the *Confessions* is found in his analysis of these possible accusations.

With regard to the first sort of lie, Rousseau admits a degree of guilt. He says that at times he may have accused himself "with too much severity." After making this admission, he dismisses its significance because it compromises his openness very little. With regard to the second sort of lie, Rousseau admits that he has practiced it but denies that it constitutes a crime. None of his embellishments or additions have violated the truth; they have merely given it charm. Of this sort of departure from the truth he concludes, "I am wrong to call it a lie." These two types of lie have no effect whatsoever on the success of the *Confessions*.

The third sort of lie is more serious. Rousseau says that he omitted

2. Later in the First Walk Rousseau further complicates the relationship between the two works by referring to "my first *Confessions*," implying that the *Reveries* are his second confessions (I, 1001).

from the *Confessions* stories that would have shown his "happy qualities." To illustrate and correct this omission, he tells two stories about
incidents in his childhood in which he lied to protect friends from
punishment that they would have incurred for injuring him. The focus
of these stories is Rousseau's compassion, which is remarkable in that
these are cases in which he himself has been injured. He feels compassion for the pain that the sight of his suffering inflicts on the people
who cause it. These stories about Rousseau's failure to accuse when he
could have done so with justice balance to a degree his story about the
false accusation of Marion. Accordingly, they remedy a slight but real
defect in the *Confessions*.

A second aspect of these stories is that they show Rousseau as a liar
as well as a compassionate boy. In relating the incidents, Rousseau
drops his normal motto, "*Vitam impendere vero*" (To stake one's life on
the truth) (I, 1024), and adopts the new motto, "*Magnanima menzogna!
or quando e il vero/Si bello che si possa a te preporre?*" (Magnanimous lie!
what truth could be so beautiful as to be preferred to you) (I, 1037).
Thus, while accusing himself of lying in the *Confessions*, Rousseau cor-
rects the lie by adding two true stories and disposes of the accusation by
using these stories to defend magnanimous lies. In the end he appears
to excuse the *Confessions* as much as he accuses it.

These last words of Rousseau's on the *Confessions* are a dazzling
display of the complex relations among factual truth, moral truth, and
philosophic truth. They reopen the question of whether the *Confessions*
succeeded in combining these forms, but they do not answer it. They
are a powerful warning to Rousseau's readers not to dismiss or accept
his claims unreflectively, an invitation to a cautious attempt to appraise
Rousseau's success in each of his goals for the *Confessions*.

The *Confessions* as the Epistemological Foundation of Rousseau's System

Rousseau's system is based on the assertion that man is naturally
good and has been corrupted by society. This assertion entails a claim
that the scientific progress on which humans pride themselves moves
them further and further from the experience of their own nature.
Thus Rousseau asserts a more or less radical split between civilized self-
consciousness and knowledge of the natural condition. If this split were
complete, Rousseau's system might be true but he could not know it.
For him, or anyone else, to become aware of this split, he must have

overcome it at least in his own consciousness. The *Confessions* is in part the story of how someone learns about the split between nature and convention.

The decisive moments in the account of Jean-Jacques's rediscovery of nature occur in Books VII and VIII. Prior to this point Rousseau has shown his education leading him away from nature. This is true, not only in the general sense that his imagination is becoming more active, but also in the specific way his vanity takes on a desire for public distinction. His absorption in the opinion of others turns him toward the conventions of society and away from the question of their foundation in nature. The period at les Charmettes narrated in Book VI is only an apparent and temporary exception to this rule of departure from nature. For the brief period of his illness, Jean-Jacques is cured of his vanity and other artificial sentiments. He lives like a natural man, however, both in lacking these sentiments and in failing to understand the significance of this lack. He lives in a quasi-natural condition but has no awareness of its naturalness. One could say that only the Rousseau at the end of the *Confessions* is capable of describing the happiness of Jean-Jacques at this period (I, 225–26). Jean-Jacques feels it, but he does not understand it.

Only in his encounter with Zulietta in Book VII is Jean-Jacques confronted with the question of the relations among social institutions, his imagination, and nature. Zulietta's social condition is in marked contrast to her natural beauty and to Jean-Jacques's image of her. For the first time, Rousseau presents himself as being struck by a disproportion among the three factors of nature, convention, and imagination. The case of Zulietta is too personal to resolve this issue, but it leaves Jean-Jacques in a condition of troublesome doubt which makes him receptive to the discovery of its general resolution.

This discovery comes in Book VIII with the famous "illumination," or inspiration, on the road to Vincennes. This experience, which gives birth to Rousseau's system, has both rational and arbitrary aspects. Jean-Jacques's rediscovery of nature is rational and conscious in that it is the result of reflection on the specific question posed by the Academy of Dijon, "Has the restoration of the sciences and arts tended to purify morals?" Because of the rational form of the question, it is logically possible that someone other than Rousseau might answer it correctly. It is equally possible that Jean-Jacques himself might develop his system on presentation of a different question, such as "What is the origin of inequality among men; and is it authorized by natural law?"[3] According to this view, the circumstances of Jean-Jacques's reading of a particular question are merely occasional causes that could be replaced by any number of others. As Diderot explained years later when asked about his role in the composition of the *First Discourse*, "If the impertinent question of Dijon had not been proposed, would Rousseau have been less capable of writing his discourse?"[4] Thus, to be rationally intelligible, Rousseau's system must be independent of the circumstances of its discovery.

At the same time, Rousseau consistently emphasizes the accidental character of the discovery, as if it could have been avoided altogether. There is the accident of reading the proposed question. There is the accident of Jean-Jacques's encounter with Zulietta, which puts him in a condition of openness to the discovery of his system. There is the accident of his unique character and education, which makes him react to Zulietta in a singular way. Rousseau presents the discovery of his system as contingent on a whole series of accidents. Although certain purely rational factors such as regular discussions with Condillac and Diderot contribute to his discovery, they do not sufficiently explain it according to Rousseau's own account.

To emphasize the arbitrary, accidental character of Jean-Jacques's discovery may seem to undermine its validity, but Rousseau argues the opposite. If his system is correct in asserting that civilized humans are radically removed from naturalness, the rediscovery of nature must depend on a fortunate or fateful accident rather than systematic thought alone. Some of Rousseau's writings can be understood as attempts to precipitate such fateful accidents in his readers. To be sure, not all readers can be convinced. Each reader who is convinced must have been predisposed to the discovery by one Zulietta or another. Again, while this might be regarded as reducing Rousseau's system to psychological factors alone, it can also be viewed as a declaration of the truth of his argument.

In the terms in which the *Confessions* presents it, the epistemological foundation of the discovery of nature must retain this ambiguity. The nature of Rousseau's system does not allow him to present it as the necessary outcome of every course of reflection. Accordingly, he pre-

3. This is the question of the *Second Discourse*.
4. Quoted in Trousson, *Socrate*, p. 119.

sents it as both true and of an arbitrary, fortunate origin. The consequent uneasiness is not overcome either by the external evidence available to test the system or by the narrative of the *Confessions*. Everything
depends on the uniqueness of Jean-Jacques's nature and his education.[5] At most, Rousseau can claim to have shown that his system may
be solidly grounded.

The *Confessions* as an Account of the Life According to Nature

Rousseau's second philosophic project in the *Confessions* is to provide an account of human nature, or at least to give an important "piece
for comparison" that can contribute to such an account. This topic can
be considered independently of the epistemological grounding of the
system because it concerns only its comprehensiveness and intelligibil-
ity. The *Confessions* contributes to Rousseau's account of human nature
in two major ways: It shows the formation and development of artificial
characteristics, and it reveals the extent to which these artificial characteristics can be overcome. Both aspects are connected with Rousseau's
presentation of himself as an extraordinary human. His unusual natural characteristics and almost universal experience make him a particularly good test case for examining some of the extreme directions
that denaturing can take. The same attributes also allow him to claim
that he represents a virtually unique case of the overcoming of denaturing. He is both an exemplary unnatural man and an exemplary natural
man.

Accidents play a decisive role in Jean-Jacques's departure from nature and in his return. In Book I the first experiences of imaginary
activity, sexuality, indignation, and vanity are each presented as the
result of mistakes made by his father or teachers. Each is presented as
an irreversible departure from nature. At the same time, the development of the artificial sentiments set in motion by these experiences is
presented as subject to alteration. For example, Jean-Jacques's first
sexual experience predisposes him toward masochism, but his later
experiences turn him to his imagination for satisfaction. At least part of
the reason for this change is his accidental failure to meet more than
one Mlle Goton. A similar variability is seen in his indignation and
vanity. As a rule, when one of these sentiments is strong, the other is

5. See the comparison of Rousseau and Hegel in Chapters 1 and 5.

proportionately weak. This is true in two ways. First, indignation at affronts to him, such as his experience with M. de Montaigu at Venice, leads him to reject the pursuit of public recognition. Second, compassionate indignation against injustice to others turns him into something like a citizen who feels a fierce pride rather than vanity. In the end, these two feelings seem to unite in his project for posthumous glory as a benefactor of humanity, but even this merger is effected only by the accidental inspiration on the road to Vincennes.

Among the artificial sentiments or faculties, it is imagination that pursues the most constant path. Throughout Part One, Rousseau shows this first faculty changing from a reflective power to a creative one through the intermediate stages of productivity and generation. Even though the imagination can be checked at a particular stage, such as a period of illness, it increasingly dominates Jean-Jacques's existence. Finally, the imagination could be said to point in the direction of a cure for itself, when Jean-Jacques constructs his belief in a universal conspiracy which puts an end (tentatively in the *Confessions*) to his imaginary hopes and fears and restricts him to the tranquil imaginary pleasure of botany and recollection. The imagination can in certain circumstances end by destroying the tormenting hopes and fears that it began by creating. In other words, the effects of the imagination can be overcome by means of the imagination.

Jean-Jacques's returns to quasi-natural wholeness are also conditioned by accidents. The clearest example is the period at les Charmettes, in which a physical "revolution" with an accidental origin temporarily cures him of artificial hopes and fears. His final return to nature on St. Peter's Island is brought about by the accident of the conspiracy against him. Even if one regards the conspiracy as largely a figment of his imagination, his banishment from country after country is real.[6] Thus Rousseau's teaching about the possibility of a return to nature is ambiguous. First, the strength and charm of the artificial passions make it impossible for civilized humans even to desire a return to a natural condition. While the prospect of wealth, satisfaction of vanity, love, and the multitude of other objects of civilized hopes remains, the abandonment of these desires has no immediate attraction. Rousseau shows, however, that there are certain accidents that can end

6. For an account of the conspiracy which is not altogether sympathetic to Rousseau, see Ronald Grimsley, *Jean-Jacques Rousseau: A Study in Self-Awareness* (Cardiff: University of Wales Press, 1961), pp. 186–234.

these hopes and restore humans to a quasi-natural happiness, against their wills, as it were.[7] In a few extraordinary people, perhaps only in one extraordinary person, the imagination can develop to such an extent and in such a direction that these salutary accidents are more likely to occur. It should be kept in mind, however, that Rousseau begins his description of his ultimate happiness and self-sufficiency in the *Reveries* by saying, "The most sociable and the most loving of humans has been proscribed [from society] by a unanimous accord" (I, 995). He does not seek a return to nature; it is forced on him. Furthermore, as the *Confessions* shows, if the opportunity for a new project, such as legislation for Corsica, arises, the natural self-sufficiency may disappear. The longing for wholeness which Rousseau stimulates so well in his audience is likely to remain unfulfilled for all but the most extreme cases.

This picture of the departure from and return to nature corresponds to and adds to the pictures in *Emile* and the *Second Discourse*. Rousseau's case study of himself illustrates the growth of artificial sentiments in a civilized human and then throws into relief the important features of the healthy development recommended in *Emile*. It also illustrates the possibilities of domestic life, citizenship, and independence on the fringes of society which are available to humans who find themselves in the corrupt social position described at the end of the *Second Discourse*. Thus, although the *Confessions* may not lay the most solid foundation for Rousseau's system, it complements and adorns the edifice of the system as it is revealed in the other theoretical writings.

The *Confessions* as a Moral Fable

The picture of Jean-Jacques's departure from and return to nature is a part of the moral fable of the *Confessions* as well as a complementary part of Rousseau's system. With the account of his own life, Rousseau gives a persuasive image of human experience. Jean-Jacques may be too idiosyncratic and at times too unattractive to be an exemplary figure. Nevertheless, the description of his experiences does transform the readers of the *Confessions* by exposing them to a new way of looking at a life. As I asserted in Chapter 1, the success of Rousseau's description is indicated by the enduring popularity of autobiographies. To the extent

7. Another method of returning to nature by accident is described in the *Reveries* (I, 1003–6).

that this new way of looking at a life is now taken for granted, Rousseau's *Confessions* has caused or signaled a "revolution in the universe."

Intrinsic to Rousseau's autobiographical enterprise is an emphasis on feelings, the interior life, and a corresponding depreciation of external actions including speeches. It cannot be denied that Christian confessional literature brought to the fore some aspects of interior life long before Rousseau, but Rousseau's "human" autobiography stresses the richness of internal life rather than the struggle between sinfulness and grace.[8] What Rousseau means by "confession" is different from what Augustine means because of this new understanding of internal life. It is this new understanding that makes Rousseau "the Columbus of a new internal world."[9]

Rousseau's new understanding of the internal life leads to a new judgment about the purpose of its revelation. For Augustine, confession is evidence of repentance and acknowledgment of God; for Rousseau it is a token of sincerity and acknowledgment of oneself. Rousseau offers sincerity, frankness, and openness as the standards for judging a life, and the *Confessions* as the standard for judging sincerity, frankness, and openness. Those who attack Rousseau for not being open enough, for being insincere, are precisely the ones who have been most persuaded to accept Rousseau's standard of judgment. Their enthusiasm for beating Rousseau at his own game betrays their lack of reflection about whose game they are playing and why they are playing it.

Rousseau's revolution extends beyond the praise of sincerity. The terrain of the internal world he reveals has its own distinctive features. Its specific contours are given by the imagination, which Rousseau presents as the source of the charms and afflictions of human life. The imagination's primary products are the feelings of sexuality, vanity, and indignation. Rousseau's philosophic teaching about these artificial sentiments is neither widely accepted nor widely understood. Nevertheless, his view that feelings and faculties like these are the most important aspects of life is widely shared. Rousseau's moral fable encourages readers to dwell on their feelings, to seek parallels with his presentation in their own lives, and to cultivate parallels where they did not exist before. Rousseau may not have settled the debate about the precise

8. Herder distinguishes between Rousseau's "human" autobiography and Augustine's "pious" one; see Mounier, "Reception," p. 105.

9. Havelock Ellis, *From Rousseau to Proust* (Boston: Houghton Mifflin, 1935), pp. 32–33.

nature of these feelings, but he has in large part succeeded in setting the terms of the debate. His account of the origin of faculties and feelings invites one to pay special attention to the early experiences that elicit them and gives them their form. The openendedness of the potential development of these characteristics entails the understanding of human life as an ongoing process subject to change. By teaching the importance of the particular experiences that give feelings their shape, it also encourages a view of life as radically individual. Rousseau's insistence on his own uniqueness may well make his readers wonder whether nature did not break the mold after making each of them.

Thus the decisive elements in the orientation toward human life given by the *Confessions* are new perspectives about sincerity, the imagination, feelings, and individuality. The novelty in Rousseau's presentation of the importance in these elements can be seen with reference to the exemplary figures Rousseau sought to replace. Jesus does not speak of the charms of an embellishing imagination. Cato spends little time dwelling on his feelings. The ironic Socrates may praise wisdom, but not sincerity. It is Jean-Jacques who is the champion and exemplar of these characteristics. By focusing on them, he turns attention away from other qualities such as Christian charity, Roman courage, and philosophic wisdom. The significance of Rousseau's attempt to focus attention in new directions is also revealed in his opposition to these three exemplary figures. Rousseau's revision of the Sermon on the Mount reveals his attempt to turn people's attention to this world. His presentation of the richness of the inner life, the capacity of the imagination, and the possibilities for wholeness or completeness are meant to show that a turn away from Heaven need not be an abandonment of high aspirations in a quest for mere preservation or power. Rousseau attempts the daunting task of showing that a life that takes its bearing by nothing higher than itself need not be a base one. Perhaps the greatest merit of this attempt is Rousseau's awareness of the gravity of the issues at stake and his insistence on exposing false solutions to the problems he poses.

Rousseau's treatment of Cato shows the magnitude of his project as well as its limitations. It is clear that he regarded his reattainment of natural wholeness as superior to Cato's virtue when judged according to the natural standard. Cato nonetheless remains the greatest of humans when judged from the standard of social utility. The moral fable of the *Confessions* has a limited value from this standpoint. Rousseau's presentation of himself as a lover of solitude who enjoys innocent pleasures and occasionally rises above himself to champion justice is an attainable object of emulation for corrupt civilized humans who cannot be citizens. It is on this point that Rousseau's project appears to be most moderate, but it is also on this point that serious questions can be raised. It is not clear whether the moderation Rousseau wishes to encourage can resist the powerful longings for individual and social wholeness he stimulates. His presentation of these longings can give birth to demands for their fulfillment which cannot be satisfied.

To judge the final success of the *Confessions*, it is necessary to consider the significance of the longing for natural wholeness which Rousseau presents as the deepest human desire. This is the point at which the moral fable joins the philosophic teaching, because the life of natural wholeness is the standard Rousseau uses to judge everything else. As I argue in Chapter 2, it is this standard that justifies the judgment of Socrates as superior to Cato yet ultimately calls Socrates' life into question. In the end it is the adequacy of this standard by which Rousseau's philosophic system and moral fable both stand and fall.

The judgment of Socrates is somewhat ambiguous. On one hand, Rousseau's attack on the natural basis of human reason leads him to interpret the philosophic life as a manifestation of artificial pride. On the other, in at least one context Rousseau admits that he is not sure he has disposed of Socrates' submission to public opinion properly (IV, 1053). Perhaps one of the reasons for Rousseau's hesitation in dismissing Socrates is his own desire to give a rational account of a justification for the lives of natural humans and citizens which are not based on reason. Someone who wishes to be philosophic will find it hard to dismiss the exemplar of philosophy. Rousseau insists on the separation between reason and nature, or reason and happiness, but he also tries to combine the things he has split asunder.

By attempting to be both a philosopher and a poet, Rousseau attempts to serve the causes of both reason and happiness as he understands them. His desire to combine philosophy and practical effectiveness without subordinating one completely to the other can be contrasted with the understanding of philosophy given by Nietzsche. In *Schopenhauer as Educator* Nietzsche says: "I profit from a philosopher *only* insofar as he can be an example. That he is capable of drawing whole nations after him through his example is beyond doubt; the history of India, which is almost the history of Indian philosophy, proves it. But this example must be supplied by his outward life and not merely in his books—in the way that is, in which the philosophers of

Greece taught, through their bearing, what they were and ate, and their morals, rather than by what they said, let alone by what they wrote."[10] The extent to which Rousseau shares this view of philosophers as examples rather than as thinkers is indicated by his enterprise in writing an autobiography that presents his feelings more than his thoughts. His attempt to be both an example and a thinker who tries to understand the system of nature shows that he did not completely abandon the standard set by Socrates.

The *Confessions* shows the most far-reaching elements of Rousseau's thought in relation to the most personal incidents of his life. The work forges a link between the reflective concerns of a philosopher and the practical cares of all people. Rousseau's ability to capture his readers' feelings was appreciated by Stendhal, who declared, "I must try to undo the prejudices that J. J. Rousseau has given me and he has given me plenty."[11] Rousseau's appeal to feelings is indeed the source of many prejudices, but his efforts to reason as well as to form prejudices make his books among the best antidotes to prejudice. His accomplishment in the *Confessions* confirms his claim to have written "a precious book for philosophers."

10. Friedrich Nietzsche, in *Untimely Meditations*, trans. R. J. Hollingdale (Cambridge: Cambridge University Press, 1983), pp. 136–37.

11. Quoted in *The Private Diaries of Stendhal*, trans. and ed. Robert Sage (New York: Norton, 1962), p. 50.

Bibliography

D'Alembert, Jean Le Rond. *Preliminary Discourse to the Encyclopedia of Diderot.* Trans. Richard N. Schwab and Walter E. Rex. Indianapolis, Ind.: Bobbs-Merrill, 1963.

Augustine. *The Confessions of St. Augustine.* Trans. E. B. Pusey. London: J. M. Dent, 1970.

Baczko, Bronislaw. "Moise législateur. . . ." In *Reappraisals of Rousseau.* Ed. Simon Harvey et al. Totowa, N.J.: Barnes and Noble, 1980.

————. *Rousseau: Solitude et communauté.* Trans. Claire Brendhel-Lamhaut. Mouton: Ecole Pratique des Hautes Etudes et Mouton, 1974.

Barber, Benjamin R. "Rousseau and the Paradoxes of the Dramatic Imagination." *Daedalus* 107,3 (1978): 79–92.

Barth, Karl. *Protestant Thought: From Rousseau to Ritschl.* New York: Harper and Brothers, 1959.

Barthes, Roland. "From Work to Text." In *Textual Strategies: Perspectives in Post-Structuralist Criticism.* Ed Josué V. Harari. Ithaca, N.Y.: Cornell University Press, 1979.

Berman, Marshall. *The Politics of Authenticity.* New York: Atheneum, 1970.

Brée, Germaine. "Michel Leiris: Marginale." In *Autobiography: Essays Theoretical and Critical.* Ed. James Olney. Princeton: Princeton University Press, 1980.

Brown, Peter. *Augustine of Hippo.* London: Faber & Faber, 1967.

Buchner, Margaret Louise. *A Contribution to the Study of the Descriptive Technique of J. J. Rousseau.* Baltimore, Md.: Johns Hopkins University Press, 1937.

Burgelin, Pierre. *La Philosophie de l'existence de J.-J. Rousseau.* Paris: Librairie Philosophique J. Vrin, 1973.

Burke, Edmund. *The Works of the Right Honourable Edmund Burke.* London: Henry G. Bohn, 1845.

Cameron, David. *The Social Thought of Rousseau and Burke: A Comparative Study.* Toronto: University of Toronto Press, 1973.

Cantor, Paul A. *Creature and Creator: Myth-Making and English Romanticism.* Cambridge: Cambridge University Press, 1984.

Cassirer, Ernst. *The Question of Jean-Jacques Rousseau.* Trans. and ed. Peter Gay. New York: Columbia University Press, 1954.

———. *Rousseau, Kant, and Goethe.* Princeton, N.J.: Princeton University Press, 1945.

Chedreville, François, and Roussel, Claude. "Le Vocabulaire de l'ascension sociale dans le livre II des *Confessions*." *Annales de la Société Jean-Jacques Rousseau* 36 (1963–65): 57–86.

Cohler, Anne M. *Rousseau and Nationalism.* New York: Basic Books, 1970.

Condillac, Abbé Etienne Bonnot de. *Essai sur l'origine des connaissances humaines.* Paris: Editions Galilée, 1973.

Courcelle, Pierre. *Les Confessions de St. Augustin dans la tradition littéraire.* Paris: Etudes Augustiniennes, 1963.

Darnton, Robert. "Readers Respond to Rousseau: The Fabrication of Romantic Sensitivity." In *The Great Cat Massacre and Other Episodes in French Cultural History.* New York: Basic Books, 1984.

De Man, Paul. *Blindness and Insight.* New York: Oxford University Press, 1971.

Derrida, Jacques. "L'Archeologie du frivole." Introduction to *Essai sur l'origine des connaissances humaines,* by Abbé Etienne Bonnot de Condillac. Paris: Editions Galilée, 1973.

———. *Of Grammatology.* Trans. Gayatri Chakravorty Spivak. Baltimore, Md.: Johns Hopkins University Press, 1976.

Duffy, Edward. *Rousseau in England.* Berkeley: University of California Press, 1979.

Eigeldinger, Marc. *Jean-Jacques Rousseau et la réalité de l'imaginaire.* Neuchâtel, Switzerland: Editions de la Baconnière, 1962.

Ellis, Havelock. *From Rousseau to Proust.* Boston: Houghton Mifflin, 1935.

Ellis, Madeleine B. *Rousseau's Socratic Aemilian Myths.* Columbus: Ohio State University Press, 1977.

———. *Rousseau's Venetian Story.* Baltimore: Johns Hopkins University Press, 1966.

Fackenheim, Emil. *The Religious Dimension in Hegel's Thought.* Boston: Beacon Press, 1967.

Fayolle, Roger. "Les *Confessions* dans les manuals scolaires de 1890 à nos jours." *Oeuvres et Critiques* 3,1 (1978): 63–86.

Gadamer, Hans-Georg. *Truth and Method.* London: Sheed and Ward, 1975.

Gagnebin, Bernard. "L'Etrange Accueil fait aux *Confessions* de Rousseau au XVIIIe siècle." *Annales de la Société Jean-Jacques Rousseau* 38 (1969–71): 105–26.

Goldschmidt, Victor. *Anthropologie et politique: Les Principes du système de Rousseau.* Paris: Librairie Philosophique J. Vrin, 1974.

Gossman, Lionel. "The Innocent Art of Confession and Reverie." *Daedalus* 107,3 (1978): 59–78.

Gouhier, Henri. *Les Méditations métaphysiques de Jean-Jacques Rousseau.* Paris: Libraire Philosophique J. Vrin, 1970.

Gourevitch, Victor. "Rousseau on Lying: A Provisional Reading of the Fourth Reverie." *Berkshire Review* 15 (1979): 93–107.

Grimsley, Ronald. *Jean-Jacques Rousseau*. Totowa, N.J.: Barnes and Noble, 1983.
———. *Jean-Jacques Rousseau: A Study in Self-Awareness*. Cardiff: University of Wales Press, 1961.
———. *The Philosophy of Rousseau*. Oxford: Oxford University Press, 1973.
———. *Rousseau and the Religious Quest*. Oxford: Clarendon Press, 1968.
Groethuysen, Bernard. *J. J. Rousseau*. Paris: Editions Gallimard, 1949.
Guéhenno, Jean. *Jean-Jacques Rousseau*. 2 vols. Trans. John Weightman and Doreen Weightman. New York: Columbia University Press, 1966.
Hartle, Ann. *The Modern Self in Rousseau's Confessions: A Reply to St. Augustine*. Notre Dame, Ind.: University of Notre Dame Press, 1983.
Hendel, Charles W. *Jean-Jacques Rousseau: Moralist*. Indianapolis, Ind.: Bobbs-Merrill, 1962.
Hoffman, Paul. "La Memoire et les valeurs dans les Six Premiers Livres des *Confessions*." *Annales de la Société Jean-Jacques Rousseau* 39 (1972–74): 79–92.
Howarth, William L. "Some Principles of Autobiography." In *Autobiography: Essays Theoretical and Critical*. Ed. James Olney. Princeton, N.J.: Princeton University Press, 1980.
Huizinga, Jakob Herman. *Rousseau: The Self-Made Saint*. New York: Grossman, 1976.
Kelly, Christopher. " 'To Persuade without Convincing': The Language of Rousseau's Legislator." *American Journal of Political Science*, 31,2 (1987): 321–35.
Kessen, William. "Rousseau's Children." *Daedalus* 107,3 (1978): 155–66.
Leduc-Fayette, Denise. *J. J. Rousseau et le mythe de l'antiquité*. Paris: J. Vrin, 1974.
Lejeune, Philippe. *Le Pacte autobiographique*. Paris: Editions du Seuil, 1975.
MacCannell, Juliet Flower. "History and Self-Portrait in Rousseau's Autobiography." *Studies in Romanticism* 13 (1974): 279–98.
Marty, Olivier. *Rousseau de l'enfance à quarante ans* Paris: Nouvelles Editions Débresse, 1975.
Masson, Pierre Maurice. *La Religion de J. J. Rousseau*. Paris: Librairie Hachette, 1916.
Masters, Roger D. *The Political Philosophy of Rousseau*. Princeton, N.J.: Princeton University Press, 1968.
May, Georges. *L'Autobiographie*. Paris: Presses Universitaires de France, 1979.
Mercier, Sebastien. *De J. J. Rousseau considéré comme l'un des premiers auteurs de la révolution*. Paris: Buisson, 1791.
Miller, Arnold. "Rousseau's *Confessions* in Russian Critisicm: The Pre-Soviet Period." *Oeuvres et Critiques* 3,1 (1978): 115–23.
Momigliano, Arnoldo. *The Development of Greek Biography*. Cambridge, Mass.: Harvard University Press, 1971.
Mounier, Jacques. "La Reception des *Confessions* en Allemagne de 1782 à 1813." *Oeuvres et Critiques* 3,1 (1978): 101–13.
Okin, Susan Moller. *Women in Western Political Thought*. Princeton, N.J.: Princeton University Press, 1979.
Olney, James. "Autobiography and the Cultural Moment: A Thematic, Historical, and Bibliographical Introduction." In *Autobiography: Essays Theoretical and Critical*. Ed. James Olney. Princeton, N.J.: Princeton University Press, 1980.

————. "Some Versions of Memory/Some Versions of *Bioi*: The Ontology of Autobiography." In *Autobiography: Essays Theoretical and Critical*. Ed. James Olney. Princeton, N.J.: Princeton University Press, 1980.

Orwin, Clifford. "Compassion." *The American Scholar* 49,3 (1980): 309–33.

————. "On the Sovereign Authorization." *Political Theory* 3,1 (1975): 26–44.

Pascal, Roy. *Design and Truth in Autobiography*. Cambridge, Mass.: Harvard University Press, 1960.

Peyre, Henri. *Literature and Sincerity*. New Haven, Conn.: Yale University Press, 1963.

Raymond, Marcel. *Jean-Jacques Rousseau: La Quête de soi et la rêverie*. Paris: José Corti, 1962.

Roussel, Jean. "Le Phénomène de l'identification dans la lecture de Rousseau." *Annales de la Société Jean-Jacques Rousseau* 39 (1972–74): 65–77.

Rousset, Jean. "'Qu'est-ce que le talent du comédien?'" *Annales de la Société Jean-Jacques Rousseau* 37 (1966–68): 19–34.

Saussure, Hermine de. *Rousseau et les manuscrits des Confessions*. Paris: Editions E. de Boccard, 1958.

Schwartz, Joel. *The Sexual Politics of Jean-Jacques Rousseau*. Chicago: University of Chicago Press, 1984.

Shklar, Judith N. *Men and Citizens: A Study of Rousseau's Social Theory*. Cambridge: Cambridge University Press, 1969.

————. "Rousseau's Images of Authority." In *Hobbes and Rousseau: A Collection of Critical Essays*. Ed. Maurice Cranston and Richard S. Peters. Garden City, N.Y.: Anchor Books, 1972.

Starobinski, Jean. "The Accuser and the Accused." *Daedalus* 107,3 (1978): 41–58.

————. *Jean-Jacques Rousseau: La Transparence et l'obstacle suivi de sept essais sur Rousseau*. Paris: Gallimard, 1971.

————. *L'Oeil vivant*. Paris: Gallimard, 1961.

————. *La Relation critique*. Paris: Gallimard, 1970.

Stendhal. *On Love*. Trans. H. B. V. New York: Grosset and Dunlap, 1967.

Strauss, Leo. *Natural Right and History*. Chicago: University of Chicago Press, 1953.

————. "On the Intention of Rousseau." In *Hobbes and Rousseau*. Ed. Maurice Cranston and Richard S. Peters. Garden City, N.Y.: Anchor Books, 1972.

Temmer, Mark J. *Art and Influence of J. J. Rousseau*. Chapel Hill: University of North Carolina Press, 1973.

Trilling, Lionel. *Sincerity and Authenticity*. Cambridge, Mass.: Harvard University Press, 1972.

Trousson, Raymond. *Socrate devant Voltaire, Diderot et Rousseau*. Paris: Lettres Modernes Minard, 1967.

Voltaire. *Voltaire's Marginalia on Rousseau*. Ed. George R. Havens. New York: Burt Franklin, 1971.

Weintraub, Karl J. "Autobiography and Historical Consciousness." *Critical Inquiry* 1 (1975): 821–48.

Williams, Huntington. *Rousseau and Romantic Autobiography*. Oxford: Oxford University Press, 1983.

Index

Works by Rousseau are indexed only when they are mentioned in the text or substantively in the notes. Characters in works others than the *Confessions* are followed by a parenthetical notation of the work in which they appear.

Library of Congress Cataloging-in-Publication Data

Kelly, Christopher, 1950–
   Rousseau's exemplary life.

   Bibliography.
   Includes index.
     1. Rousseau, Jean-Jacques, 1712–1778—Contributions in
political science. 2. Rousseau, Jean-Jacques, 1712–1778.
Confessions. I. Title.
JC179.R9K45 1987   320'.01   86-32961
ISBN 0-8014-1936-0 (alk. paper)